THIS
BURNING
LAND

THIS BURNING LAND

LESSONS FROM THE FRONT LINES OF THE TRANSFORMED ISRAELI-PALESTINIAN CONFLICT

GREG MYRE AND JENNIFER GRIFFIN

WILEY

John Wiley & Sons, Inc.

Published by John Wiley & Sons, Inc., Hoboken, New Jersey
Published simultaneously in Canada

For general information about our other products and services, please contact our Customer Care Department within the United States at (800) 762-2974, outside the United States at (317) 572-3993 or fax (317) 572-4002.

Wiley also publishes its books in a variety of electronic formats. Some content that appears in print may not be available in electronic books. For more information about Wiley products, visit our web site at www.wiley.com.

Library of Congress Cataloging-in-Publication Data:

Myre, Greg, date.
  This burning land : lessons from the front lines of the transformed Israeli-Palestinian conflict/Greg Myre and Jennifer Griffin.
     p. cm
Includes bibliographical references and index.
ISBN 978-0-470-55090-8
1. Arab-Israeli conflict, 1993—Personal narratives.   2. Arab-Israeli conflict, 1993—Social aspects.   3. Interviews–Israel.   4. Interviews–Palestine.   5. Myre, Greg, 1960   6. Griffin, Jennifer, 1969-   7. Asymmetric warfare–Israel.   8. Asymmetric warfare–Palestine.   9. Asymmetric warfare–Case Studies. I. Griffin, Jennifer, 1969- II. Title.
  DS119.76.M97 2011
  956.9405'4—dc22

                                                                    2010048270

Printed in the United States of America
10 9 8 7 6 5 4 3 2 1

To our parents,
John and Carole,
Griff and Carolyn

"In this burning country, words have to be shade."
—Yehuda Amichai, Israeli poet

"To our land, and it is a prize of war,
the freedom to die from longing and burning."
—Mahmoud Darwish, Palestinian poet

CONTENTS

AUTHORS' NOTE

This book is based on our reporting and personal experiences during the time we were based in Jerusalem, from 1999 until 2007. During this period, Jennifer filed well over one thousand stories for Fox News, and Greg wrote roughly fifteen hundred stories for the Associated Press and the *New York Times*. This book was a joint effort. Jennifer wrote the introduction and the afterword. Her first-person accounts throughout the book are in italics. Greg's accounts are in regular type.

CHRONOLOGY

December 1987: The first Palestinian uprising, or intifada, begins. Hamas is founded. The fighting lasts nearly six years.

October 1991: With the Cold War over, Israel, the Palestinians, and Arab states meet at the groundbreaking Madrid Conference. It marks the first such gathering to discuss solutions to decades of hostilities.

September 1993: Israeli and Palestinian leaders sign an interim peace agreement on the White House lawn with the goal of reaching a full peace accord within five years.

April 1996: The frequent low-level fighting between Israel and the Lebanese guerrilla group Hezbollah heats up. After seventeen days of heavy shooting, the United States helps broker a truce, but larger issues go unresolved.

May 2000: Israel unilaterally withdraws troops from southern Lebanon, ending nearly two decades of occupation.

July 2000: Israel and Palestinians hold two weeks of peace talks at Camp David, hosted by President Bill Clinton, but do not reach a deal. In September, Israeli opposition leader Ariel Sharon visits the Temple Mount–Noble Sanctuary in Jerusalem, angering Palestinians. The second Palestinian uprising begins the following day with riots at the Jerusalem holy site.

January 2001: Israelis and Palestinians negotiate in the Egyptian Red Sea resort of Taba. They say they are closer than ever to a deal, but come up short. Days later, Sharon is elected prime minister in a landslide as Israelis turn to him to end the Palestinian uprising. The peace talks collapse.

September 2001: Al Qaida carries out terror attacks on 9/11 in the U.S. Israel aligns itself with the U.S. war on terrorism.

March 2002: Palestinian suicide bombings peak. Sharon orders a massive invasion of the West Bank, known as Operation Defensive Shield. Israel establishes hundreds of roadblocks and checkpoints to limit Palestinian movements.

June 2002: Israel begins building its West Bank separation barrier.

March 2003: The United States invades Iraq, deposing Saddam Hussein.

June 2003: President George W. Bush introduces the Road Map peace plan, but Israeli-Palestinian fighting continues.

2005: After five years of daily violence, the Palestinian uprising winds down. Sharon withdraws all Israeli soldiers and settlers from Gaza, ending 38 years of Israeli presence in the territory. Hamas claims victory, and fires rockets into southern Israel just days after the Israeli pullout. In Iraq and Afghanistan, the U.S. military is increasingly bogged down by insurgencies.

January 2006: Hamas wins the Palestinian election, setting the stage for a showdown with the rival Fatah movement.

July 2006: The Lebanese group Hezbollah stages a cross-border raid against Israeli troops, provoking a thirty-four-day war. The fighting ends in a standoff, similar to their battle a decade earlier. Hezbollah celebrates what it considers a moral victory, while Israelis view the war as a psychological defeat.

June 2007: Hamas defeats Fatah in Gaza, taking full control of the territory. Fatah retains control in the West Bank.

2008: Israel unleashes a major offensive, Operation Cast Lead, on December 27 to halt Palestinian rocket fire coming out of Gaza. The campaign lasts three weeks, leaving 1,400 Palestinians dead and inflicting major destruction.

May 2010: Israeli commandos kill nine Turkish citizens during a raid on a flotilla in the Mediterranean attempting to break an Israeli blockade and deliver aid to Gaza. The episode causes an international outcry. Israel responds by easing, but not lifting, the blockade.

September 2010: President Barack Obama sponsors a new round of Israeli-Palestinian peace talks despite widespread skepticism about the chances for a breakthrough.

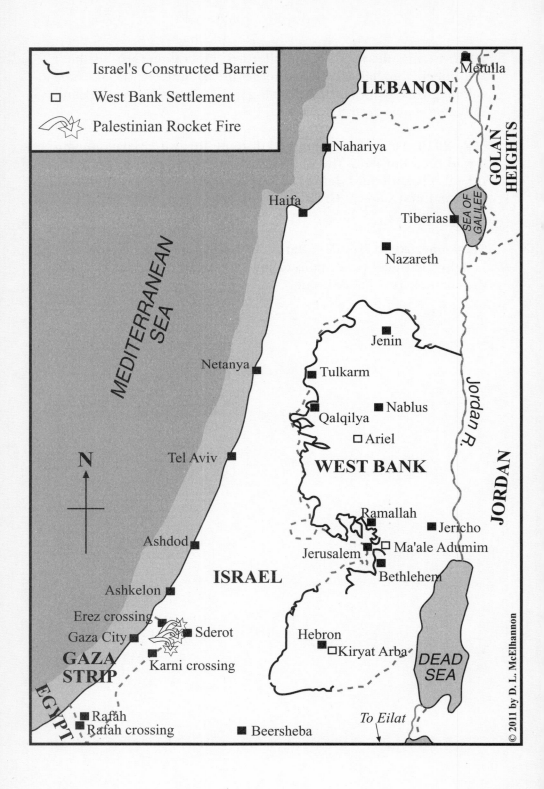

INTRODUCTION

Jennifer Griffin

The phone rang with urgent news from the Gaza Strip, and I immediately grabbed my two most essential items: my flak jacket and my breast pump. For years, my husband, Greg Myre, and I had covered wars across several continents, but now we were trying to do it while juggling the demands of our two young daughters. On this sticky morning of June 10, 2003, we both went scrambling into action. Israeli attack helicopters had just fired several missiles at a silver Mitsubishi SUV carrying Dr. Abdel Aziz Rantisi, one of the most prominent leaders of the radical Islamist group Hamas. Dr. Rantisi was a pediatrician but was much better known for his fiery calls for Israel's destruction than for making house calls to check for strep throat. The first missile narrowly missed the vehicle being driven by his son, Ahmad. The second struck the hood just as they passed through a busy intersection in Gaza City not far from the Mediterranean Sea. Shrapnel hit the doctor's chest and left leg, yet he managed to flee on foot before the next round of missiles turned his car into a fireball, killing three

Palestinian bystanders, paralyzing his son, and sending a thick plume of black smoke curling into the sky.

Both Greg and I knew the drill as we raced to get to Gaza from our home in Jerusalem. Greg, a correspondent with the *New York Times*, needed only a pen, a notebook, and his laptop computer, and he was set for days. I needed a bit more gear for my work with Fox News. My flak jacket had fluorescent yellow gaffer tape on the front and the back that read "TV." It was a prayer that the men with the guns had at least a minimal respect for the press. My milk pump came in a chic black leather case that hung from my shoulder like a purse and would not have looked out of place on the streets of Manhattan. It had a name to match: "Pump in Style." We kissed our girls—Annalise, then two, and Amelia, then six months and still nursing—and left them with our babysitter, Rose Espanol. Off we went. Some couples take a break from their kids with weekend getaways in the country. Greg and I went to Gaza.

Within a couple of hours, we were at Shifa Hospital in Gaza City, where the wounded Dr. Rantisi remained defiant from his hospital bed. Pointing to the sky, he proclaimed, "We will continue with our holy war and resistance until every last criminal Zionist is evicted from this land." In the streets, Dr. Rantisi's seething Hamas supporters fired their automatic rifles into the air, promising "an earthquake" and chanting "Allahu Akbar," or "God is Greatest."

This particular trip to Gaza marked our first night alone since Amelia had been born. We spent it at the Beach Hotel, where the terrace was covered with brilliant bougainvillea and overlooked the sea. We dined on seafood served in clay pots at the hotel's outdoor restaurant. We were serenaded by the rhythmic thumping of Israeli helicopters and the buzz of unmanned drones guided by Israeli air force officers at a base deep inside Israel. We worked well past midnight with our editors in New York.

This visit to Gaza, like dozens of others, came with certain guarantees: our days would be long and exhausting, and we would spend them coated in sweat and dust. Our Palestinian hosts would offer us more cups of sugary tea and cardamom-laced coffee than any human bladder could endure. We would hear gunfire and quite possibly air strikes. There would be countless frustrations, including prickly phone lines that always seemed particularly balky when deadlines loomed. Yet when the moon rose over the Mediterranean, we would have a story worth telling, and that was the payoff that kept luring us back.

The following day, we prepared to leave Gaza and reenter Israel at the Erez Crossing. This was almost always a maddening process that involved multiple security checks by Israeli soldiers and hours of waiting. Security was particularly onerous this time because the Israeli military was on high alert, expecting retaliation from the Palestinians.

The crossing included a half-mile-long walkway that served as a no-man's-land between the borders. It resembled a cattle passage with security cameras staring down from the thirty-foot-high concrete walls. At the Israeli end of the passage, travelers were required to undergo high-tech body scans as soldiers checked and rechecked luggage for explosives. Bomb-sniffing dogs seemed to share their masters' suspicion, if not disdain, for journalists. On one occasion, a highly trained canine walked directly to the suitcase of a European reporter and urinated on it.

As our wait dragged on, I called David Baker, an aide in the Israeli prime minister's office, and asked whether he could speed up our passage. I played all of my cards, stressing that my packets of breast milk were rapidly going sour in the heat and dust of Gaza. I could sense him blushing down the phone line, but he promised to do what he could. I then marched over to the Israeli soldiers behind the passport counter and insisted that they refrigerate my milk. This was clearly a new experience for them. Their faces registered surprise, but they complied without a word. And we continued to wait.

Eventually, our cell phones rang almost simultaneously with news from our offices in Jerusalem. A Palestinian suicide bomber, disguised as an Orthodox Jew, had just blown himself up on a Jerusalem bus, killing sixteen Israelis on Jaffa Street, the busy commercial strip near our offices. We again pressed the soldiers, begging them to let us back into Israel so we could report on the attack, but the soldiers did not budge.

We were still stranded a couple of hours later when an Israeli air force jet fired a missile at a sedan traveling along a busy street in Gaza City, killing seven Palestinians and wounding twenty-five. That settled it. Instead of trying to get out of Gaza, we asked the Israeli soldiers to return our passports—and my milk. We turned around and reentered Gaza.

As Greg helped lower the flak jacket over my head, the tears started rolling down my cheeks. I had once again broken a pledge to my mother that we would not be together in a place where there was fighting. Some risk-averse couples do not take the same flight when they have young children. We tried to stay out of war zones on the same day, but news kept getting in the way. As the sun set, my milk went sour, Amelia made do with a bottle of formula, and we were looking at another long night in Gaza.

During our more than seven years in Jerusalem, we zigged and zagged from Israel to Gaza to the West Bank to cover the relentless bloodshed. This trip to Gaza stood out because it encapsulated so much of the chaos and the insanity of the Israeli-Palestinian conflict. Time and again, we would reach the scene of one violent act, only to be redirected to yet another.

This particular episode in Gaza was significant because it came just a week after President George W. Bush launched a major attempt to restart Israeli-Palestinian negotiations. It was impossible to ignore the huge chasm between the diplomatic vision and the facts on the ground. I was at Jordan's Red Sea resort of Aqaba as Israel's prime minister, Ariel Sharon, and his Palestinian counterpart, Mahmoud Abbas, flanked President Bush on the beachfront for the unveiling of the Road Map. It was intended to pave the way for a Palestinian state and a comprehensive peace deal. Despite the fanfare, it seemed doomed from the start. I expressed this to a Fox White House correspondent traveling with President Bush.

"Yes, but President Bush is really serious this time. I have never seen him so serious," the veteran correspondent said.

"Yes, but the president has never met the Al Aksa Martyrs Brigades," I replied, referring to one of the many Palestinian armed factions. "They control the streets in the West Bank, and they're not listening to anyone."

With contributions from the Al Aksa Martyrs Brigades, the Road Map quickly proved to be a dead end. Collectively, the thousands of shootings, bombings, and air strikes dramatically reshaped the conflict during the last decade, and that is the focus of this book.

For more than sixty years, this feud has continually evolved without being solved. It has played out over a longer period of time, burned with greater intensity, and defied more international attempts at a resolution than any other dispute in the world. The last decade was not merely the latest chapter. It marked a period of fundamental changes that have thrown into question some of the most basic assumptions about the conflict.

At the dawn of the new millennium, a solution seemed within reach. The conventional wisdom held that the Israelis and the Palestinians would eventually negotiate a deal dividing the territory between the Mediterranean Sea and the Jordan River, creating two states living side by side in peace. Many Israelis were anticipating peace, security, and normality in daily life that the country had never known since its founding in 1948. Many Palestinians were convinced that statehood was finally on the way as they acquired the trappings of a nation, including their own security forces, an airport in Gaza, and a cavernous parliament building that was rising on the edge of East Jerusalem.

Yet in this moment of hope, the two sides began their most protracted battle ever, then waged a completely lopsided war that neither one could win outright. With its powerful, high-tech military, Israel could steamroll the Palestinians with raw force or unleash a missile strike at an individual militant on a crowded Gaza City street. Yet Israel, a country dominated by current and former military officers, kept bumping up against the limits of its military muscle.

If military dominance was the sole ingredient for ending this conflict, it would have concluded with Israel's lightning victory in the Six-Day War of 1967. Instead, Israel has increasingly found itself cast as the neighborhood bully, facing increasing international criticism from opponents who question the very legitimacy of the Jewish state. As a country, Israel is more powerful than at any point in its history. Yet Israeli diplomats spend so much of their time addressing these attempts to isolate the country that they now refer to it simply as BDS—shorthand for "boycotts, divestment, and sanctions." Rather than Israel becoming a quiet, prosperous nation that goes about its business in a routine way, many Israelis continue to feel that they are under siege and are still wrestling with existential angst.

As the superior power in this asymmetric battle, Israel can dictate the shape and the terms of the conflict with the Palestinians. Israel can impose a blockade on Gaza, send tanks rumbling into cities in the West Bank, and effectively set the rules for Palestinian commerce and travel. The one thing Israel cannot do unilaterally is end the war.

The Palestinians have far fewer choices, but the one thing they can do unilaterally is keep the fighting going as long as they are not satisfied with their plight. They have successfully kept their cause in the international spotlight for decades, and they continue to frustrate Israel. Their problem has often been their choices. The suicide bombers launched from the West Bank and the rockets unleashed from Gaza produced harsh Israeli military responses that crippled Palestinian society, ruined much of their economy, and pushed the prospect of statehood ever farther into the future.

The daily fighting has subsided, at least for now, but has left its scars. A full-fledged peace agreement in the coming years is now much less plausible than at any time in a generation. Even if the atmosphere for negotiations improves, it is not possible to simply dust off peace plans that have been sitting on the shelf.

Consider the conditions that existed when President Bill Clinton was trying to negotiate a deal in the 1990s compared to those that faced his wife, Secretary of State Hillary Clinton, when she relaunched peace talks in the fall of 2010:

- President Clinton worked with leaders like Israeli prime minister Yitzhak Rabin and Palestinian leader Yasser Arafat, who were strong advocates of the peace process and were considered capable of delivering on a deal. In contrast, Secretary Clinton dealt with an Israeli prime minister, Benjamin Netanyahu, who had a long history of deep skepticism toward the negotiations and led a conservative coalition. On the Palestinian side, President Mahmoud Abbas supported the talks but was a relatively weak leader who had no authority in the Gaza Strip, which was run by Hamas.
- The fighting since 2000 has claimed a huge toll, leaving some some six thousand Palestinians and more than one thousand Israelis dead. The intensity of the fighting hardened attitudes on both sides, encouraging more radical views and pushing aside moderate ones. In this environment, U.S. influence has waned. Washington may still be essential to brokering a deal, but the Israelis and the Palestinians now have far less faith in America's ability to shape events and forge an agreement.

- There is now almost complete segregation of the Israelis and the Palestinians. Before the fighting, nearly 150,000 Palestinians from the West Bank and Gaza entered Israel daily to work, study, and shop. These interactions did not inspire brotherly love, but they did humanize the other side and made it harder for Israelis and Palestinians to demonize one another. In recent years, the most common point of contact has often been between Israeli soldiers and Palestinian civilians at checkpoints.

- Israel has remade the physical landscape, and it is now more difficult to create a viable Palestinian state. Israel has built a barrier stretching for hundreds of miles in the West Bank and has effectively sealed off Gaza. In addition, Israel has continued to expand its West Bank settlements. When President Clinton first brokered talks between the Israelis and the Palestinians in the early 1990s, the West Bank settler population was a little more than one hundred thousand. Today, some three hundred thousand settlers live there.

- The Palestinians are bitterly divided among themselves. They elected a radical Islamic movement to lead them and then split into rival fiefdoms. Fatah runs the West Bank and seeks negotiations with Israel. Hamas controls Gaza and refuses to have any contact with Israel, unless it involves rockets. Both Palestinian factions have become steadily more entrenched in their separate territories and have shown no sign of forming the united front that is needed to effectively negotiate with Israel. President Clinton was welcomed as a hero when he visited Gaza in 1998. Secretary Clinton would not even consider such a trip; U.S. diplomats stopped going to Gaza years ago.

- Back in the 1990s, many Israelis entertained the notion that their country might finally win acceptance as a permanent part of the broader Middle East. Today, the Israelis feel extremely isolated in their region and see little prospect that will change. In addition, Israelis are in a period of relative stability and prosperity and feel no sense of urgency about making a deal with the Palestinians or others in the region. Many Israelis have turned inward and psychologically walled themselves off from thinking about the Palestinians and the Arab states.

President Barack Obama and his secretary of state face the same paradox that has confronted every administration since that of Harry Truman: the Israeli-Palestinian conflict cannot be solved, and yet it cannot be ignored.

President Clinton personified the president who was determined to solve the conflict, and although he came close, he ultimately fell short and left office with the region ablaze. George W. Bush began his presidency intending to keep his distance. He was ultimately dragged into the feud, yet also left office with nothing to show for his efforts.

President Obama has sought a fresh start. Yet Israelis see him as much less sympathetic than President Bush and more likely to put pressure on Israel. The Palestinians, having had their hopes dashed so many times, are not inclined to trust the promises of any U.S. president. If there is a silver lining, perhaps it is that expectations are so low. The best anyone can hope for is to manage the conflict—keeping the violence to a minimum, encouraging dialogue, and bolstering moderates on both sides. Americans like to believe that all problems can be solved, but there is no near-term solution for the Israelis and the Palestinians. The ultimate prize, a full-fledged peace treaty, has receded beyond the horizon.

We learned many hard lessons from our years in the Middle East, but Greg says that most of what he needed to know, he could have grasped at age seven. It was 1968 and he was living in Little Rock, Arkansas. On a scorching summer's day, he went knocking on neighborhood doors with his brother, Keith, and three friends to raise money for the giraffe fund at the Little Rock Zoo. They raised a whopping thirty dollars, and when they went to the zoo to pour the money into the kitty, a photographer took their picture as they squinted into the sun.

The news cycle was a bit slow in Little Rock during a summer heat wave, and this landed them on the front page of the *Arkansas Democrat*. Right next to that photo was an Associated Press story from Amman, Jordan. "Israeli Attack Feared," the headline said. Israeli troops were massing and could be seen on "the hills overlooking the [Jordan] valley." Israel's foreign minister, Abba Eban, said that his government would consider negotiating directly with the Palestinians if it could not reach a comprehensive peace deal with all of the Arab states. Despite the ritual nod to negotiations, the underlying message was clear: expect more fighting. A monumental war had been fought a year earlier in 1967, yet nothing was settled. It was just a prelude to many more years of quarreling, a concept that even a seven-year-old could grasp.

It took us decades to reach Jerusalem and put this theory to a test. In the meantime, we prepared by taking a tour of some of the world's nastiest conflicts. Greg joined the Associated Press immediately after graduating from Yale University in 1983 and four years later was sent to South Africa at a time when the black majority was rising up against the country's white rulers.

He was two years into that assignment in 1989 when he went to cover the first legal African National Congress rally in a generation at Soweto's main soccer stadium. Several of Nelson Mandela's prison comrades had just been freed as a precursor for the release of Mandela himself. Some seventy thousand cheering black South Africans crammed into the stadium. I was also there. I had taken a year off as an undergraduate at Harvard and was an intern at the *Sowetan*, the country's largest black newspaper. I was in one of the media booths, and Greg, the only person in the stadium wearing a red St. Louis Cardinals baseball cap, came in looking for a phone line. He made his call and then found excuses to stay until he managed to get my phone number.

We spent most of the next two decades chasing wars. We roamed all over Africa, Asia, the former Soviet Union, and the Middle East. We were always game to board an antiquated airplane, take a rickety bus, or drive all night through the desert as long as there was a good story at the other end. As reporters, we kept gravitating to war in general, and the Middle East in particular, for the same reason Willie Sutton was attracted to banks.

In all our travels to convulsed lands, a recurring theme was clear: traditional wars featuring armies from two nations appear to be a thing of the past. Almost every modern conflict now features a national army versus a much smaller group of militants that is seeking to drive out an occupier, overthrow a government, or establish a separate homeland. As a rule, these conflicts are often waged at a relatively low level and drag on inconclusively for years. They are rarely, if ever, settled by decisive victories on the battlefield. When they end, it is by political compromise. We saw this time and again in Africa, from South Africa to Mozambique, to Namibia, to Angola. And in Somalia, we witnessed what happened when there was no compromise.

The same was true in Afghanistan, where we spent our first few weeks of wedded life in Kabul in 1994, during one of the most anarchic periods in the country's civil war. Rockets rained down on the city, night and day. We worked from a house with no electricity, running water, phones, or glass in the windows, all casualties of the war. We bathed in small buckets of hot water boiled in tea kettles. We hunkered down in the basement at night in what had been one of the city's finer neighborhoods. We watched the Taliban emerge to impose their primitive beliefs on the country, and we returned several years later after the Taliban were dislodged by the U.S. military. None of these developments ended the war; they simply marked new stages in an open-ended conflict.

In fact, the only major conflicts in recent years featuring two national armies were the U.S. wars against Iraq, in 1991 and 2003. Yet soon after Saddam Hussein was driven out of Baghdad in the second U.S. invasion, the fighting turned into the same kind of asymmetric warfare we had been witnessing elsewhere.

In the fall of 1999, we wrapped up a three-year assignment in Moscow and landed on a cool October evening at Ben-Gurion International Airport outside Tel Aviv to begin a new posting in Jerusalem. It was one of those rare rosy moments in the Middle East that made us think we might actually be covering peace and not another war.

Compared to our previous posts, Jerusalem felt like a pillar of stability. There had been no major spasms of violence for three years. The city was overflowing with tourists. Coexistence was the spirit of the day. We figured we would enjoy a few comfortable years in Jerusalem and perhaps witness the historic end of the Israeli-Palestinian conflict.

Our delusions were reinforced as we set out to explore. Every weekday, Palestinian commuters from the West Bank and the Gaza Strip streamed into Israel. When the weekend came, Israelis did not hesitate to drive into the West Bank to gamble at the flourishing Oasis Casino in Jericho, have a lamb kebab lunch in Bethlehem, or buy garden supplies at a small neighborhood shop in Jenin. As we drove around, we were sometimes unsure whether we were in Israel or the West Bank because the boundary was unmarked on most maps and on the roads.

The Israeli military occupation still governed many aspects of Palestinian life. Yet soldiers and checkpoints were scarce. Occasionally, we saw Israeli soldiers sitting under a palm tree on the side of the road and wondered whether we were obliged to stop. Most often, we simply drove past, unable to stir them from their torpor. Where, exactly, was this conflict everyone talked about?

We spent our first few weeks in Jerusalem at the American Colony Hotel, founded by nineteenth-century American missionaries and a longtime haunt of journalists, diplomats, aid workers, and spies. Walking down the paved-stone hallways after dinner one night, we stopped to read the framed, yellowed newspaper clippings of the region's tortured history. A *New York Times* story from 1929 described the Muslim uprising at Jerusalem's ground zero. Jews call it the Temple Mount, the holiest place in Judaism. Muslims call it the Noble Sanctuary and believe it is where the Prophet Muhammad rose to heaven.

From the September 29, 1929, edition of the *Times*, the headline shouted, "47 Dead in Jerusalem Riot, Attacks by Arabs Spread." The article read, "Centering on the ancient remnant of Solomon's Temple, known as the Wailing Wall, sacred shrine to Jews all over the world, the trouble started in Jerusalem at noon yesterday. Crowds of armed Arabs attacked the Jews who formed themselves into defense units. Rioting spread and soon got beyond control. Hospitals were crowded with the injured. The authorities who proclaimed martial law barred the populace from the streets after six o'clock at night." A separate clipping from the *Times*, which was published a few weeks later, featured photos of the fighting. A young Arab boy in Jerusalem wore a bandage around his head to protect a recent wound. A synagogue in Hebron was in ruins, one of the attacks that drove Jews from the ancient city.

Seventy years later, in 1999, the clippings looked like relics. The Israelis and the Palestinians were negotiating almost daily as part of the interim Oslo agreement signed six years earlier by Israeli prime minister Yitzhak Rabin and Palestinian leader Yasser Arafat on the White House lawn. The Israeli and Palestinian security forces were partners that carried out joint patrols on the streets of Gaza and the West Bank.

We felt all the more confident in our assessment because we had seen one historic peace breakthrough while in South Africa. Having witnessed black and white South Africans negotiate an end to apartheid, we believed, naively, that the Israelis and the Palestinians were on a similar trajectory.

We were wrong. Within a year of our arrival, we found ourselves covering some of the worst fighting ever between the two sides. For a while, we and many others thought the upheaval would be temporary. How could either side opt for nihilistic violence when the solution seemed within reach? Khaled Abdel Shafi, a member of a prominent Gaza family and the head of the United Nations Development Program in Gaza, said in 2007 that "for years, we kept thinking it can't get worse. But it keeps getting worse. So we've stopped saying this now. Things can always get worse."

During our time in Jerusalem, a typical day could often be summed up in three words: hot, sunny, apocalyptic. Throughout Israel and even in the most ravaged parts of Gaza and the West Bank, normality usually prevailed at daybreak, with parents dropping their kids at school, heading to work, and grabbing a shot of caffeine somewhere along the way. Both Israelis and Palestinians greeted the dawn with the hope that the day would be uneventful, but with the knowledge that something terrible could happen at any moment. By nightfall, something awful usually had taken place, and it was often accompanied by talk of Armageddon.

For us, like the Israelis and the Palestinians, conflict became a way of life. And this brings us to another fundamental reason for this book. We wanted to explore one simple question: what is it like to live in a place of permanent conflict? Israelis and Palestinians have lived their entire lives in a state of friction. In ways large and small, this has shaped their worldviews, their psychologies, and their life choices. Some choose to be full-time participants, making it their obsession. Others seek to avoid the conflict, only to find themselves dragged into it in ways they never expected.

Even as temporary residents, we felt the conflict's gravitational pull. We were constantly whipsawed between its worst cruelties and the great warmth we felt from both the Israelis and the Palestinians, particularly toward our children. A single day could take us from death, destruction, and gun battles in the West Bank to birthday parties and play dates in our Jerusalem neighborhood. After one day of mayhem, I went to pick up Amelia from her Israeli pre-school, where she had served as the "Shabbat Mommy" on a Friday. She had tied a kerchief around her head and recited the *bracha*, or blessing, while her partner broke the challah bread. We didn't have the heart to tell her she was not Jewish.

Our kids seemed, for the most part, oblivious to the upheaval around them. Yet it did seep in. One day Annalise was playing in the park with one of her best friends, Benny Anderson, the son of *Washington Post* correspondents Molly Moore and John Ward Anderson. Annalise grabbed a cell phone, held it to her ear, and said to Benny, "There has been an explosion in Tel Aviv." And Benny responded without looking up, "Have you sent a photographer yet?"

On one occasion, our children were even responsible for a scoop. A few weeks after Israel's prime minister, Ariel Sharon, fell into a coma in 2006, he needed emergency surgery. Shortly after the operation began, rumors started to circulate that Sharon had died. I called Maya Rivkind, our weekend babysitter. Her father was a prominent Israeli surgeon, Dr. Avi Rivkind, who was operating on Sharon. As the nation waited to see whether he would survive, I asked Maya for her dad's cell phone number. I called, and Dr. Rivkind picked up on the first ring. He had just walked out of the operating theater and assured me that Sharon had survived. I had the news even before the hyper-competitive Israeli media did.

In such an intimate feud, we had access to a great many people. One day might bring an interview with an Israeli government minister, and the next day we might find ourselves in the home of a Hamas leader in Gaza. More than a dozen suicide bombings went off within a couple of miles of our home or office, and we were often at the scene only moments after the attack. The following day, one of us might be talking to the families of the victims, while the other would be interviewing the family of the Palestinian bomber. We were in Palestinian towns when Israeli tanks and helicopters carried out lethal strikes. Palestinian gunmen were always eager to talk, even if they insisted on wearing ski masks to conceal their identities. We spoke with Palestinian informants, or collaborators, who shared their secrets in helping the Israeli security forces track down Palestinians sought by Israel. We were in the blood-slicked hallways of hospital emergency rooms on both sides, and then there were the funerals; there were always more funerals.

The staggering history, the religious passions, and the daily dramas often merged into one grand epic. Sam Kiley, an excitable British reporter who was with the *Times* of London, once asked an Israeli about an incident a day earlier. "Well, you have to look back at several centuries of history," said the Israeli.

Sam, who never hesitated to speak his mind, cut off the interviewee. "We're not going back several centuries," Sam interjected. "We're not going back to 1948 or even 1967. We're going to talk about yesterday. What happened yesterday?"

No matter where you begin, the Israelis and the Palestinians were always willing to share their stories. As much as they fight, they love to talk even more. Everyone wanted to tell his or her story, and in a place with so much pain and history, these were almost always compelling tales. In all of our years in the Middle East, neither Israelis nor Palestinians ever said, "No comment."

American journalists are generally posted to Jerusalem for three or four years, and on such a grinding beat, most are ready to move on when their tour is up. We stayed more than seven years and left only with great reluctance. It was not an endurance test. We loved it and made many dear friends on both sides of the bitter divide.

We left Jerusalem as the fortieth anniversary of the 1967 war was approaching, and the newspaper headlines were painfully familiar. Israel's "Home Front Command to Get Public Ready for 'All-Out War,'" the *Jerusalem Post* reported. With a few tweaks, the newspaper stories from decades earlier were virtually interchangeable with the current ones. It was a sad way to leave, after arriving with so much optimism. During those years, we never discovered the solution to the conflict, but we were always gripped by it.

1

"GO TO THE TEMPLE MOUNT"

Ariel Sharon had no intention of setting foot on the Temple Mount. In the fall of 2000, the Israeli coalition government was teetering, and Sharon, the opposition leader, sensed an opportunity to speed up its collapse and position himself to be the next prime minister. It was the post he had long coveted, but it seemed beyond his reach, due to the many controversies that had swirled around him for decades. As Sharon plotted, he considered some modest gestures, such as a news conference near the Temple Mount, the most important and sensitive holy site in the region. It is revered by Jews, as well as by Muslims, who call it the Noble Sanctuary. Sharon's brief stroll to the shrine would be one of the most significant events in a decade of dramas that further entrenched one of the world's most enduring conflicts. Yet the spark for that walk came about in a casual, almost accidental way, the product of one brief transatlantic phone call with his best friend. That friend, Israeli journalist Uri Dan, happened to be one of the first people we had met when we arrived in Jerusalem a year earlier, in the fall of 1999.

In our early days in Jerusalem, Uri invested considerable time in trying to persuade us that everything we thought we knew about the Middle East was wrong. At that point, a full-fledged peace agreement between the Israelis and the Palestinians seemed within reach. Uri disputed this. There had been virtually no fighting for the previous three years, and violence between the two sides appeared to be fading into the past. Uri said it was not. And Sharon, Israel's most prominent hawk, looked to be in the twilight of his long and checkered career. On this last point, Uri was most adamant of all. Sharon, he insisted, was a man with a future.

A charming, dapper chain-smoker with an elfish grin and a perpetual tan, Uri built his long career on an allegiance to Sharon that bordered on religious faith. The bond between the two men was built on one unshakable belief. The Jews and the Arabs had been fighting for generations, and in the minds of these two men, no resolution was on the horizon. The year 2000 was perhaps the most hopeful time ever in the Israeli-Palestinian feud, but Uri Dan and Ariel Sharon saw no reason to be optimistic. As they viewed it, the Arabs had never genuinely accepted the presence of Israel, and it would be a grave and foolish risk to let Yasser Arafat lead an independent state of Palestine on Israel's borders. The Israeli men believed it was always dangerous to let your guard down when dealing with the Palestinians or the Arab world, and no document masquerading as a peace treaty was going to put to rest this long history of animosity. They accepted the conflict as a permanent feature of life in the Middle East, part of the world they were born into, and part of the world they would leave behind. Their goal was to steadily improve Israel's position in this endless struggle. Perhaps a solution would gradually emerge at some distant date, but they saw no point in entertaining that notion in their lifetime. In their minds—and in the minds of a fair number of Israelis and Palestinians—if you did not accept the enduring nature of the conflict, then you did not understand the conflict at all.

This idea, and their friendship, had a long history. Uri first encountered Sharon in 1954 when Uri was a nineteen-year-old correspondent for a military newspaper, and the future Israeli leader was a young lieutenant colonel commanding the secret paratrooper Unit 101, which carried out commando raids in the West Bank. Uri, a natural reporter even in his teens, tracked down the unit and showed up unannounced. Sharon was greatly annoyed that a journalist had pierced the secrecy surrounding the unit, and he grilled Uri about who had tipped him off, to no avail.

"Many years later Sharon told me that his friendship for me began that night, when I refused to reveal my sources. He liked that," Uri said.[1] Uri, in turn, was so enamored with Sharon's gift for leadership that he devoted his professional life to chronicling Sharon's every military and political battle for a half-century. Uri wrote three books about Sharon, defended him at times when he was a political pariah, and ceaselessly championed Sharon's hard-line views in columns that appeared in Israeli newspapers and the *New York Post*.

Because the *New York Post* and the Fox News Channel both belonged to Rupert Murdoch's media galaxy, Uri saw it as only natural that he should offer Jennifer his take on the mysteries of the Middle East. His analysis was always colored by his unwavering loyalty to Sharon. Yet his war stories were good ones, even if they were largely dramas from the past and came from a man so old-fashioned that he still composed his articles with a pen and a notepad.

Uri did not hesitate to remind us of his most famous remarks about Sharon, made initially in 1972, when Sharon was an army general who had been passed over for the position of army chief of staff. "Whoever doesn't want Sharon as chief of staff will get him as defense minister," Uri wrote in the Israeli newspaper *Maariv*. Sure enough, Sharon became defense minister nearly a decade later, although he was ultimately forced to resign for his role in orchestrating Israel's 1982 invasion of Lebanon, which targeted Arafat's Palestine Liberation Organization. A Lebanese Christian militia allied with Israel massacred hundreds of Palestinians in two refugee camps, Sabra and Shatila, near Beirut. This generated an international outcry and massive antiwar protests in Israel. Ultimately, an Israeli government inquiry found that Sharon bore indirect responsibility for not preventing the killings. Sharon's career was in ashes, and his many critics said he was finished as a politician. Yet Uri still saw a bright future and offered a second prophecy to complement the earlier one: "Whoever doesn't want Sharon as defense minister will get him as prime minister."

These remarks sounded dated, if not ridiculous, by the time Uri recounted them to us. Sharon was then seventy years old, a widower twice over, and was not exactly the picture of health as his waistline expanded with age. One reporter watched Sharon work his way through an entire tube of Pringles potato chips as they conducted an interview.[2] As one wag put it, Sharon managed to soldier on in the rough-and-tumble of Israeli politics because he was "psychosomatically healthy." He was still a war hero to some Israelis, but he had many more critics, and the prevailing Palestinian view was that he was the devil.

Uri was not shy in boasting about their friendship. Once, with Sharon sitting next to him, Uri told us how Sharon would often wrap up his sixteen-hour working days with an after-midnight phone call so they could rehash the crisis of the day. "Sometimes I fall asleep while he's still talking," Sharon chimed in. And when Sharon traveled, Uri was almost always part of the entourage, assuming the contradictory roles of journalist and confidant. Whenever Sharon met with foreign leaders, Uri was usually nearby and would pull out his pocket-size camera and snap a couple of quick photos. Then Uri would ask the host leader to sign the menu of the meal that he had shared with Sharon. This tradition carried on even after Sharon became prime minister. On trips to Washington, Sharon occasionally escorted Uri into the Oval Office and presented "my best friend" to President George W. Bush.

We had not been in Israel long when Uri arranged for Jennifer to interview Sharon. At the time, it was more a courtesy call than a news event. Sharon was not in great demand. Jennifer viewed it as an opportunity to stockpile material for a future piece on Sharon that might run when he retired, or perhaps even for his obituary. Sharon volunteered to come to the Fox office on Jaffa Street in Jerusalem. He patiently recounted familiar stories while sitting on a small, rickety metal chair that had never been intended for someone with his frame.

Sharon had rehabilitated himself politically since the Lebanon debacle nearly two decades earlier. His comeback included several cabinet posts, and by 1998, he was Israel's foreign minister. With great reluctance, he was forced to negotiate with his archrival Arafat in talks hosted by the United States at Wye River Plantation on Maryland's Eastern Shore. With considerable pressure from the Clinton administration, the bitter enemies reached a very limited interim deal, known as the Wye River Memorandum. Israel was to hand over security control to the Palestinians in several areas, and the Palestinians were to fight terrorism. As part of the process, there was talk of getting the sides together for a group handshake. In the carefully choreographed world of diplomacy, a handshake between Ariel Sharon and Yasser Arafat is about as sexy as it gets. Uri was nearby, having dinner at Legal Sea Foods in Washington, when he spoke by phone to Sharon. Uri asked Sharon whether he would actually allow himself to be photographed clasping hands with Arafat. "Shake the hand of that dog?" Sharon huffed. "Never."

The Wye River Memorandum happened. The handshake didn't.

Diplomacy marched on, and in the summer of 2000, Clinton invited Israeli prime minister Ehud Barak and Arafat for negotiations at Camp David, Maryland, in search of a comprehensive deal. These talks came nearly seven years after the sides had signed their first interim agreement, known as the Oslo Accords, which was sealed with a handshake between Arafat and Israeli prime minister Yitzhak Rabin on the lawn of the White House in September 1993. The agenda at Camp David included core issues that had divided the two sides for more than a half-century: the borders of the two states, the fate of Palestinian refugees, the prospect of dividing Jerusalem, as well as the question of sovereignty over Jerusalem's most contested religious site, the Temple Mount–Noble Sanctuary.

In a photo session at the beginning of the talks, Barak and Arafat played to the cameras as they prepared to enter the guest house in the wooded compound. Both men were overtly polite as they simultaneously reached the front door, extending their arms and trying to guide the other inside with body language that said, "No, I insist, you go first." Clinton cajoled and twisted arms as the delegations remained secluded at Camp David, where, two decades earlier, President Jimmy Carter had negotiated the historic peace agreement between Israel and Egypt. For the Israelis and the Palestinians, it was standard practice to leak the details of their negotiations every time one of the participants took a bathroom break. Yet this time, the parties were tight-lipped as they conducted the most detailed talks ever.

Sharon remained in Israel as the talks took place. As the opposition leader in parliament, he was generally ignored by the media. Still, he told anyone willing to listen that a peace agreement with the Palestinians was rash and unrealistic and would leave Israel far less secure.

When the Israelis and the Palestinians emerged from Camp David after two weeks of talks, they were closer to a deal than they had ever been, but each side said that the other had stopped a few steps short. Almost immediately, the recriminations began. Barak and the Israelis described their offer as "extremely generous" and believed it was rejected because that was the instinctive Palestinian response to all Israeli offers. For many Israelis, the Palestinians had once again fulfilled Israeli statesman Abba Eban's aphorism: "The Arabs never miss an opportunity to miss an opportunity."

Barak did not hesitate to lambaste Arafat. "At Camp David, Mr. Arafat well understood that the moment of truth had come and that painful decisions needed to be made by both sides. He failed this challenge," Barak wrote. "At the deepest level Arafat does not accept the . . . right of the State of Israel to exist as a Jewish state."

Arafat and the rest of the Palestinian leadership said that Israel failed to address essential Palestinian needs and that the proposal would not have given the Palestinians a viable state. He argued that the Palestinian territory in the West Bank would not have been contiguous, that the Palestinians would not have full sovereignty in East Jerusalem, and that the proposal did not sufficiently address the status of millions of Palestinian refugees. Arafat said that if he had accepted the terms, he would have suffered the same fate as Yitzhak Rabin, who was assassinated by a Jewish ultranationalist in 1995, just two years after he signed the interim peace deal with Arafat. "If I will betray [my people], no doubt [some]one will come to kill me," Arafat said.[3]

Barak's peace offer at Camp David was not in writing, and the two sides had different interpretations afterward. Yet participants said it was clear that the Israeli leader was offering a compromise on the Temple Mount–Noble Sanctuary. For religious Jews, relinquishing control of Judaism's holiest site was sacrilege, and for ardent nationalists such as Sharon, it was tantamount to treason.

Sharon and his supporters held press conferences and issued statements arguing that such a deal would be a disaster for Israel. Yet Sharon was largely ignored. Uri suggested that Sharon might be able to attract more attention if he held a weekly news conference in the cobblestone plaza facing the Western Wall. The retaining wall had been part of the Second Temple in King Herod's Jerusalem. Ever since the temple's destruction by the Romans in 70 CE, this one surviving wall, on the western side of the compound, has been the holiest place for Jewish prayer. Sharon took note of his friend's idea but did not immediately act on it.

Despite the failure at Camp David, Israeli and Palestinian negotiators continued to meet, holding secret sessions during August and September. The talks were held even though Barak's coalition government was increasingly shaky. Sharon was already anticipating its demise, and in September he traveled to New York to express his deep misgivings about the Camp David negotiations to Jewish leaders in the United States. Such trips to the United States are part of a regular pilgrimage for Israeli politicians of all parties.

While in New York, Sharon was already charting his next moves. Sharon called Uri for one of their daily chats and reached Uri as he was traveling in a car with a fellow Israeli journalist on their way to dinner in Jerusalem. They took Sharon's call on the car's speaker phone. Sharon had finally warmed to Uri's idea from a few weeks earlier. "When I get back, I plan to hold a press conference at the Wall," Sharon said, referring to the Western Wall.

This should have pleased Uri, but he and his colleague had moved on and upped the ante. "No, no, no, Arik," Uri said, referring to Sharon as he was universally known in Israel. "That's not enough. You must go all the way to the Temple Mount." Uri and his colleague then proceeded to make their case for Sharon to take the far more dramatic step of going to the Temple Mount.

Sharon was not a religious man, and Israeli politicians had long steered clear of the shrine because it is such an explosive site. The sensitivity is both political and religious. In political terms, any visit by an Israeli politician is sure to inflame Muslims. In religious terms, most rabbis say that it is forbidden for Jews to ascend the Temple Mount, due to the possibility they will inadvertently tread atop the "holy of holies." This was the inner sanctuary in each of the ancient Jewish temples that was reserved for special visits by the high priest. Yet if Sharon visited, he would surely attract extensive media coverage and could convey several messages simultaneously. He could show the depth of his opposition to Barak's Camp David proposal, burnish his reputation as Israel's leading security hawk, and restate Israel's claim that Jerusalem—all of Jerusalem—belonged to the Jewish people.

An Ariel Sharon press conference at the Western Wall plaza, where thousands of Jews pray daily, might have drawn a bit of media attention. Most likely, it would have been a one-day story that would have appeared on the evening television news and merited a modest mention buried inside newspapers the next day.

Uri's provocative suggestion had the potential, however, to thrust Sharon back into the center of the debate. It would be a major drama for Sharon to take a few extra steps and lumber up the wooden walkway from the Western Wall plaza to the Temple Mount–Noble Sanctuary above. The thirty-five-acre religious shrine, with its paved stones and soaring cypress trees, rises above Jerusalem. It hosts two seventh-century shrines: the iconic Dome of the Rock, with its golden top, and the much larger, if less spectacular, Al Aksa Mosque. Muslims believe this was the place where the Prophet Muhammad ascended to heaven on a winged steed. These two shrines are also built on top of the ruins of the Jewish temples. This is the most bitterly contested piece of real estate in the entire Israeli-Palestinian conflict.

Israel has claimed sovereignty over the site since capturing it in the 1967 Arab-Israeli war. Israelis stunned themselves by taking it, and Muslims were equally shocked that they had lost it. Israelis had been denied access to the site since the 1948 Arab-Israeli war that divided Jerusalem, and its return to Israeli hands was seen as a modern miracle. Yet even in that euphoric moment in 1967, Israel's leaders understood that Jewish control of the holy site would be a major source of conflict. The Second Temple had been destroyed nearly two thousand years earlier, and the Islamic holy sites had been in place for thirteen hundred years. Israel could declare the site its own and allow worshippers to pray at the Western Wall. Yet any action on the Temple Mount–Noble Sanctuary itself would be seen by Muslims as a desecration. The Israelis grasped this and kept a Muslim religious trust, the Wakf, in charge of the site on a day-to-day basis. The vast majority of daily visitors have always been Palestinian Muslims. Israel still claims sovereignty, however, and it will be incredibly difficult for any Israeli leader to relinquish this claim over Judaism's holiest site. Israeli police have always been on duty at the entrances and the exits and are often present on the grounds as well. Foreign tourists and Israeli Jews are allowed to visit but are strictly instructed not to interfere with the Muslim worshippers. Any Jews who begin to pray are quickly escorted away by Israeli police.

Several days before Sharon's planned visit, Barak invited Arafat to his private home in the small Israeli community of Kochav Yair, northeast of Tel Aviv. Given the hostility of the last decade, it may be difficult to comprehend how dramatically different the atmosphere was in 2000. Arafat was driven to Barak's home for an extended talk on the most sensitive issues, and it barely raised an eyebrow. The venue was unusual. Direct talks between Barak and Arafat were relatively rare, and the meeting was not announced in advance. Still, Israeli and Palestinian negotiators met so often that it was no big deal when word of the meeting came out afterward. Along with their aides, Barak and Arafat talked late into the night in an attempt to work through issues that had stymied them at Camp David.

It was not a formal negotiating session, and Barak, the decorated Israeli general, and Arafat, the lifelong revolutionary, never had a warm relationship. Yet those present said it was by far the most relaxed meeting the two men ever had. Two months earlier at Camp David, they had barely conversed. During the dinner, the Israeli leader placed a call to President Clinton to say how well the discussion was going. With Arafat close enough to hear Barak's side of the call, the Israeli leader told Clinton that "I'm going to be the partner of this man even more so than Rabin."[4]

For the Palestinians, the one sour note of the evening was Sharon's impending trip to the religious shrine. Arafat went with Barak onto his balcony and urged the Israeli leader to prevent Sharon's visit on the grounds that it would inflame the Palestinians. "I told Bill Clinton, I told the European Union, I told the Vatican, I told the Arabs, I told Barak himself in his house, we were in his house, 'please don't let Sharon go there,'" Arafat said later.[5]

Barak did not envision Sharon's visit causing an uproar and declined to intervene. Barak saw it as an internal Israeli political matter. From his perspective, Sharon's goal was to solidify his hold on the Likud Party in the face of a potential challenge by Benjamin Netanyahu, who was returning to Israel after spending a year in the United States.

The disagreement did not spoil the night. When Arafat left, he kissed Barak on both cheeks, something he had not done before, according to participants. Reflecting the upbeat mood, the two sides agreed to send negotiators to Washington for further talks with the Clinton administration, which was revising proposals made at Camp David.

The Palestinians made several additional pleas to block the visit. Saeb Erekat, the chief Palestinian negotiator, said that he warned Shlomo Ben-Ami, Israel's acting foreign minister, about the potential consequences. Jibril Rajoub, the senior Palestinian security chief in the West Bank, told the *Jerusalem Post* that "the visit is a provocation which will trigger bloodshed and confrontation. . . . Sharon is putting oil on fire."

On Thursday, September 28, 2000, Sharon, dressed in a dark suit and wearing wraparound sunglasses, trudged up the wooden walkway to the Temple Mount, surrounded by hundreds of members of the Israeli security forces with the same wraparound shades. Jennifer and her TV crew were nearby.

I was several months pregnant with our first child and was feeling woozy. Journalists were not allowed to follow Sharon up to the shrine, and while I waited, I felt increasingly unsteady in the heat and noise that surrounded Sharon's tense walkabout. In between filming stand-ups with my crew, I had to sit down repeatedly to catch my breath.

On top of the Temple Mount–Noble Sanctuary, Sharon strolled around the expansive grounds. He did not enter either of the two Muslim religious shrines and was largely lost in a sea of security guards. On the fringes, angry Palestinians and the Israeli police exchanged shoves. Soon the Palestinians began hurling stones from the top of the platform down toward Jewish worshippers below. Sharon did not linger. He made his point and exited on the same wooden walkway he entered. I, meanwhile, found myself spending most of my time doubled over—partly from morning sickness, partly as cover from the hail of Palestinian stones.

The next day at the traditional Friday prayers, Palestinian preachers worked the already agitated worshippers into a frenzy. The young men stormed out of the mosque and immediately started to throw rocks, chairs, and any other objects that were not nailed down. Israeli riot police, standing shoulder to shoulder behind their clear fiberglass shields, confronted the Palestinians just outside the shrines and fired back with tear gas, rubber bullets, and, eventually, live fire. As the Palestinian mob spread across the grounds of the shrine in several directions, young men rained down rocks on the Jewish worshippers at the Western Wall. I was wearing a flak jacket over my expanding belly and was again nearby in the Old City with my crew. We navigated our way through the narrow streets, taking cover in side alleys and door wells. The threats included Israeli tear gas and rubber bullets, Palestinian stones, and piles of trash that had been set aflame by the rioters.

The Palestinians and the Israeli police battled for hours, and the fighting on the Temple Mount–Noble Sanctuary and surrounding areas left seven Palestinians dead and about two hundred injured. The fighting instantly spread to the West Bank and Gaza. Israeli and Palestinian policemen, who had been carrying out joint patrols for years, suddenly began shooting at one another. Multiple battles erupted daily. The stone throwing and the gun battles soon escalated into Palestinian car bombings and Israeli helicopter strikes. The Palestinian uprising was launched.

Uri Dan's final book, *Ariel Sharon: An Intimate Portrait*, was published shortly after Sharon fell into a coma in January 2006. Uri wrote of Sharon's excursion to the Temple Mount but made only a brief, veiled reference to his part in encouraging it. Uri wrote that a day after the visit, Sharon's son, Omri, "shot angry looks at me. I suppose he thought that I was the instigator of the visit to the Temple Mount. The fact is that Ariel Sharon made his decision alone."

Yet later that year, Uri proudly recounted his role in Sharon's visit to us shortly before he died of lung cancer in December 2006, at age seventy-one. The Israeli journalist who was in the car and who participated in the conversation with Uri and Sharon also confirmed the episode, although he asked not to be named. In Uri's mind, he had helped persuade Sharon that dramatic action was needed at a crucial moment. And to Uri's way of thinking, the Palestinian response to Sharon's visit unmasked their true intentions and showed that the Palestinians could not be trusted to make peace.

If Sharon had not walked up the ramp to the Temple Mount, would the last decade have been fundamentally different? Perhaps the peace talks would have continued in an environment that was not so overheated, and a breakthrough could have been reached.

Maybe Sharon never would have become prime minister, a less confrontational atmosphere would have prevailed, and the Palestinian uprising could have been avoided or at least contained.

Yet there is an equally strong case suggesting that the Israelis and the Palestinians would not have reached an agreement, no matter how tranquil the atmosphere. Seven years of negotiations had already taken place. The Palestinians had not received the statehood they expected. Their frustration was at the boiling point before Sharon took his walk, and if that episode had not led to the uprising, something else easily could have.

The Israelis and the Palestinians always have competing narratives, and Sharon's visit was a classic example of how these very different interpretations of events fuel the conflict. For Palestinians, Sharon had been a reviled figure for nearly a half-century, and he was directly challenging the Muslim claim of sovereignty over the third holiest site in Islam. Given this bitter history, combined with the place and the timing of his visit, Sharon skillfully pressed the Palestinian hot buttons, producing a highly charged response that could not be easily contained. Sharon's visit was an extreme provocation and generated an outpouring of anger. To this day, many Palestinians believe the uprising could have been avoided if Sharon had stayed away from the holy site and if the Israelis had made additional concessions at the peace talks.

Yet many Israelis believe that the Palestinian uprising was not only inevitable but was planned by Arafat and the Palestinian leadership as a way to pressure the Israelis in the negotiations. Even Israelis who disagreed with Sharon's visit defended his right to make it. For decades, foreign tourists and Israelis had visited the Noble Sanctuary on a daily basis without incident. How come, they asked, the Palestinians could not tolerate one brief visit by Sharon?

"I was reading intelligence reports from early 2000 that said Arafat was going to use violence if he didn't get what he wanted," said Chuck Freilich, a senior member of Israel's National Security Council from 2000 to 2005 and later a lecturer at Harvard University's John F. Kennedy School of Government. "I think it goes back to the fact that Arafat wanted a peace process, not a peace agreement. When he had to make hard choices, he turned to violence."

Ami Ayalon, who had completed a five-year term as head of the Shin Bet security service, Israel's equivalent of the FBI, shortly before the uprising, had a very different take. "Yasser Arafat neither

prepared nor triggered the intifada. The explosion was spontane-
ous against Israel, as all hope for the end of occupation disappeared,
and against the Palestinian Authority, its corruption, its impotence.
Arafat could not repress it," he said.

The first Palestinian intifada, from 1987 to 1993, was universally viewed by Palestinians as a success. Those street protests,
marked primarily by stone-throwing clashes, gave the Palestinians
a renewed sense of pride, brought the Israelis to the negotiating
table, and led to the Oslo Accords. Given that history, Arafat and the
movement he led for decades, Fatah, were proud to embrace the
second intifada and claim after-the-fact sponsorship. "The Fatah
movement is proud of launching the intifada and leading it," said
Marwan Barghouti, the Fatah leader in the West Bank who was the
most prominent figure at street protests during the early days of
the uprising. "The intifada expresses the will of the masses. It did
not begin with an order and will not end with an order."[6]

Sharon's visit and the ensuing violence did not immediately tor-
pedo the negotiations. The Israelis and the Palestinians continued
to talk for another four months, even as the fighting intensified and
Barak's coalition government disintegrated. From the perspective
of Arafat and the Palestinians, rejecting the Camp David proposal
and embracing the uprising seemed to make sense, at least initially.
Barak responded by sweetening the offer he had made at Camp
David. Arafat and many of his fellow Palestinians believed that time
and the tide of history were on their side, and the intifada was a way
to speed up the process.

Yet Arafat's approach was not sustainable. It was a mistake that
both sides have often made over the years, opting for short-term
tactics that seem to provide temporary advantage, at the expense
of a long-term strategy dedicated to resolving the conflict. The
improved Israeli offer had more to do with the desperation of
Barak and Clinton, both of whom badly wanted an agreement as
their days in power dwindled. Once they were gone, Arafat would
have to deal with their replacements, who had no interest in negotiating with him.

Sharon, meanwhile, was suddenly unstoppable. He had been
considered unelectable ever since 1982, when he led Israel into
the quagmire of Lebanon, pursuing Arafat all the way to Beirut.
Sharon's obsession with Arafat had been his downfall. Now, in a
supreme irony, Arafat's backing of the Palestinian uprising elevated

Sharon to new heights in the eyes of Israelis. Sharon won a land-slide election victory over Barak on February 6, 2001, barely four months after the Temple Mount visit undertaken at the prodding of Uri Dan. Just as Uri had predicted, Israelis turned to Sharon when they felt threatened.

"The Jews were awakened by the bombs, and they looked around and said, 'Who will save us?'" Uri said. "Let's have a man like [Sharon] leading the war against Arafat and his terrorism. Yasser Arafat made Sharon the prime minister of Israel."

For decades, Sharon demonstrated an extraordinary ability to influence the Israeli-Arab conflict. He often managed through the sheer force of will. Time and again, his actions and their impact greatly exceeded his authority. In the 1973 Mideast War, his command of Israeli forces in the Sinai Peninsula helped turn the tide of that war after Israel was caught off-guard by the Egyptian and Syrian invasion. In the 1982 Lebanon war, he unleashed a massive military operation as defense minister before others in the Israeli government realized the full extent of his plans. And for years, he was the engine for settlement building in the West Bank and the Gaza Strip, often proceeding without government approval. Sharon's Temple Mount excursion followed in the same tradition, setting off a remarkable chain of events that continue to shape the conflict.

In the months and years that followed, both Israelis and Palestinians would opt for hard-line leaders over moderates, making a resolution of the conflict ever more difficult. As the fighting intensified and positions hardened, the battles would take on a perverse logic of their own. Palestinian suicide bombings terrorized Israel but ultimately undermined the Palestinian cause. The Israelis conducted massive military operations that subdued Palestinian militants but also inflicted widespread civilian casualties and harmed Israel's international standing. Both sides would greatly overestimate what they could achieve. The Palestinians believed the uprising would take them on the path to statehood, only to find that it set them back. The Israelis would repeatedly bump up against the limits of their military power, crushing the Palestinian uprising only to find themselves dragged down by the same unresolved political problems.

Perhaps the most important legacy of Sharon's Temple Mount excursion was in demonstrating how swiftly Israeli-Palestinian peace efforts could be undermined and how difficult it is to restart them. It took the Israelis and the Palestinians fifty years to hold full-fledged negotiations on the conflict's core issues. With just a little nudge from his good friend Uri Dan, Sharon took a short walk to the most combustible place in the Middle East, lighting a fire that would burn for years.

2

PREPARING FOR WAR

When I gave birth to our two daughters at the Hadassah Mount Scopus hospital in the eastern part of Jerusalem, we could not help but notice a jarring paradox on both occasions. First, Arabs and Jews mix easily in Israeli hospitals. No matter how tense the streets, hospitals were one of the few places, and at times the only place, where all were welcome. In April 2001, just two days before the arrival of our first girl, Annalise, the violence was raging, and I went to the West Bank city of Ramallah to interview the family of a Palestinian suicide bomber. I sensed the baby was on its way, but I wanted to finish this one last story. On my way home, I felt the weight of every step as I waited in line with Palestinians to cross an Israeli military checkpoint and return to Jerusalem.

The next day, I filed my report. Then I called our handyman to put the last touches on the nursery as my nesting instinct kicked in. A day later, the conflict seemed to melt away as we stepped inside the hospital that overlooked Jerusalem's Old City. It was in a Jewish neighborhood surrounded by Palestinian ones, and a sign at the hospital entrance told patients and visitors to hand over their weapons. There was an armed guard manning a metal detector to make sure they did. The guards also checked for any signs of sandwiches and unleavened bread because it was Passover and the hospital was kosher.

Everyone seemed to check their hostilities at the door as well. Walking the halls, we heard almost as much Arabic as we did Hebrew. In the nursery, Muhammad and Moshe were both popular names for newborns. Annalise was a pale, bald infant and was impossible to miss in a crowded nursery that featured a sea of olive-skinned babies, most sporting thick manes of black hair, and some already in urgent need of a haircut. The Jewish and Arab children were indistinguishable. We had no idea how the parents could locate their own without checking the wrist bracelets. If you could replicate the atmosphere in Israeli hospitals, Arabs and Jews would have made peace decades ago.

Yet when we were in the hospital for the birth of Amelia, in December 2002, reality bit before we made it out the door. Like all parents in Israel, whether Muslim or Jew, Christian or Druze, we received a certificate good for one free protective tent designed to keep an infant safe during a chemical or biological weapons attack. Adults and older children have government-issued gas masks, but the masks are too frightening for an uncomprehending newborn, who would feel the sensation of suffocation. So the infants get tiny, airtight tents that look as if they were made for a Barbie doll camping expedition. Welcome to life in Israel. It is no exaggeration to say that on the day you are born, you begin to prepare for war.

This was a sad commentary on life in the Middle East—but not so sad that we actually bothered to pick up the free tent, courtesy of the Israeli government. Covering the daily bloodletting and raising two small children stretched us to the limit. It was hard enough meeting our daily deadlines and keeping our house stocked with Pampers. Suicide bombs and diaper rash were both clear and present dangers. A chemical weapons attack felt vague and theoretical.

That changed soon enough. By the time Amelia was two months old, the U.S. invasion of Iraq was imminent. While most of the world opposed the U.S. war plan, the vast majority of Israelis backed it, even though it rekindled terrible memories. During the first Gulf War in 1991, Iraq had fired thirty-nine Scud missiles into Israel, sowing panic and inflicting dozens of injuries. The great fear in 2003 was that a desperate Saddam Hussein would unleash a new barrage of Scuds, this time laced with the biological or chemical weapons he was presumed to be hiding.

Soon Israelis were standing in long lines to receive new gas masks and baby tents. Hardware stores were filled with Israelis sweeping the shelves clean of duct tape, plastic sheeting, jerricans, flashlights, and other essentials needed for hermetically sealed "safe rooms" in their homes.

In schools, teachers sought to ease anxieties with practice drills that herded small children into the "popcorn room," a secure, sealed room made child-friendly with snacks, videos, and a comforting name.

On Israeli television, children's programs featured puppets wearing gas masks. For adults, news programs answered queries such as whether it was safe for a mother to breast-feed when wearing a gas mask. The answer: no, because the baby would not be protected. Many Israelis began to carry their gas masks everywhere. Even on my short trip to work, I had my mask dangling from one shoulder and my trusty Medela breast pump slung over the other.

Greg was more cavalier. Living in Jerusalem, he felt that we had immunity. Saddam's Scuds were so wildly inaccurate that targeting Jerusalem meant any one of the city's Arab neighborhoods or Islamic holy sites was just as likely to be hit as an Israeli apartment complex. In 1991, Saddam had directed his fire at Israel's coastal cities, such as Tel Aviv, but spared Jerusalem, presumably for this reason.

Greg's office gave him a gas mask, however, just as mine had done. This put us in the awkward position of having masks for ourselves but no protection for our daughters or our babysitter, Rose Espanol. Guilt quickly got the best of us, and in short order, Greg joined the long lines to pick up gear for the entire family.

As the war in Iraq unfolded, the Israeli fears were never realized. Saddam did not fire any missiles at Israel before he fled the Presidential Palace in Baghdad in the spring of 2003. Yet the episode was another reminder of the ceaseless threats Israel has faced since the country's founding and that continue to shape the national character. Israelis have learned to cope with the possibility of war the way Californians deal with earthquakes or Floridians handle hurricanes. You just learn to live with the threat because otherwise you would be paralyzed.

3

THERE WILL BE A BOMB

We knew a Palestinian suicide bomber was on his way. We did not have any inside information, nor did we need any. It was Saturday, March 9, 2002, and the violence had become so intense and the bombings so frequent, we were certain a young Palestinian man with a bomb vest strapped to his chest would be headed toward an Israeli city at any moment, if he was not already on the way. The only real question was whether the Israeli security forces would stop him before he could find a crowd and flip his detonator switch.

We were exhausted from working around the clock and on this rare day off chose to do absolutely nothing. The daylight hours on Saturday were as close as we could get to a respite. With Israel observing the Sabbath, the country was shut down, and there were few targets for armed Palestinians. Yet a grim pattern had developed. When the sun set on Saturday, marking the end of Shabbat, Israelis immediately returned to the streets. Shops and restaurants reopened. And a Palestinian attack was virtually guaranteed.

Because Jerusalem was bombed more than any other city, this greatly discouraged our going any place where crowds gathered. We also knew that any attempt at a Saturday night diversion would likely be interrupted by a phone call bringing news of an attack that would put us to work. Even on occasions when we ventured out for dinner or a movie, we kept an iron grip on our cell phones. We did not dare set them on the vibrate mode and risk missing an urgent call.

It was a terrible feeling, sitting at home and knowing that something awful was going to happen. Yet we stayed in our apartment on Marcus Street that night with our daughter Annalise, who was approaching her first birthday. By ten o'clock, she was asleep, and it was looking like a blissfully uneventful evening.

At the same time, twenty-seven-year-old Sharona Rihani and several of her girlfriends entered the Moment Café, a popular hangout for young Israelis that was two blocks from our apartment and just across the street from the prime minister's official residence, Agion House. The Moment Café was a self-consciously hip place that seemed more in tune with young, modern, and secular Tel Aviv than with ancient, traditional, and religious Jerusalem. The café was on Gaza Street, and one advertising flyer offered discounted drinks for "residents of the Gaza Strip and environs," although it was doubtful that an actual Palestinian from Gaza had ever set foot in the place. On one occasion, the restaurant sent out party invitations that featured a graphic with a bomb and a lit fuse. Underneath it read, "The Moment you've all been waiting for." Even in the worst of times, many young Israelis coped by turning to gallows humor.

Rihani and her friends had spent the day at the beach, one of the few public places considered reasonably safe. On the way back to Jerusalem in the evening, the women decided to have dinner and drinks. As they reached the Moment Café, a security guard searched their purses for weapons. Rihani told the guard, "Please check all the people and all the bags. I don't want to die this evening." The café was tiny and packed, and several women squeezed around one table, while Rihani and two others went to the bar. They ordered drinks and were just settling in when Rihani dropped some things from her purse. She bent down to pick them up, unaware of the enormous significance of this small act.

The security guard had ignored Rihani's advice and stepped away for a moment. At that instant, suicide bomber Fuad Horani of Hamas reached the entrance to the café, stepped inside, and detonated the explosives wrapped around his torso. Everyone in the restaurant was thrown violently to the floor. Tables and chairs were hurled about, glass rained down on the victims. The bomb ripped out the ceiling, leaving behind dangling wires. The café instantly filled with thick black smoke. Rihani was so stunned, she was not aware of her own serious wounds. "I didn't feel anything," she said.

At our home, the thunderclap shook our second-floor apartment, rattling the windows and rolling over the entire building like a tsunami. Greg and I stopped in our tracks. Before the reverberations stopped, we knew precisely what had happened. The sirens were immediate. The commotion woke Annalise, who began to cry. Our cell phones began ringing. We passed our daughter back and forth as we both tried to start working. It was a drill we knew too well. While we were still scrambling around our apartment, we heard the front door to the building slam shut. It was Yoram Cohen, our upstairs neighbor and the owner of the Moment Café. He somehow knew it was his café that had been bombed, and he sprinted down the street to get there. I grabbed my cell phone and headed in the same direction to meet up with my crew. The satellite truck was on its way, and I needed to get to the scene. I ran all the way there. With Annalise wailing, Greg turned on his computer and called the Israeli police to begin piecing together the initial details and filing a series of urgent one-sentence bulletins for the Associated Press, his employer at the time.

Amid the bedlam inside the café, Rihani struggled to escape. "I crawled out, and I went between the bodies on the floor," she said. "My only thought was how to get out of the place." Choking on the smoke and bumping into bodies and furniture in the dark, Rihani made it to the sidewalk on her hands and knees. With sirens screaming and blue police lights flashing, rescuers descended on the café by the dozen. They reached Rihani and placed her in the back of an ambulance. Only then did she become aware of the gashes to her legs and shoulders. She was bleeding profusely and soon passed out, with no knowledge of the full carnage. Later, when she regained consciousness at Shaare Tzedek Hospital, she learned the horror: eleven people had been killed, including five of her girlfriends.

The two women standing at the bar with Rihani were killed instantly, although their bodies showed no sign of injuries. No shrapnel or other objects had pierced their skin. The two women apparently died from internal injuries caused by the sheer force of the shock waves, something that often happened when a suicide bomber detonated in an enclosed space, such as a small café or a bus. Israeli doctors said the intensity of the explosions caused the vital organs of the victims to rupture or collapse. Rihani could have easily suffered the same fate, but she believed she was partially shielded because she was bending down to recover the contents of her purse.

After so many bombings, a choreographed chaos unfolded instantly, not only at the café, but throughout Israel and the West Bank. The converging ambulances and police cars drowned out the moaning and shrieking of the stunned and bloodied survivors. The screams died down, but the crowd grew. We always worried about a second bomb being set off as the crowd gathered. Police cordoned off the streets with yellow tape in a futile attempt to keep back news crews. Television news vans, including mine, were usually at the scene within minutes. Yet on this night, I had difficulty locating my colleagues because the streets were so packed. Eventually, my cameraman Yaniv Turgeman found me.

Greg and I both tried calling our babysitter, Rose, but the mobile phone lines were jammed. As was often the case, the country's cell phone circuits crashed under the load of Israelis frantically calling relatives and friends to see whether they were alright. Yet Rose was so well schooled in this horrible drill that she knew exactly what to do. The Moment Café bombing took place between our apartment and hers, which was just a few blocks away, on King George V Street. She ran toward our apartment, but as she neared the bomb site, an Israeli policeman grabbed her by the arm. The policemen detained her momentarily but let her go, concluding that a middle-age Filipina was probably not involved.

Nearby, white sheets were placed over the dead, while the wounded were whisked to several Jerusalem hospitals. The commingled smells of smoke, chemical explosives, and burned flesh saturated the cool Jerusalem night air. The Israeli police and the Shin Bet security service immediately searched for forensic evidence, with shards of glass crunching beneath their every step. Mixed in among them were middle-age Jewish volunteers who were a fixture at every bombing. Jewish religious law mandates the burial of every body in its entirety, and the volunteers of ZAKA, a Hebrew acronym for Disaster Victim Identification, collected slivers of human flesh and drops of spilled blood, which they placed in small plastic bags. The ZAKA volunteers, most of them with thick gray beards and fluorescent lime vests, dropped to their knees to pick through ruined restaurants, outdoor food markets, and crumpled buses, systematically covering every inch in the blast zone. They even climbed into trees, where the branches had been denuded of leaves by the explosion, but which had snared scraps of human remains that were hurled skyward.

The frenetic energy radiated out from the bomb site. The emergency room at Shaare Tzedek Hospital and other hospitals in Jerusalem buzzed as the staffs treated more than fifty wounded on this night. On the outskirts of Tel Aviv, an hour from Jerusalem by car, Israel's lone forensic institute, the National Center for Forensic Medicine, kicked into overdrive. After every bombing, the staff worked through the night to identify the dead, many of whom had been maimed beyond recognition, and match up dozens, if not hundreds, of body parts.

The Palestinian group responsible for the bombing usually boasted of its responsibility within minutes of the blast, and the Islamist faction Hamas claimed this one. Often the groups filmed a statement by the bomber shortly before his attack. The video would be handed out to news organizations, but word of mouth spread the bomber's identity at the speed of light through the Palestinian territories. Crowds immediately gathered at the family home, and candy was occasionally passed out as well-wishers expressed support to the family of the "martyr." This routine changed abruptly, however, when Israel temporarily revived an old practice of tearing down the homes of Palestinian attackers. Instead of the festive air resembling a street party, the bomber's family would scramble to borrow a truck and urgently pack the family belongings, including the furniture, knowing the Israeli forces could arrive at any moment to demolish the home and everything inside.

In the aftermath of a bombing, the Palestinian leadership under Yasser Arafat issued brief statements condemning the killing of all civilians but did not act against the individuals or the groups involved. In Israel, the government and the security forces held emergency meetings to plan a response, which could range from a warning to a coordinated air strike and ground raid by the military.

Although Jerusalem was bombed regularly and cafés were a frequent target, the Moment Café had seemed comparatively safe. It was not on one of the main downtown thoroughfares where the bombers struck most often. The café was clustered with several other shops, but it was in a predominantly residential area, making it an unlikely target. In addition, the café had a security guard, although he had been absent at the crucial moment. Most significantly, the café was catty-corner from the prime minister's residence, meaning that neighborhood security was extremely heavy. "I'm going to the safest place in the city, right across from the prime minister's house," Livnat Dvash, twenty-eight, had told her mother, who asked her daughter not to go out that night because she thought it was too dangerous. Dvash was among those killed.[1]

The story never ends with the bombing. The next day brings funerals, because Jewish law requires immediate burial. Then there are witness accounts of the random acts that spared some lives and claimed others. Perhaps weeks or even months later, Israel will track down and capture or kill the Palestinians who orchestrated the bombing. In this case, Abdullah Barghouti of Hamas was arrested and then convicted two years later, in 2004, for organizing the Moment Café bombing and several other deadly attacks in Jerusalem. Overall, he was found guilty and sentenced to life in prison for planning six suicide bombings that killed sixty-six people and wounded hundreds.

More time would pass, and another remarkable story would emerge.

The day after the bombing, with Rihani still sedated, a visitor came to her hospital bed bearing flowers. His name was Sharon Barashi, and it was the first time they met face-to-face. Barashi, a car salesman, had recently sold Rihani's father a Volkswagen Passat. Rihani assisted her father with the paperwork and had spoken to Barashi several times by phone. On the night of the bombing, Barashi, who lived near the Moment Café, heard the explosion and the ambulances rushing to the scene. Later, he was watching television as survivors were interviewed at the hospital. As one woman spoke, he recognized the voice as Rihani's and caught a fleeting glimpse of her.

Barashi called Rihani's father to ask about her condition and followed up with a hospital visit the next day. As Rihani began a long, painful recuperation that involved multiple surgeries and frequent counseling, the two had no additional contact. Four months after the bombing, though, and long after Rihani had been released from the hospital, she called Barashi. They began dating. A year later they were married. They soon had two children, a boy and a girl, and moved to a Jerusalem suburb. Rihani continued to work for a government ministry, where she had been employed before the bombing. Her husband got a new job selling Mercedes-Benzes in Jerusalem, and they lived a typical middle-class Israeli existence.

Yet the bombing was still with Rihani every day. Despite the surgeries, a tiny piece of shrapnel remained lodged in her hip, too small and difficult to remove, although it caused her pain. She underwent years of counseling but still had nightmares of the bombing. The memories remained so vivid that she rarely went to restaurants, parties, or other social events, which often triggered flashbacks. Even a casual walk at night could be unsettling, her husband told me.

I contacted Barashi in the spring of 2007, five years after the bombing. He initially said that he and his wife would talk to me at their home, but in several subsequent conversations, he kept putting me off. He finally acknowledged that the bombing was still too traumatic for his wife to discuss. He graciously agreed to speak to me, and we had several conversations, but only when he was at work and away from his wife. "She deals with it, but it is not easy," said Barashi. "Anything can bring back the terrible memories."

4

"HAMAS DOESN'T NEED TO RECRUIT"

We thought we had heard every possible rationalization for Palestinian suicide bombings, none of them persuasive. Yet a wizened old man with a long white beard and an even longer view of history urged us to reconsider. "Take these suicide bombers," he began. "People call them irrational. I don't think they're irrational. They're ideologically motivated people who are willing to sacrifice their lives for a goal they consider of paramount importance. There's nothing irrational about this. They're rational. You see, sometimes people look irrational, but actually, they are effectively pursuing a goal."

How could that be, when decades of violence had consistently harmed the Palestinian cause? Israel could always hit back harder, and much of the world, particularly the West, considered suicide attacks indefensible. The old man was insistent and eloquent. Israel was becoming soft and middle-class, he explained, and its will to fight was eroding. Israel was willing to consider a range of concessions in hopes of putting the conflict to rest. The Israelis were looking for "peace now," he said, playing off the liberal Israeli group of the same name. The Palestinians wanted total victory in the future.

"Everybody's out to make as many bucks as possible and live well and play on the golf course," the old man said dismissively of Israeli society. In contrast, the Palestinians were looking to pocket concessions now and continue fighting for more with each new generation. "The Palestinians are doing fine. They're doing great. They will win out in the end," the old man argued. "They are very, very stubborn, and they have a very long horizon, and they are saying, 'OK, these [Jewish] people are here for a few dozen years, but maybe after 100, 150, 200 years, they'll be gone.'"

The old man was not a Muslim sheik brandishing the Koran and preaching the virtues of martyrdom. He was Professor Robert Aumann, an Israeli-American who won the Nobel Prize for Economics in 2005 and the head of the Center for the Study of Rationality at the Hebrew University in Jerusalem. His specialty is game theory, and when examining the different ways the Israeli-Palestinian feud might play out, he saw little hope of a solution and much to criticize about the Israeli approach. "We have to stop this panicked lunging for peace," Aumann said of his fellow Israelis during our interview at the university. "The Palestinians are rational. We are the ones acting irrationally as a group."

"Rational" was not a word that leaped to mind a few years earlier, back in 2001, when I ventured into Gaza City's Jabaliya Refugee Camp to ask a senior Hamas leader, Nizar Rayan, about the suicidal shooting attack carried out by his son. Rayan was one of the most prominent Hamas leaders, and he looked the part with his intense eyes, a commanding presence, and a beard almost as thick as Aumann's. When Rayan was not making regular and forceful calls for attacks against Israel, he taught religious studies at the Islamic University in Gaza City.

Two days earlier, his son Ibrahim Rayan, seventeen, and a fellow Hamas gunman staged a nighttime raid on the Jewish settlement of Elei Sinai in northern Gaza. Firing automatic rifles, they gunned down an Israeli couple and wounded fifteen more residents, including two toddlers, as they shot at every Jew in sight until they in turn were killed by the Israeli security forces. The episode was unusual

because it was extremely difficult for Palestinian gunmen to penetrate a heavily fortified Jewish settlement in Gaza. The settlements
had fences topped with razor wire and soldiers who stood guard
around the clock. The shooting was also significant because it was
so rare for a family member of a Hamas leader to actually carry out
an attack.

Despite the possibility of an Israeli reprisal, Nizar Rayan was
not difficult to find. He was holding court beneath a traditional
funeral tent set up alongside a sandy, trash-filled street in the refugee camp. Friends kissed him on the cheek and expressed condo-
lences that sounded more like congratulations. Filled with paternal
pride, Rayan smiled and showed me a Palestinian newspaper with a
photo featuring the crumpled body of his dead son. "I feel good,"
said Rayan, dressed in sandals and wearing a simple white robe.
"Look, he was still holding his weapon after he was martyred."

Rayan explained that his family had lost its home in the 1948
war between Israel and its Arab neighbors. The family had been
forced from what is now Ashkelon, a coastal town in southern Israel,
just a few miles north of the Gaza Strip. Although this had happened a decade before Rayan was born, he still planned to get the
house and the land back. Rayan said that his son's shooting attack
"brought me closer to my home and will be followed by similar
actions until the end of Israel."

I asked Rayan, who had four wives and many children, whether
he wanted his other sons to become "martyrs" as well. Without hesitation, Rayan called to his four-year-old boy, Abdel Khader, who
ran over and jumped into his father's lap.

"Where is Ibrahim?" the father asked.

"In paradise," the boy said.

"What do you want to be when you grow up?" the father asked.

"A martyr, like Ibrahim," said the boy. The father patted the
head of his son, who then ran off to resume playing with his young
friends. At that point, I was out of questions. Words failed me as
Rayan celebrated the death of one son and smugly demonstrated
that he had brainwashed another.

More than seven years passed, and on New Year's Day 2009,
Abdel Khader, then age twelve, became a martyr. In the course of
an intensive three-week bombing campaign in Gaza, the Israeli air
force targeted Rayan and dropped a one-ton bomb that obliterated
the four-story apartment building where he lived in Gaza City. The

bomb killed Rayan, all four of his wives, and eleven of his twelve children, including Abdel Khader.

So there it is. Aumann, the conservative, hyper-rational, Israeli Nobel Laureate, and Rayan, the fanatical, firebrand Hamas leader in a Gaza refugee camp, both viewed suicide attacks as a way forward for the Palestinians. Whether you agree or not, both men tapped into one of the defining features of the conflict: acts that seem totally irrational to outsiders often seem to make sense to insiders. From afar, the suicide bombings appeared incomprehensible and nihilistic. Yet for many in the Middle East, they were a regular topic of long, sober debates, and the underlying premise was that they had been enormously influential in shaping the conflict during the last decade.

Some Palestinians saw the bombings as a way to gain international attention, to counter Israel's superior military might and instill fear in Israeli civilians. These Palestinians, many of them radical Islamists, did not share the traditional Western notion of victory and defeat in war. They knew they were not going to beat Israel on the battlefield in the short term. Yet they wanted to deliver the most painful blow possible and believed they would chip away at Israel's will to fight in the long term.

Palestinian factions also had their own narrow motives for the attacks. Hamas employed the bombings effectively to raise its own standing, and other Palestinian groups tried to match Hamas. It often seemed as if the radical Palestinian factions were largely competing with one another, with little or no concern about the larger impact on the Palestinian people.

The Israelis, meanwhile, waged a constant internal debate about the best way to stop the bombings. They questioned whether the tough tactics discouraged Palestinian attacks or had the unintended consequence of creating more would-be bombers.

It feels like a long time ago, but as recently as 2000, Islamic extremists, including the Palestinian ones, rarely carried out suicide bombings. In the broader Muslim world, the pioneers were

Hezbollah, the Lebanese Shiite Muslim group, which unleashed several major attacks in the 1980s. Al-Qaeda began to strike at U.S. targets in the 1990s. Yet these attacks were rare, and, before the new millennium, Islamist groups could not even claim to be the most prolific suicide bombers. That title belonged to the Liberation Tigers of Tamil Eelam, the group that fought for a quarter-century for an independent homeland in Sri Lanka. They were ultimately defeated by the Sri Lankan army in 2009.

The general pattern in the Muslim world was also true for the Palestinians. The first Palestinian uprising, from 1987 to 1993, was defined by daily rock throwing and a good deal of shooting. The only suicide bombing came in April 1993, near the end of this intifada. During the Israeli-Palestinian negotiations, from 1993 through 2000, there were nineteen Palestinian suicide bombings carried out by extremist groups such as Hamas and Islamic Jihad, which opposed talks with Israel.

Yet the second Palestinian uprising that began in 2000 was much more intense from the start. The stone throwers were quickly overtaken by militants with automatic rifles and bombs. "In the previous uprising, Palestinians would say, 'I want to go and fight,'" Palestinian psychiatrist Eyad Sarraj told me. "Now they are saying, 'I want to fight and die.'" Dr. Sarraj was one of the most respected figures in Gaza. He was an outspoken opponent of suicide bombings, yet was also perhaps the most articulate Palestinian voice when it came to explaining why violence had become so much a part of Palestinian society. He founded the Gaza Community Mental Health Program, the first Palestinian psychiatric center to study and treat Palestinians for the effects of violence. He was equally at home in Britain, where he and his British wife spent a good deal of their time, and in Gaza, where he treated those traumatized by the bloodshed.

When we sat down in his Gaza City office in November 2000, there had not been a single suicide bombing since the uprising began two months earlier, and the bombing campaign would not start in earnest for months to come. Yet even at this early stage, Dr. Sarraj had diagnosed a change in Palestinian attitudes, and he forecast what lay ahead. "The power of the martyr is an overwhelming symbol now," Dr. Sarraj told me. "Many youths have seen their fathers humiliated by the Israelis, and they see the Palestinian Authority as helpless. Only the martyr has an image of strength and power—someone who conquers death." Previously, it was mostly Palestinian teenagers and young, unmarried men in their early twenties who were prepared to take up arms, he said. Now he regularly saw men in their thirties, married with children, who talked about becoming martyrs. "They tell me it's better to die once with honor than to die every day from fear and despair."

The first suicide bombings of the second intifada did not come until it was nearly three months old. On December 22, 2000, a Palestinian attacker killed himself and wounded three Israeli soldiers at a roadside café deep inside the West Bank. Within months, the Palestinians began to launch these attacks with assembly-line regularity, and the Palestinian public was hugely supportive.

On Palestinian television, videos of suicide bombings played in an endless loop, set to somber songs praising the bomber. On Muslim holidays, a few Palestinian parents dressed their children up as suicide bombers, with mock bomb belts and the green headbands of Hamas. Young men wore similar costumes when taking part in street rallies. Whenever a bomber blew himself up, his "martyr poster" was produced overnight and plastered on buildings throughout his neighborhood. "The Koran is very clear on this: the greatest enemies of the Islamic nation are the Jews," Sheik Ibrahim Madhi, one of the better known and more radical sheiks in Gaza, said during a sermon on Palestinian television in 2001. "Nothing will deter them except for us voluntarily detonating ourselves in their midst."[1]

Initially, the bombers were veteran members of the most radical groups, Hamas and Islamic Jihad. Yet over time, the bombers came from an increasingly broad range of backgrounds and appeared to be driven by a variety of motives. Some were social outcasts who saw a suicide bombing as a way to achieve fame. One bomber was a divorced woman whose husband had left her when he found out she could not have kids. Another would-be bomber was an extremely short teenager who said he was lashing out against the taunting of his fellow Palestinians. While many bombers were deeply religious, some were not or had turned to religion only shortly before the bombing. Although many were poor and barely literate, a significant number were middle-class and well educated.

At the peak of the bombing campaign in 2002, Dr. Sarraj noted that children were behaving very differently than they had during the first uprising. In the first go-round, Palestinian children played a sort of cowboys-and-Indians game that they called "intifada," Dr. Sarraj recalled. It featured an Israeli soldier, with sticks representing his guns, against Palestinian kids with stones. "Many of the children at the time preferred to play the Jew, basically because the Jew with the guns represented power. This game has entirely disappeared. If you ask a child in Gaza today what he wants to be when he grows up, he doesn't say that he wants to be a doctor or a soldier or an engineer. He says he wants to be a martyr."[2]

"The people who are committing the suicide bombings in this intifada are the children of the first intifada, people who witnessed so much trauma as children," he added. "Desperation is a very powerful force. It propels people to actions or solutions that previously would have been unthinkable. What is unthinkable today becomes accepted tomorrow."[3]

The watershed year for suicide bombings, among the Palestinians and Muslim extremists elsewhere, was 2001. The Palestinian bombings became increasingly frequent as the year wore on. Then came the Al-Qaeda attacks in the United States on September 11 and the group's subsequent bombings around the globe. This was followed by the wave of suicide bombings in Iraq that started in the months following the U.S.-led invasion in 2003. A few years later, the Taliban launched a major suicide bombing campaign in Afghanistan. In Pakistan, once-rare suicide bombings became regular events.

There are a couple of ways to interpret this. The trend could burn itself out and fade away. The groups that embraced the bombings— the Palestinians, insurgents in Iraq, the Taliban in Afghanistan, and Al-Qaeda in many places—have not achieved their goals. These groups have inflicted great damage but have also undermined their causes. This could reduce their frequency over time.

There is, however, another argument. Recruiting suicide bombers turned out to be much easier than previously thought. Almost any group with a grievance can quickly put together an army of volunteer bombers. Until 2001, the stereotypical suicide bomber was fairly well defined, and the September 11 plane hijackers in the United States fit this mold. They were motivated by a blend of extreme religious and political beliefs and had completely devoted themselves to their cause for years. Most were educated men well into their twenties or even their thirties. They were sophisticated enough to live in Western countries without arousing suspicion and intelligent enough to carry out an elaborate plan with great precision.

There was a similar pattern initially with the Palestinian bombers. Most were men in their twenties who were card-carrying members of radical groups. The Palestinian bombers who executed the deadliest attacks tended to be older and better educated than the average bomber, according to one study.[4]

In short, the bombers were not a random assortment of lunatics. "Most terrorists as individuals are psychologically normal," said Jerrold Post, a former CIA official and the author of the book *The Mind of the Terrorist: The Psychology of Terrorism from the IRA to al-Qaeda.* "Terrorists do not fit into a specific category. Indeed, terrorist groups expel emotionally disturbed individuals since they are a security risk. The concepts of abnormality or psychopathology are not useful in understanding terrorism."

Palestinian kids have few local heroes to emulate. There is a dearth of famous athletes, singers, actors, or millionaires. But young men who join militant groups are treated with great respect, Post noted during a 2008 speech in Israel. "A youngster who belonged to Hamas or Fatah was regarded more highly than one who didn't belong to a group and got better treatment than unaffiliated kids. These kids' heroes are [martyrs] just like other kids' heroes are football players. We are talking about very normal psychologies here."

Among Palestinians, volunteers flooded in after the bombing campaign began and were quickly shipped out. Some bombers were dispatched only days or even hours after walking in off the street. Contrary to popular belief in the West at the time, it did not require years of religious indoctrination in the mountain caves of Afghanistan or at mosques in the slums of Gaza to create a suicide bomber. In fact, it took no training at all. All you needed was a radical ideology and a presence at the local mosque, where large numbers of applicants materialized. The hard-core professionals may have been more deadly than the walk-ins, but the latter group made up for this in numbers.

During the bloodiest years of the Palestinian intifada, from 2001 to 2004, "there were many Palestinian cells working in almost every city," said Micky Rosenfeld, a spokesman for the Israeli police.

So many Palestinians were volunteering that it was difficult for Israeli intelligence to develop profiles on all of the small units. "The bomber could be an eighteen-year-old whose brother was killed a day earlier. He goes to the mosque, hooks up with Hamas, and they give him a ready-made bomb belt. He makes a video that night, and off he goes the next day." At one point, Hamas held a fair for would-be suicide bombers, and it drew some five hundred people in five hours. "There were tables with bomb belts," Rosenfeld said. "It was mostly young men who showed up, but there were also women."

On the Palestinian side, Dr. Sarraj echoed this analysis. "Hamas doesn't need to recruit. One of my colleagues told me about a patient who became very depressed when he was passed over as a suicide bomber—he had missed his chance to be a martyr."[5]

5

THE CHASE

Micky Rosenfeld is a direct, no-nonsense man, and it required a bit of prodding to get him to tell me about his eventful days in the Yamam, a police counterterrorism force that is one of the most elite and secretive units in the Israeli security forces. The Yamam does not advertise itself and is virtually unknown, compared to Shin Bet and Mossad. Yet the Yamam was at the white-hot center of events when the Palestinian uprising was at its worst. When on duty, Yamam members eat, sleep, and live at a base near Tel Aviv. The instant they receive intelligence about a possible Palestinian attack, members have three minutes to get ready. They may dress in civilian clothes or official uniforms, depending on the operation. They may pile into either a large GMC van or a helicopter, depending on where they are headed. "Yamam is a unit that's ready twenty-four hours a day," said the wiry Rosenfeld, who was a member from 1994 to 2003. "You get woken in the middle of the night and get dressed. You go to intercept terrorists before they reach Israel. When word arrives, you know they are leaving or have left already."

Yet the information that Yamam members received was often fuzzy, and the teams often did not know exactly where they were racing to or who they were looking for. "You get the intelligence on the way. But it's not like you know that a terrorist is in a specific apartment," Rosenfeld said. "Only if you're really lucky do you get intelligence that is 100 percent precise. Before you know exactly where they are, you head to the area, and the intelligence is updated minute to minute." That intelligence could come from Palestinian informants passing on tips. It might be information gleaned from a cell phone conversation that was being monitored. Or it may simply be the description of a car. "We have a GPS, night vision goggles, and a bullet in the barrel," he said.

Rosenfeld then described one remarkable day in February 2003, a time when Palestinian factions were often attempting multiple attacks on the same day. Shortly after daybreak, his unit was at its base when word came that militants in the West Bank city of Nablus were planning to enter Israel for an attack. Rosenfeld's unit, which included twelve men and a bomb-sniffing dog, scrambled aboard their helicopter and flew to the Palestinian city in less than a half-hour. They were entering the largest Palestinian city in the West Bank and needed detailed information on their target; in this case, they had it. They were dropped off and quickly encircled a four-story residential building in a built-up area.

"We try to close in on a target from 360 degrees, but it's not always easy," Rosenfeld said. "We operate stage by stage, with very specific orders. First, we call on a loudspeaker for the residents to leave the building." Such a call often drew out civilians, although it rarely brought the surrender of Palestinian militants, many of whom were prepared to fight to the death. In this case, Palestinian gunmen gave their answer with a burst of automatic rifle fire, and the Yamam squad responded in kind. A major gun battle erupted, and the Yamam unit stormed the building. Five Palestinian gunmen were killed in the shootout, while members of Rosenfeld's team emerged unscathed.

"We prefer to wait and lay an ambush on a road if we know the route," said Rosenfeld. "It's much more dangerous to penetrate a building. But there were so many terror attacks at this time, the government decided we would do whatever it took, and therefore we would go in if we had to. Our operations became much more dangerous."

The Yamam team was full of adrenaline as the members got in their helicopter and left Nablus to return to their base. But the day was still young. While on the short flight back, they received intelligence that a would-be Palestinian bomber was about to leave the West Bank town of Bethlehem in a taxi for Jerusalem, a trip that took only a few minutes under normal conditions. In response to the frequent attacks, Israel had barred virtually all Palestinian vehicles. A limited number of Palestinian taxi drivers had permission to pass through Israeli checkpoints, however, and these taxis offered a bomber perhaps his best chance of making it into Israel undetected.

The helicopter was diverted toward Bethlehem, which is on the southern border of Jerusalem. The chopper landed, dropped off the Yamam team on the side of the road, and then disappeared. "It was gone within thirty seconds," Rosenfeld said. The unit then broke into three teams. One set up a roadblock to stop the taxi. A second took up positions to block possible escape routes. The third team consisted of snipers. "Then we just waited silently for the taxi to come," he said. When it did, the Yamam members sprang into action, stopped the taxi, and immediately grabbed the would-be bomber, who had his explosive in a bag. Not a shot was fired, and no one was hurt.

It was not even lunchtime, and Rosenfeld's unit had enjoyed a rather full day. The team members were flown back to their base to be debriefed by commanders, but their work was not done. That evening, the police received word that an attacker would be coming out of Hebron, to the south of Jerusalem. The unit went back in the helicopter around 7 p.m. and was dropped off alongside a road near Hebron. In an operation similar to the one earlier in Bethlehem, the Yamam teams waited in the dark. When the taxi materialized, they pounced and seized another would-be bomber and his explosive.

One day. Three West Bank cities. Three potential attacks stopped. "The goal is to bring the terrorist in alive," Rosenfeld said. "It's a lot more complicated to do this, but it's far more valuable because of the intelligence you can gather by interrogating him. In both Bethlehem and Hebron, the terrorist was brought in without any shots being fired, and our team was safe. That was a good day."

The Israeli security forces say they have thwarted the vast majority of Palestinian attacks during the last decade. Rosenfeld's tale depicts a roaring success: operations that were lightning fast and precise, with militants who were captured or killed and no civilians harmed. Sometimes the work was so swift and clean that Palestinians in the neighborhood were unaware that the Israelis had come and gone. The prevention of Palestinian attacks became so common, it often merited only a small mention in Israeli newspapers. Sometimes, the security forces chose not to publicize their work at all because they planned follow-up raids. "There are more cases you don't hear about than those you do," said Rosenfeld, who became a police spokesman after leaving the Yamam. The day after Rosenfeld's team foiled the three planned attacks, there was no fanfare. The shootout in Nablus garnered a brief mention in the media, but there was no information on the two planned bombings that had been averted.

Israel has waged four conventional wars against its Arab neighbors, beginning with the 1948 war at its founding and concluding with the 1973 Yom Kippur War with Egypt and Syria. Since then, Israel's clear military superiority has discouraged Arab states from carrying out conventional attacks involving large numbers of ground troops, tanks, aircraft, and heavy artillery guns. As Israel's military power continues to grow, such wars become less likely with each passing year. Yet the threats facing Israel have not disappeared; they have mutated. Israel has been embroiled in an ongoing series of asymmetrical battles against small militias. This scenario, featuring a traditional national army against bands of militants, is not unique to Israel; it has been one of the defining features of war around the world in recent decades.

The Israelis faced the same challenges the U.S. military would encounter in its wars in Afghanistan and Iraq. The Israelis and the Americans had almost limitless military might compared to their enemies, but all of these tanks and planes are of little or no use when trying to identify and stop a lone bomber dressed in civilian clothing. What is required is up-to-the-second intelligence, and developing such a network takes time.

Yet the Palestinian uprising came during a period when the Israeli security forces were becoming much less active in the Palestinian areas. As part of the interim peace agreement in 1993, Israel withdrew troops from Palestinian cities in the West Bank and Gaza. Violence was sporadic during the years of peace negotiations that followed, and Israel no longer had such a pressing need for the network of Palestinian informants it had built up over decades. In addition, Israel was permitting large numbers of Palestinians to enter the country daily from the West Bank and Gaza to work, shop, and study. Palestinians in Gaza had to go through Israeli security at the border crossing, but there were virtually no checkpoints or other barriers for a Palestinian coming into Israel from the West Bank.

For all of these reasons, Israel was extremely vulnerable to attack, despite its long history of battling terrorism. "At the beginning of the second intifada," Rosenfeld said, "it was relatively easy for the Palestinians with bombs to come out of the West Bank and enter Israel."

With Palestinian attacks mounting in September 2001, one year into the intifada, I visited a major police center in Jerusalem, known as the Russian Compound. In one overworked section, the police hotline was flooded with calls from members of the public who had seen people or unattended packages that struck them as suspicious. In a country where most men and women serve in the military, few doubt their own expertise in security matters, and there was no shortage of tips. At this time, police were receiving roughly 400 calls a day, up from 150 when the uprising began.

A group of harried police officers sat before a bank of telephones that never stopped ringing and radios that never stopped squawking. The officers dispatched policemen to search every area where a suspicious person or a potential bomb was sighted. In the vast majority of cases, the leads did not pan out, but streets were routinely cordoned off and traffic disrupted until the bomb squad and its robotic sapper could be called in. "The workload has doubled, but the number of police hasn't," complained Avi Sabag, the officer in charge of the center.

The first year and a half of the Palestinian uprising, from September 2000 to March 2002, was extremely bloody. Yet Israel drew a red line it was reluctant to cross. The Israeli military did not want to send large numbers of troops back into Palestinian urban areas that had been handed over to the Palestinian Authority during the 1990s.

Ehud Barak, the prime minister when the intifada began, wanted to carry on with the fragile negotiations. His successor, Ariel Sharon, who took over in March 2001, six months into the intifada, favored much tougher military measures. Sharon held back during his first year in office, however, in an apparent attempt to soften his image as a bulldozing general who always favored the military option. When Israeli troops did tiptoe a few hundred yards into the open fields of northern Gaza in early 2002, the United States immediately complained, and Sharon pulled back the Israeli forces instantly. "When Sharon became prime minister, he had a reputation to live down," said Chuck Freilich, who served as the deputy chief of Israel's National Security Council. "He wanted to establish new credentials with Washington."

No one accused Israeli troops of passivity. Far from it. They waged daily shootouts with Palestinian gunmen on the fringes of West Bank cities. Small groups of Israeli soldiers slipped into the center of Palestinian towns to make nighttime arrest raids, grabbing suspected militants in their beds. Apache attack helicopters swooped down to fire missiles that killed wanted militants on the street or in their homes. The troops were in action every day and night. Yet they did not linger in Palestinian cities, and Israel clearly did not want to make them a permanent presence there.

During this period, Raed Karmi was one of the Palestinians who attracted the attention of the Israeli military. A young, gangly militant, Karmi quickly emerged as the most prominent figure in the ragged West Bank town of Tulkarm. He led the local branch of the Al Aksa Martyrs Brigades, an offshoot of Yasser Arafat's Fatah movement. The Al Aksa Martyrs Brigades consisted of motley bands of gunmen that formed in every major Palestinian town. Their ranks often included members of the Palestinian security forces and local thugs who had specialized in activities such as car theft before the uprising began. Al Aksa's signature attack was a roadside ambush, and the gunmen menaced Jewish settlers throughout the West Bank. Karmi's group was particularly deadly.

On the gray, overcast day of January 14, 2002, Karmi was walking along an empty side street in his hometown. As he strode beside a low stone wall, no higher than his waist, a small bomb hidden at the base of the wall was detonated from afar, killing Karmi with a spray of shrapnel.

I raced to Tulkarm, bouncing over dirt tracks because the Israeli military had closed off all of the main roads. I arrived a couple of hours after the bombing, and Karmi's angry colleagues, their automatic rifles dangling from their shoulders, immediately directed me to the site. The damage was so minor that without their guidance, I never would have found the spot. The bomb left only a small divot on the side of the road, as if someone had scooped up one shovel's worth of dirt. Nearby, a small patch of soil had been dampened and darkened by Karmi's blood, and his colleagues placed a small circle of rocks around the stain. Quite literally, the Israelis had been watching every step he took.

At the town morgue, Karmi's body was on a gurney, and his followers streamed in to kiss their fallen leader, who had a green bandanna wrapped around his head. One Al Aksa fighter daubed the still-damp blood from Karmi's body and smeared it on his own military-style vest in homage to his colleague. The preceding weeks had been the least violent since the Palestinian uprising began more than a year earlier, but Karmi's death enraged his supporters, and they vowed revenge in a call that echoed far and wide, well beyond Tulkarm.

To keep militants on the run, Israel's military has waged a relentless campaign of targeted killings. They have been among the military's most controversial actions. Some were carried out with stunning precision. Others were performed clumsily. Either way, the consequences were impossible to predict.

Israel planned and carried out Karmi's killing in a most meticulous manner. Yet his death was a case study in the ripple effect of Israel's military actions. His killing ended the period of relative calm and led many Palestinians to argue that Sharon and the Israeli security forces wanted to ramp up the conflict. Within days, Palestinian attacks soared, and the next several months would produce the bloodiest fighting ever between the Israelis and the Palestinians.

The Palestinian suicide bombings increased drastically during the next few months and reached their peak with sixteen separate bombings in March 2002. For Sharon and his cabinet, the final straw was a March 27 blast at the Park Hotel in the coastal city of Netanya that killed thirty people and wounded more than a hundred as they sat down for the traditional Seder dinner to mark the beginning of Passover. The following evening, Sharon's cabinet met through the night and approved a massive incursion that began when Israeli troops stormed into the West Bank on Friday morning, March 29.

Operation Defensive Shield was one of the most important events of the last decade and one of the largest Israeli military undertakings ever directed against the Palestinians. It marked the moment when Israel went from limited, targeted attacks against the Palestinians to the use of full-scale, blanketing force intended to break the back of the uprising. Any pretense of reconciliation was tossed aside as Israeli troops entered every major Palestinian city in the West Bank.

Sharon declared Arafat an "enemy of the state" and said that Israel would "act to crush the Palestinian terrorist infrastructure, in all its parts and components." In the first hours of the incursion, the Israeli forces besieged Arafat's compound in Ramallah, just north of Jerusalem. Arafat would effectively remain a prisoner of his ruined compound until the final days of his life, two and a half years later. His Palestinian Authority had always been weak and corrupt but could at least pretend to be a state in waiting. With Operation Defensive Shield, the Palestinian Authority crumbled like a house of cards, and Arafat could do little besides rant from the sandbagged front steps of his headquarters, known as the Muqata.

As the Israeli forces entered each Palestinian town, they were met by Palestinian gunmen, and shootouts raged, day and night. Yet with its overwhelming force, the Israeli military needed only a few weeks to retake control throughout the West Bank. The Israeli tanks chewed up the roads. Water lines were ruptured, and electrical lines were torn down. Major Palestinian government buildings were reduced to piles of concrete and rebar. Hundreds of Palestinian militants and civilians were killed.

The heavy fighting did not last long, but the consequences for the Palestinians were devastating and enduring. In the wake of Operation Defensive Shield, Israel established hundreds of new checkpoints and roadblocks inside the West Bank, making it extraordinarily difficult for the Palestinians to move between cities. Israel also began to build the West Bank separation barrier as part of its web of tough security measures.

Since the operation, Israel has sent its soldiers wherever it wants and keeps them there as long as it likes. For the Palestinians, no sense of normality can be restored to their lives, and no solution to the larger conflict is possible until Israel rescinds the many measures that began with Operation Defensive Shield.

Yet in the view of most Israelis, the operation was a major success. By almost any measure, Israeli life started to get better after
Operation Defensive Shield. Israel became much safer or, at least,
less dangerous. The Palestinians carried out more than fifty suicide
bombings in 2002, which was by far the worst year ever. The suicide bombings, combined with other Palestinian attacks, killed 451
Israelis that year.

Israel's West Bank incursion, combined with the construction of
the West Bank barrier, the arrests of thousands of Palestinians, and
severe restrictions on the movements of all Palestinians, reduced
the bombings by more than half, to twenty-five in 2003.

The bombings fell to fourteen in 2004, then dropped to seven
in 2005 and four in 2006. Since then, Palestinian suicide bombings
have been extremely rare.

Whenever the occasional Palestinian bomber has slipped into
Israel in recent years, Israel has responded swiftly and harshly.
Israel bans virtually all Palestinians from entering Israel for days
or even weeks. Given the measures Israel is prepared to take, there
is no realistic possibility that the Palestinians will be able to carry
out the kind of intensive bombing campaign they managed from
2001 through 2004. If the bombings do pick up again, Israel is
positioned to crack down immediately.

Many Israelis point to Israel's military actions as proof of the
need for a tough, relentless campaign against terrorism. They argue
that Israel is much better off killing and capturing as many terrorists as possible, even though this can increase the motivation of
the remaining Palestinian militants and create new recruits. Before
Operation Defensive Shield, Palestinian bombers could operate
with relative freedom. When a would-be bomber left his hometown
in the West Bank and headed toward an Israeli city, he often faced
only a single layer of Israeli security, such as a checkpoint. And he
could probably avoid it by taking a back road or simply walking
along dirt paths through the hills.

All of that changed with Operation Defensive Shield. During the
incursion, Israel arrested thousands and gathered valuable intelligence. The military broke up Palestinian cells that had been carrying
out attacks and destroyed the bomb-making labs that were set up in
private homes. In addition, Israel established a multilayered defense

system. This meant that a bomber was likely to encounter an Israeli checkpoint as he tried to leave his hometown. If he made it out, he could expect to find another roadblock somewhere on the road to Israel. Then there would be beefed-up security along the border with Israel. One senior Israeli security official estimated that before Operation Defensive Shield, Palestinian terrorists spent 90 percent of their time making bombs and planning attacks and 10 percent on the run from Israeli forces. After the operation, he said, the figures were reversed.

"At the beginning of the intifada, we expected the Palestinian Authority to maintain control in their areas," said Rosenfeld, the former Yamam member turned police spokesman. "But when everything turned to chaos, we realized we couldn't rely on it to protect Israeli lives."

6

THE INVISIBLE HAND

It would be easy to overlook Sami. He is a paunchy, middle-age Arab man with a crew cut and several days' worth of stubble on his cheeks. He chain-smokes Rothmans cigarettes and wears rumpled pants, an untucked shirt, and a sad look that seems permanently embedded in his dark eyes. He lives in a dingy walk-up apartment in the working-class Israeli town of Bat Yam. Despite its fortuitous location on the Mediterranean coast just south of Tel Aviv, the town has little charm. Row after row of stucco apartment buildings are each as bland as Sami's. If you set eyes on Sami for the first time and were told that he once belonged to one of most secretive and lethal branches in Israel's security services, you might find it difficult to suppress a chuckle. Yet Sami would not let me publish his last name because his work was so sensitive, he believed that it still endangered his safety, although he had been retired for years.

As improbable as his story sounds, Sami's everyman appearance was the perfect disguise for his clandestine work. Sami was a collaborator, or informant, part of an invisible army of Palestinians who supply the Israeli security services with crucial information that can be gleaned only by well-placed Palestinians living among fellow Palestinians. Time and again, collaborators provided the Israeli military and police with the precise, real-time information that allowed them to ambush a would-be suicide bomber while he was in motion toward an Israeli city. These informants stealthily marked cars belonging to Palestinian militants so that Israeli helicopters could swoop in for missile strikes on congested Gaza streets. The collaborators surreptitiously directed Israeli ground troops on raids through labyrinthine Palestinian refugee camps in the middle of the night to snatch those on Israel's most wanted list.

Working as a collaborator is a thankless job that places one's life expectancy on the short end of the actuarial charts. And once a Palestinian signs up, there is no turning back. It is akin to entering the U.S. Witness Protection Program after testifying against the mob. The pay is minimal, and the risks last a lifetime. Israel puts the collaborators in harm's way in order to assist with its security. Palestinian militants do not hesitate to kill fellow Palestinians who are suspected of cooperating with Israel and thereby betraying the Palestinian cause. Despite the considerable downside for informants, the Shin Bet seems to have little trouble recruiting them and maintains a roster of collaborators that surely runs into the hundreds.

We wanted to understand the psychology of the collaborators. What motivated these Palestinians to help Israel capture and kill Palestinian militants? It was not clear whether the collaborators secretly sided with Israel, whether Israel pressured them into the job, or if they were simply doing it for the money.

We picked up fragments, and, every once in a while, a ray of light would shine on this shadowy world. In Sami's case, I knew he lived somewhere on Herzl Street, one of the main thoroughfares in Bat Yam, although I did not have an address. I drove there one evening and began asking around. After several false leads, I found Sami's apartment. He was not there, but his wife, Nadia, invited me in for tea and said I could wait for him. Sami arrived shortly afterward, surprised to see a stranger on his living room couch. As an unexpected bonus, one of Sami's friends dropped by, and he, too, acknowledged that he was a former collaborator. He insisted on the pseudonym Muhammad.

Under normal circumstances, neither of these men would want anything to do with a journalist, but Sami had recently been involved in a bizarre episode that briefly and unhappily resurrected his career as an informer. The incident filled him with bitterness, and he was ready to talk.

Sami's story began at age seventeen when he left his hometown of Jenin in the West Bank and traveled to Lebanon to join Yasser Arafat's Fatah movement, which operated there in exile during the 1970s. Sami was trained as a guerrilla fighter and dreamed of destroying the Jewish state. Yet during his four years in Lebanon, from 1976 to 1980, there were no opportunities to kill Israelis. Instead, Sami became an unwilling participant in Lebanon's nasty civil war. "I was a fighter, and there was a war between the Muslims and the Lebanese Christians," he said. "Somehow I didn't die there, so all of this time since then is just bonus time."

The Arab-versus-Arab bloodbath left Sami deeply disillusioned, and he returned home to Jenin and married Nadia in 1981. Even as he pursued a more mundane existence, Sami stayed in touch with some of his old Fatah comrades, corresponding by mail. Many of his letters went to Tunisia, where Arafat and his movement regrouped after the Israeli forces drove them out of Lebanon in 1982. Sami's letters to Tunisia eventually attracted the attention of the Shin Bet, and the Israelis arrested him in 1987 for his ties to Fatah, which was outlawed at the time. While Sami was behind bars, Israeli security officials periodically tried to persuade him to become an informant.

Israel has tremendous leverage over the lives of Palestinians, and the security forces do not hesitate to invoke this pressure to recruit informers. Palestinian prisoners were prime targets. After the second intifada began, Israel began large-scale round-ups of Palestinian militants and detained roughly ten thousand Palestinians at any given time. The cases against them ranged from stone throwing to mass killings. If Israel was rocked by Palestinian attacks that originated from Jenin, the Shin Bet would round up suspects in that town or simply approach Palestinian prisoners from Jenin who were already in custody. The Shin Bet would then make an offer: provide us with intelligence from your hometown, and we will release you; otherwise, you could languish in jail indefinitely. Most Palestinian prisoners rejected such Israeli offers, but some accepted.

Israel also leaned on Palestinians who had work permits for Israel that needed to be renewed regularly. Before the second intifada, tens of thousands of Palestinians had these prized permits that allowed them to commute to jobs in Israel that paid much better than similar work in the West Bank or Gaza. Israel cut back drastically on the permits after the fighting began. When crossing into Israel, any Palestinian with a permit could be pulled aside by an Israeli security official and told in a less-than-subtle fashion that sharing the names of neighborhood militants was the best way to ensure that a work permit was renewed.

Most often, Israel paid a modest sum, perhaps the equivalent of one hundred dollars a month, for a typical collaborator, according to Palestinian security officials who have investigated such cases. Yaakov Perry, the director of the Shin Bet for seven years in the 1980s and the 1990s, wrote in his autobiography that payments should be small because "sudden riches arouse suspicion."[1] Yet with just one small payment, Israel effectively owned a collaborator for life. If the collaborator changed his mind and wanted to quit, the Shin Bet could simply threaten to expose the collaborator to his fellow Palestinians. In reality, Israel would have little interest in revealing its helpers, but few informants were willing to call the bluff.

The methods may not be pleasant, but for Israel, the payoff is high. "Good intelligence is the most important thing in fighting terrorism," said Gideon Ezra, a member of Israel's parliament who served more than three decades in the Shin Bet and was second in command before leaving in 1995. The army carries out many of its operations at night in densely packed neighborhoods that are poorly lit, with unmarked streets. Without intelligence, "the army is a bit blind and deaf. The minute a suicide bomber has a bomb, he is a weapon that is already in flight. Only good and accurate information can stop him."

Sami said he repeatedly rebuffed Israeli overtures to recruit him, and he was released after more than four years in prison. When he returned to Jenin in the early 1990s, however, he was shocked by what he described as Fatah's thuggish tendencies. "A Fatah cell was established to kill collaborators," he said. "People were accused of being collaborators and were being killed. I didn't agree with the violence. A person could be sitting with his family and then be dragged away and shot. I thought that should stop."

Despite witnessing this swift demise of suspected collaborators, Sami said that he initiated contact with an Israeli military officer and volunteered. "I told him, 'If there is room for me, I will join.'" He still had contacts in Fatah, and he observed events in Jenin, which has long been a breeding ground for extremists. The intelligence network was still a bit crude in those days, and Sami simply used public pay phones to call in his reports to his Israeli handlers. Yet after a couple of years, Palestinian militants in Jenin grew suspicious of Sami, and people who were suspected of being collaborators in the town were receiving vigilante justice at an alarming rate. "I started to feel danger," Sami said. "I had been in security in Fatah, so I knew how it worked. I saw people watching me and following me. I felt they were about to take me away."

One evening in 1993, gunmen came to his street at dusk, according to Sami, who had a one-year-old son at the time. "They surrounded my house, they had masks and weapons." He was sure they were about to kill him, so he grabbed his young son and said the boy was sick and needed a doctor urgently. Sami walked down the main road, carrying his son in his arms, effectively using the child as a shield. Sami went directly to the house of a fellow informant, who had weapons. When he reached the house, Sami was welcomed in and wasted no time. "I called my Israeli contact person, who said, 'Don't leave.' He sent a car to pick me up, and I was driven to Israel." Sami had little choice but to leave his son behind, along with the rest of his family.

When Sami reached the Israeli town of Afula, his Israeli handler bluntly explained that his old life was over. "He told me I would have to stay in Israel," Sami said. "He gave me money and told me to buy new clothes and shave. He sent me to a hotel where I checked in under an assumed name. I was there sixty-five days, and then he gave me an apartment."

Sami had no option but to build a new life, on his own, in the northern Israeli port of Haifa. The city is mostly Jewish but has a large Arab minority, and relations between the two communities are generally decent. For nearly a decade, Sami remained in Haifa, living on a stipend from the Israelis, while his family remained in Jenin. They were less than an hour away by car but lived in another world. Finally, in 2002, Sami moved to Bat Yam, and his family came to Israel to join him at the apartment on Herzl Street. In addition to Sami's wife, Nadia, four of their six children and five of their grandchildren lived there. Money was tight, and the apartment was cramped. The large family home in Jenin was just a memory for Sami. At least, the family was together and had seemingly escaped the turmoil of the West Bank. But as we witnessed time and again, escaping the conflict often seems impossible. Even when you try to walk away from it, the conflict comes and finds you.

. . .

One day in February 2007, a would-be Palestinian suicide bomber from the West Bank, Omar Abu Roub, entered Israel with the intent to wreak havoc in or around Tel Aviv. He slipped into Israel, but, for reasons that were not clear, he did not immediately seek a target. He may have had second thoughts, and Israeli police also speculated that he thought his bomb had malfunctioned.

Whatever Abu Roub's thinking, he hid the bomb in a trash can and contacted a young Palestinian acquaintance named Emad— who happened to be Sami's son. In most places, such a coincidence would strain credulity, but the Israelis and the Palestinians are so few in number and live in such close proximity that strange connections crop up with regularity.

The would-be bomber, Abu Roub, and Sami's son, Emad, knew each other from time spent together in an Israeli jail for relatively minor offenses. When Abu Roub called, he failed to mention why he was in town, and Emad said afterward he had no idea that his former cellmate was taking a brief respite from his suicide-bombing mission.

Emad cordially invited Abu Roub to the apartment on Herzl Street, and the two young men sat down for coffee. Sami was napping at the time but was awakened by the sound of the visitor. Furthermore, he immediately sensed something suspicious about the guest. It was extremely difficult for a West Bank Palestinian to reach Israel. How did he get here, and what was he doing? Sami had been well trained. He promptly did what good Palestinian collaborators do—he surreptitiously called the Israeli police.

Within minutes, the police burst through the front door. They grabbed the men in the apartment and then began overturning furniture, tearing doors off their hinges, pulling drawers out of dressers, rifling through kitchen cabinets, and leaving plates, glasses, and clothes strewn throughout the apartment as they frantically searched for a bomb. "The house was a total mess," said Nadia. "The police threw everything on the floor and broke many things."

The police arrested Abu Roub and Emad. The officers were not persuaded by Emad's seemingly far-fetched story about an unexpected call from a former jail mate on a suicide-bombing mission. After a brief interrogation, Abu Roub then led police to the trash can where his explosive was hidden. Soon after that, Abu Roub and

Emad once again found themselves sharing a jail. This was hugely distressing for Sami. In his view, he had once again come to the aid of the Israelis and felt that he deserved credit for sparing them a potentially deadly attack. Instead, his son was in jail, and his good deed had turned into a nightmare.

To make matters worse, Israeli television got wind of the story and rushed to the scene, splashing Sami's face on television. Sami did not appreciate the publicity, and his Jewish neighbors were less than thrilled to learn that Sami's son had invited a would-be bomber into their apartment block. "The other residents saw me on television, and now they don't want me in the building," Sami lamented. "And I can't afford to move."

The next morning it got worse. Israel's largest circulation newspaper, the tabloid *Yedioth Ahronoth*, featured a screaming headline: "A Terrorist from Islamic Jihad in Apartment in Bat Yam." There was also a large photo, with a caption that read, "Shin Bet agent with terrorist." There was one glaring error. The "terrorist" pictured was not Abu Roub—it was Sami's son Emad. This development also had an adverse effect on Sami's relations with his neighbors. After two days, the police decided that Emad was not a conspirator in the bombing plot and released him, sending him back to the apartment building where he was now persona non grata.

The story did not end there. Armed with intelligence gathered from Abu Roub, the Israeli army raided Jenin shortly afterward and killed three Islamic Jihad members who had allegedly planned the bombing. Sami, meanwhile, was still trying to patch up his battered apartment three months after the raid when I stopped by. "The Ministry of Defense said they couldn't help me because they didn't cause the damage," he said. "They told me to talk to the police, but they didn't help either. I'm angry. It wasn't just a little bit of damage."

As Sami wallowed in despair, he reflected on the life he had abandoned in Jenin. "I lived well," he said. "We're a family of farmers. We had a big house, lots of land with olive, lemon, apple, and orange trees. We had a big family and lots of friends. I sold vegetables to Israelis in the northern Galilee."

"In Jenin, my living room is nearly seventy square meters," he said. "Here, my apartment is seventy square meters." The house in Jenin he recalled so fondly sat empty most of the time. Sami's wife visited once a month, for two or three days. "They leave her alone," he said. "But I can't go back."

Sami then volunteered a family tragedy to drive home his point. His younger brother died in an accident in 1996. "My family didn't even call and tell me until after his funeral because they were worried I would try to go to Jenin and something bad would happen to me."

The tales of collaborators rarely have happy endings, but Sami's friend Muhammad expressed great pride in what he had done. Unlike Sami, he displayed no bitterness or regret, although his work as an informant had permanently reshaped his life. He then proceeded to reveal some of the more effective techniques he used as a collaborator.

Muhammad grew up in Nablus, the largest city in the West Bank. Like many Palestinian men, Muhammad had once worked in Israel, making good money as a metalworker. He was not involved in politics, he said, but one day in 1982 a member of the Israeli security forces approached him. "We hear you are a good man, a strong man," the Israeli told Muhammad. The simple flattery worked. Muhammad agreed to assist the Israelis in return for a monthly payment, a standard arrangement, and he was, by his own account, very good at his new job.

One of his main missions was to go to West Bank cities looking for Palestinians who were wanted by Israel. The Palestinian streets are full of hawkers who have lungs like bellows and sell everything from vegetables to candy to cigarettes. Muhammad passed himself off as a wandering blanket salesman. His thick blankets were draped over his shoulder and fell down below his waist, concealing a small communications device attached to his belt.

In those technologically primitive days of the early 1980s, the device had a simple on-off switch. When Muhammad surreptitiously flipped the switch on, it meant that he had located a wanted man, and the Israeli forces could pinpoint his location. As Muhammad shadowed the wanted Palestinian, waiting for the Israeli soldiers to arrive, he had to make sure the soldiers didn't shoot him by mistake. "I always wore a yellow baseball hat so the Israelis would know who I was," he said.

Muhammad performed this work for more than a decade, but Israel's military began to withdraw its soldiers from most Palestinian cities in the years that followed the 1993 Oslo interim peace agreement. This meant that the Palestinian collaborators, who were already vulnerable to attack by fellow Palestinians, had no protectors. Muhammad was among a wave of collaborators allowed to resettle in Israel for their own safety.

Yet the Israelis valued his skills so highly, they did not want him to retire altogether. The Israelis acknowledged that it was too dangerous for Muhammad to continue working in the West Bank, where many people knew him, but new missions were arranged in Gaza, where he was unknown.

This meant that Muhammad needed new skills, because the Israeli military operated very differently in Gaza. In the relatively open spaces of the West Bank, troops are stationed throughout the territory, and most operations are carried out by ground forces who move around in jeeps. Gaza, however, is a much more confined space. Palestinians are packed into overcrowded towns and refugee camps. The army has always been reluctant to have soldiers operate in or around the Palestinian cities in Gaza, where they would be susceptible to ambush. As a result, many operations were carried out by helicopters or unmanned drones.

Because a typical Gaza home has ten or more residents, many of them children, a militant generally enjoys a degree of immunity in his apartment or his house. The same is true when a militant is in a mosque, an office, a shop, or any other public building. The one and perhaps only time that Israel can isolate a militant is when he is in a car, but this is by no means simple. The militant is, quite literally, a moving target. He knows he is most at risk in a car and therefore may change vehicles often.

Yet in a scenario repeated countless times, a pair of Israeli helicopters suddenly materialized in the skies over Gaza City. They hovered briefly over a busy street, just long enough to pick out the car with the militant in the middle of traffic. The helicopters each unleashed a missile or two, turning the car into a fireball, and then darted out of Gaza's air space as rapidly as they came. How did they do this?

The Israelis have many ways of gathering intelligence. Palestinian militants are often sloppy when it comes to talking on both mobile phones and traditional land-line phones. The collaborators are always lurking in the shadows. The cameras in the Israeli drones feed images to the military around the clock. Still, it takes incredibly precise intelligence for these strikes. It's analogous to locating one specific cab from the air in New York City during rush hour. Clearly, a collaborator must mark the car so that the Israeli air force can instantly identify it. It also falls on the collaborator to provide visual confirmation that only a militant—and not his whole family—is in the car.

Muhammad explained how he worked. "I would secretly follow the wanted man and find out what kind of car he traveled in. Once this was determined, I would wait for the chance to secretly spray the roof of the car with a clear substance from an aerosol can." Muhammad said he could not identify the sticky substance provided by his Israeli handlers but was certain that it served its purpose. "When the target got into the car by himself or with his bodyguards, I would call my Israeli guy and say, 'My friend is here.'"

Within minutes, the Israeli helicopters appeared on the horizon.

Although we asked on multiple occasions, the Shin Bet never discussed its methods, and we could not independently confirm Muhammad's explanations. Yet they were the most detailed and plausible accounts we ever heard.

7

DOUBLE JEOPARDY

Whenever we wanted to report on one of the controversial Israeli military practices, such as mass arrests, human shields, or detention without trial, we often called Mohammed Daraghmeh, a Palestinian reporter for the Associated Press in the West Bank city of Nablus. Mohammed is a first-rate journalist. He is brave, diligent, and accurate. Yet quite often, he did not have to do much digging to find a powerful story. He simply described what had happened to himself, his friends, and his colleagues.

Israeli soldiers stormed into Mohammed's home city in April 2002 as part of their major West Bank incursion, Operation Defensive Shield. After more than a week of heavy fighting, the Israelis effectively controlled the streets, although the Israelis continued to come under heavy gunfire, particularly at night. In an attempt to root out the remaining militants, Israel began massive arrest sweeps.

Mohammed was sound asleep in his apartment on April 16 when Israeli soldiers entered his neighborhood at 3 a.m. The troops grabbed one of Mohammed's neighbors and told him to go door to door and bring them males above the age of sixteen. The Israelis often ordered a local Palestinian resident to round up the men so that they did not run the risk of being ambushed when they knocked on doors. The Israeli military euphemistically called this the "neighbor policy" and claimed this was for the safety of everyone involved; however, the handpicked Palestinian doing the knocking and serving as a human shield did not see it this way.

Within minutes, Mohammed and about fifty other men in his neighborhood were blindfolded and had their hands bound with plastic handcuffs. In many of these roundups, the men were held in local schools or other public buildings while the Israelis searched through the entire lot, looking for the Palestinians they wanted to arrest. In this case, the men were placed in a truck, taken to an Israel Defense Force base a few miles outside Nablus, and told to sit on the floor.

"The soldiers told us not to speak to one another and not to move the blindfolds from our eyes," Mohammed said. "There was a young man there, maybe eighteen years old, who moved his blindfold a bit. I saw from below my blindfold a soldier approach the man and hit him on the head with a baton. Then a soldier came in and asked who could speak Hebrew. Someone raised his hand, and the soldier told him to translate and asked us to repeat what he said. He said, 'Bring me hummus,' 'Bring me beans,' and 'I like the IDF.'" After a while, Mohammed needed to use a bathroom, and a soldier escorted him to the toilet. "When we reached the place, I asked him how I was meant to use the bathroom with my hands tied," Mohammed said. "He told me to just do it in my pants, it wasn't his problem."[1]

He was kept at the detention center the entire day as the AP bureau chief in Jerusalem, Dan Perry, working with one of Israel's most high-powered lawyers, Gilead Sher, fought to win Mohammed's release. Sher had been one of Prime Minister Ehud Barak's senior advisers and negotiators during the peace talks with the Palestinians less than two years earlier. Now Sher found himself negotiating with the Israeli military on behalf of a Palestinian journalist.

After a day of back-and-forth phone calls, the military agreed to free Mohammed—as long as the AP guaranteed he was not a terrorist. The AP vouched for Mohammed's good character, and at around 11 p.m., a soldier came and called his name at the detention camp. Mohammad was given release papers and told to go home. This should have been cause for relief, but Mohammed knew otherwise.

He now faced the prospect of walking six miles in the middle of the night to reach his home. The Israeli military had declared a curfew in the city, and any Palestinian on the street after dark would be treated as a militant—and therefore a likely target for the Israeli troops patrolling in tanks and other armored vehicles.

Mohammed began to walk toward Nablus and could hear the crackle of automatic weapons fire long before he reached the city. When he arrived at the military's Hawara checkpoint on the southern edge of Nablus, the Israeli soldiers examined his documents and let him pass. Mohammed traveled just two hundred yards, and the gunfire became so intense he retraced his steps. He returned to the checkpoint and asked whether he could remain until the shooting stopped, but the soldiers refused. Mohammed then asked whether could go back to the detention camp, but a soldier told him, "No, it's not a hotel."

Mohammed kept pleading his case, if only to buy himself time. Eventually, though, the soldiers told Mohammed he had to leave.

"I'm afraid I'll be shot," Mohammed said.

"If you stay here, I'll shoot you," one soldier said.

Mohammed then asked what he should do if he came upon a tank. The soldier told him to walk into the city with his arms raised and his release papers in hand. He should speak to the tank crew in Hebrew, telling them, "I was just released from prison." With great reluctance, Mohammed set out from the Hawara checkpoint for a second time. He made it about three hundred yards when he encountered two tanks. He raised his hands high and uttered the magic Hebrew phrase. To his astonishment and great relief, it worked. He was allowed to pass. Yet after he traveled just a bit farther, the shooting became unbearably heavy. Mohammed stopped at the first Palestinian home he saw and banged on the door, where he was greeted by an elderly man who allowed him in to spend the night.

At dawn, Mohammed resumed his trek home on the deserted streets of Nablus. After a few miles, he was stopped once again by a tank, and this time the soldiers were not so impressed by his Hebrew. The soldiers told him to freeze, and before approaching him, they wanted to make sure he was not concealing a bomb. He was ordered to take off his jacket, his shirt, and eventually his pants. As Mohammad stood in his underwear in the middle of the street, the Israelis scrutinized his documents. Why, the soldiers wanted to know, were you released yesterday and you have still not reached your home? Mohammed tried to explain that the Israeli military had been rather active in the neighborhood overnight. The soldier cut him off. "All you Palestinians claim you are innocent, but all of you are killers," the soldier said. After nearly an hour, Mohammed was allowed to pass and was even given a stick with a white flag.

This time he made it home, to a greeting of hugs and kisses from his wife and three sons.

Six months later, Mohammed got a call from an Israeli military commander, who invited him for a talk. Nablus had been under curfew for months at this point but was still roiling. The commander explained that he was asking prominent Nablus figures what the military could do to calm things down and wanted Mohammed's input. Mohammed realized that such opportunities were rare and figured there was no point in aiming low. When the commander asked what the army should do, Mohammed was ready. "Well," he told the commander, "it would be very helpful if the army could get rid of Ariel Sharon."

Mohammed's personal story is worth telling because it is emblematic of the collective Palestinian experience. Thousands of Palestinian men from every corner of the West Bank have been detained in mass roundups in recent years, and it has alienated many Palestinian moderates and hardened their view of Israel and its military. These Israeli actions have had many unintended consequences. Israeli curfews kept Palestinians off the streets of their own cities for extended periods. Israel tended to make an exception for mosques, which were generally allowed to remain open. The Israeli aim was to show a bit of sensitivity. Yet as a result, Palestinian kids were effectively barred from the soccer fields and channeled into mosques, where they received daily doses of fiery Islamic rhetoric. Mohammed noticed that his kids had started to go to the mosque on their own because there was nowhere else to go. "I'm not against the mosques, but at this time there were lots of radical speeches, and all the Islamic movements worked out of the mosques. This is where the suicide bombers were recruited," he said.

A year after he was detained, Mohammed moved his family to Ramallah, an hour's drive to the south, where the atmosphere was better. "All my family is from the Nablus area, but it's a tough town," Mohammed said. "In Ramallah, my kids belong to clubs, there's a cinema, they play soccer and go to the swimming pool. It's far from perfect, but it's a much better place for them to be."

Covering the conflict posed different risks for various journalists. Western reporters had the great luxury of traveling freely most of the time on both sides of the divide. Israeli journalists worked in the free-for-all atmosphere that existed inside Israel, but, with few exceptions, they had little or no access to Palestinian areas. And Palestinian reporters, in turn, faced the greatest restrictions. They often had trouble leaving their hometowns, and entering Israel was virtually impossible. They also faced the greatest dangers—which came from both the Israelis and the Palestinians.

Palestinian reporters were the ones most often on the front lines at clashes and were therefore subject to Israeli military firepower. These journalists also faced threats from their fellow Palestinians. The Palestinians have an energetic press compared to much of the Arab world; however, Palestinian leaders are extremely touchy about criticism. When Yasser Arafat was alive, Palestinian journalists did not dare criticize him. Since his death, many Palestinian news organizations are seen as siding with either Fatah, the movement Arafat led, or with Hamas, the Islamist movement. Palestinian reporters acknowledged that they censored themselves as they negotiated the gray areas between journalism and advocacy. Palestinian journalists who upset Palestinian leaders were threatened, had their offices ransacked, and, on occasion, were even beaten up by thugs. It was never easy navigating these twin dangers: the Israeli military and the self-appointed Palestinian media critics.

Consider the case of Nazeh Darwazeh. On September 11, 2001, several thousand Palestinians rushed into the streets of Nablus to celebrate the Al-Qaeda attacks in the United States. Nazeh, a cameraman with the Associated Press in Nablus, took videotape of the crowd. As soon as he finished shooting, he followed his usual procedure and gave his tape to a taxi driver with instructions to take it to the AP office in Jerusalem.

Yet Palestinian officials soon learned of the street celebration. They immediately dispersed it and suppressed any local media coverage, knowing it would be a public relations disaster to exult in the mass slaughter in the United States. Nablus officials learned that

Nazeh had recorded the rally, and he was promptly summoned to the Nablus governor's office and told not to release the tape. Nazeh explained that it was already on its way to Jerusalem, and there was nothing he could do. The discussion was tense, but Nazeh left without making any concessions to the Palestinian officials. Shortly after he walked out of the governor's office, however, Nazeh received a threatening phone call from the Al Aksa Martyrs Brigades, the militant group that had killed dozens of Palestinians who were suspected of collaborating with Israel.

Nazeh knew the warning was serious, and he called the AP office in Jerusalem to explain the predicament to Dan Perry, the bureau chief. In addition, Dan received a call from Ahmed Abdel Rahman, a Palestinian cabinet member and a longtime aide to Yasser Arafat, who said that the AP needed to consider Nazeh's safety. The AP was faced with a no-win choice: run the video and place Nazeh's life at risk, or suppress it to protect Nazeh and face a firestorm of criticism from Israel and its supporters.

The AP considered several options. One was to move Nazeh and his family out of the Nablus area; however, Nazeh could easily be tracked down in other parts of the West Bank or Gaza. If he went to Israel, he would probably be safe. Yet he had no interest in moving, and doing so would make him look like a collaborator with Israel. There was even talk of assigning him to London, but Nazeh had no desire to leave his home. It soon became clear that relocating him was not an option.

The AP recoiled at the notion of censoring news. Dan Perry discussed the matter by phone with AP president Lou Boccardi at the AP headquarters in New York. Boccardi was dealing with the attacks at the World Trade Center, and he asked Dan for his recommendation. Dan said the AP should not run the tape out of concern for Nazeh's safety but should report what was on the tape. "It was an agonizing decision," Dan said afterward. "It was the most difficult of circumstances, but we really didn't have a choice." The decision had nothing to do with shielding the Palestinians from themselves; it had everything to do with protecting Nazeh from his fellow Palestinians.

The AP then wrote a story for its print wire. It described the material on Nazeh's videotape, noting that thousands of Palestinians had taken to the streets of Nablus to celebrate the news of the World Trade Center attacks, and that some passed out candy before Palestinian authorities dispersed the crowd.

The AP story also noted that about two dozen flag-waving Palestinians staged a brief celebration in East Jerusalem. Another cameraman taped that event, and the AP distributed this footage to its television subscribers around the world. The Palestinian Authority could do nothing about this footage because Israel controls all of Jerusalem.

Given the events of September 11, a couple of fleeting Palestinian street celebrations were of no consequence. Nonetheless, Israeli officials and pro-Israeli Web sites complained long and loud that the AP was willing to censor news because of threats by the Palestinians, something it would never do with Israel.

In the days that followed, Palestinian authorities in the West Bank and Gaza cracked down on Palestinian journalists. Palestinian police confiscated videotape and still photos from a few additional celebrations related to the September 11 attacks. The police briefly detained a number of Palestinian journalists and warned them not to use material showing Palestinians dancing, firing guns, or carrying posters in support of Osama bin Laden.

Nazeh faced no further repercussions from the Palestinians, but other dangers awaited him. Less than two years later, Nazeh was covering an Israeli military incursion in Nablus. During the operation, an Israeli tank turned down a narrow street and became stuck. As Nazeh filmed, Palestinians quickly approached the tank, pelting it with stones.

In the video taken by Nazeh, an Israeli soldier climbed out of the tank and stood on the street, using the tank's bulk as a shield against the gathering Palestinians. With the crowd closing in on the tank, the soldier fired warning shots into the ground in an attempt to disperse the Palestinians. The soldier did not appear to be targeting anyone in the crowd. One bullet ricocheted down the alley, however, and hit Nazeh in the head. Nazeh had filmed his own death.

8

VERSIONS OF THE TRUTH

We realized very early on in Jerusalem that we would need to learn a new language.

Hebrew would be helpful, although most Israelis spoke at least some English. Arabic would have been wonderful to master, but it was monstrously difficult, and virtually all foreign correspondents relied on translators. There was, however, one local dialect that was mandatory: the language of conflict.

In a land where everything is disputed, there is a constant battle to control the narrative. Jews point to the Temple Mount and say, "We could never relinquish the holiest site in Judaism." Some Palestinians look at the same spot, which has hosted two grand Islamic shrines for thirteen centuries, and claim that the Jewish temples were never there. If you are in the mood for argument, just bring up the 1948 Arab-Israeli war. Israelis wax poetic about the glorious birth of their state in a battle against five Arab armies and say that Palestinians fled their homes voluntarily. Palestinians call it "The Nakba," or "The Catastrophe," and insist that Jewish forces rendered them homeless at gunpoint. If you ask about a shooting that took place moments earlier, both sides will likely say the other provoked the clash and fired first.

The public relations tussle is just as central to the conflict as the actual fighting is, and both sides see themselves as "righteous victims," in the words of Israeli historian Benny Morris. Even the most mundane gestures carry weight. Simply selecting a hotel in Jerusalem can be interpreted as a partisan political statement. Many journalists favor the American Colony, a grand hotel founded by American missionaries in the late nineteenth century. Because it is in the eastern part of the city, however, and the staff is Palestinian, booking a room there can be seen as sympathy for the Palestinians. If you stay at the American Colony, you could call a Palestinian to come for lunch, but it would be bad form to invite an Israeli. About a mile away is the King David, the landmark hotel in West Jerusalem with its panoramic view of the crenellated walls of the Old City. Yet staying there could be viewed as a preference for Israel, so you would not invite a Palestinian to stop by for tea and a chat.

Regardless of the hotel selection, a journalist needs to brush up on the local vocabulary before unpacking. Both Israelis and Palestinians scrutinize language obsessively, and accepting or rejecting their lexicons is a litmus test that quickly classifies you as friend or foe. For a journalist who is trying not to take sides, it is enormously tricky. Every story is a walk through a linguistic mine-field, and a carefully crafted article can be undone by an editor in New York who casually and unwittingly inserts a phrase or even a single word that one side considers blatant bias.

When armed Palestinians are fighting the Israeli security forces, are the Palestinians "militants" or "terrorists"? Should the Israeli settlements in the West Bank be considered "Jewish communities built on disputed land," or "illegal colonies that violate international law"? The list is endless. The British Broadcasting Corporation even has a list and at one point released an abbreviated version that ran for eight pages and included twenty-five terms.

One of my AP colleagues wrote a story referring to the West Bank and Gaza as "disputed territories." This is the term the Israelis prefer. They argue that no one—not Israel, not the Palestinians, or anyone else—has internationally recognized sovereignty over the land, and the question must be resolved through negotiations.

The Palestinians, in turn, call them the "occupied territories," which they define as Palestinian land being ruled by the Israeli military.

This AP story immediately incurred the wrath of the Palestinian leadership, and the Palestinian information minister, Yasser Abed Rabbo, called Dan Perry, the AP bureau chief in Jerusalem.

"You know very well, Dan, that these territories are illegally occupied," Abed Rabbo said.

"Well, no one denies that the Palestinians stake a claim to these territories, and I certainly know why," Perry replied. "But surely given the years of occupation, you are aware that some Jews do so as well, Mr. Minister, on security grounds, religious grounds, historical grounds. So without judging the merits of either claim, it is, technically, a dispute."

"I see," Abed Rabbo said. "May I ask you a personal question then?"

"Of course," Dan said.

"Do you live in a house?" Abed Rabbo asked.

"Yes, an apartment really," Dan replied.

"I see," Abed Rabbo said. "Very good. I want it. Now, you see, it is disputed."

"We both laughed long and hard, and he wished me a good day," Dan said later. "And the fact is that I still remember what he said, and I could never quite use 'disputed' with the same assurance again."[1]

No one was immune from scrutiny. The Palestinians and Israel's liberal peace camp could talk about the Israeli "occupation," but no self-respecting Israeli hawk would use such language. Yet Prime Minister Ariel Sharon did let it pass his lips—once—in May 2003. He was defending his decision to support a U.S. peace plan, known as the Road Map, despite harsh criticism from his own Likud Party. "You may not like the word, but what's happening is occupation," Sharon told Likud members of parliament. "Holding three and a half million Palestinians is a bad thing for Israel, for the Palestinians, and for the Israeli economy." After his half-century as one of the country's leading warriors, Sharon had seemingly established his security credentials, but this moment of candor brought a firestorm of criticism from Sharon's traditional right-wing supporters, and Sharon immediately jettisoned "occupation" from his vocabulary.

Even when both sides use the same word—such as "Zionist"— they have entirely different definitions. Before moving to Jerusalem, we traveled throughout the Arab world. In Cairo, Damascus, and

Beirut, "Zionists" were a frequent topic of dinner conversation, and not in a nice way. Based on this experience, we associated Zionism with hard-line Israelis who wanted to confiscate land, build settlements, and generally make life unpleasant for Palestinians. It was an eye-opener when we arrived in Israel and quickly learned that the vast majority of Israelis, even the most liberal peaceniks, defined themselves as unshakable Zionists.

The late Faisal Husseini, one of the most prominent Palestinian figures before his death in 2001, had a similar experience. He was detained by an Israeli policeman on his first visit to Israel in 1967. At one point, the policeman said to him, "As a proud Zionist . . ." Husseini burst out laughing. "What's so funny?" the policeman asked.

"I have never in my life heard anyone refer to Zionism with anything but contempt," Husseini said. "I had no idea you could be a proud Zionist."[2]

We were conversant in this new language by the time the Palestinian uprising began. It was a safe assumption that the media would not only serve as witness, but would also become embroiled in the conflict at some point. We simply did not expect it to happen on the first day of the intifada and in my office.

When Palestinians rioted at the Temple Mount–Noble Sanctuary on September 29, 2000, a horde of photographers was present. They are an intensely competitive lot, and a day's work can be for naught if you are not the first to get your photos into the hands of an editor. After the fighting began, the AP photographers, as well as many freelancers, raced to get their material to the AP office on Jaffa Street, about a mile away, and into the hands of AP's photo editors.

As this parade of photographers streamed into our office, the editors processed the photos with great urgency. They selected the pictures, typed brief captions, and relayed them to AP headquarters in New York. There, the photos were rechecked by a second layer of editors. The photos then moved on the AP photo wire, instantly reaching thousands of newspapers around the world. With such a major story, dozens of photos from Jerusalem were sent out. In many cases, only minutes elapsed from the time the photographer had arrived at the AP bureau until the photos hit the wire.

Many pictures reflected the fury of the clashes, but one seemed to say it all. It showed a dazed young man on his knees, with blood gushing down the right side of his face, staining his white shirt. Directly behind him was an Israeli policeman with his mouth contorted in anger as he pointed his baton and approached the bloodied man. Even without a caption or a context, the photo was powerful. Yet it also appeared to capture the essence of the day. The Palestinians had launched the riot but took a pounding—seven Palestinians were killed and more than two hundred injured, while several Israeli policemen and civilians were also wounded. The caption read, "An Israeli policeman and a Palestinian on the Temple Mount."

The next morning, the photo appeared in newspapers worldwide, in many cases on the front pages. Dr. Aaron Grossman, a Jewish resident of Chicago, saw the photo in the *New York Times* and felt compelled to contact the newspaper to convey a crucial piece of information. "That 'Palestinian' is actually my son, Tuvia Grossman, a Jewish student from Chicago. He and two of his friends were pulled from their taxicab while traveling in Jerusalem by a mob of Palestinian Arabs, and were severely beaten and stabbed," Dr. Grossman wrote.

The policeman, it turned out, was rescuing Tuvia Grossman, and the officer's wrath was directed at the Palestinian assailants, who were not visible in the photo. In addition, the caption claimed that the photo was taken on the Temple Mount, but in the upper-right-hand corner was a Hebrew-language sign for a gas station. In fact, the photo was taken on a street a short distance from the Temple Mount.

Anyone who has spent time in a newsroom knows that facts are fuzzy when a story breaks. The impulse to report the news as quickly as possible and the need to triple-check the details are in utter conflict. It is a recipe for error. In this instance, many captions had similar generic wording, noting that Israeli police and Palestinian civilians were battling at the Jerusalem holy site.

The photo of the bloodied young Jewish man appeared to fall in the same category. The picture had been taken by an Israeli photographer working for Zoom 77, an Israeli photo agency. He dropped the photo at the AP office with a caption written by hand in Hebrew that inaccurately identified Grossman as an Israeli ambulance medic. The AP photo editors in Jerusalem misinterpreted the note and compounded the mistake by identifying Grossman as a Palestinian. The error came to light only when Dr. Aaron Grossman, half a world away, recognized his son the following day.

Alerted of the mistake, the AP immediately sent a correction to newspapers, but in the overheated passions of this conflict, the controversy assumed a life of its own. Many Jews in America and Israel refused to accept that the error was committed without malice. Some newspapers that ran the photo were accused of bias, although they were not responsible for the mistake. Honest Reporting, a pro-Israeli organization that accuses the U.S. media of anti-Israel bias, featured the picture under an article titled "The Photo That Started It All." The controversy dragged on for weeks and set the tone for the uprising.

The intifada spawned a cottage industry of pro-Israel Web sites that existed solely to criticize what they viewed as anti-Israeli coverage. Reporters and their editors were bombarded with phone calls, letters, and e-mails, most of them from Jewish individuals and watchdog groups in Israel and the United States. "The thing that was striking to me were the letters—hand-written, venomous, hateful, threatening," said Lee Hockstader, the *Washington Post* correspondent at the beginning of the intifada. "The writers commonly expressed the wish that I would die, preferably in very violent circumstances."

The attacks were mostly verbal but not always. When Western journalists traveled in the West Bank and Gaza, they often taped "TV" in large letters on the sides of their armored cars. The aim was to discourage anyone from shooting. It soon made the cars a target, though, particularly at some of the more radical Jewish settlements in the West Bank, where a number of Western journalists had their tires slashed.

In December 2000, several months after the fighting began, both of Lee's cars were turned into fireballs outside his Jerusalem home, although no one was hurt. The following year, Lee was covering a suicide bombing at a Sbarro pizzeria in downtown Jerusalem, where fifteen Israelis had been killed. In the aftermath, a group of ultra-Orthodox Jews gathered on the street and began chanting, "Death to Arabs." When Lee arrived, he encountered an Israeli government official who was notorious for his frequent run-ins with the foreign press. Observing the scene, the Israeli official said to Lee, "You know, if I told these people you were from the *Washington Post*, they'd tear you apart." Lee saw it as a ham-handed attempt at intimidation, rather than a serious threat, but it reflected the mood of the times.

The Palestinians had plenty of their own gripes. They believed that the Western press often portrayed the Palestinians collectively as terrorists and overlooked the underlying grievances, which included the Israeli military occupation and the absence of Palestinian statehood. Some Palestinian groups and their supporters abroad tried to mimic the Israelis with e-mail campaigns that were critical of Western news organizations, although this was done on a much smaller scale.

As the fighting got worse, so did the language war. Both Israelis and Palestinians displayed a talent for sanitizing the ways they killed one another. In tracking and killing Palestinians responsible for violence, the Israeli military initially called its work "preemptive strikes." Military wordsmiths then coined the clunky phrase "pinpoint preventive operations." That never really caught on and yielded to "focused prevention." Eventually, Israeli officials decided simple was better and described the raids as "eliminations." The Palestinians, meanwhile, stuck with one word: "assassinations."

The Israeli language tended to soften the harsh reality of military action, while the Palestinians preferred flowery Arabic to describe Palestinian violence against Israeli civilians. Hamas typically described a suicide bombing as "a heroic martyrdom operation against the Zionist entity," reflecting its refusal to mention Israel by name. Hamas glorified its *shaheeds*, the Arabic word for "martyrs," and never used the term "suicide bomber."

Some Israelis also rejected the phrase "suicide bomber" but for different reasons. They felt that it emphasized the assailant, not the victims. Israeli government spokesmen occasionally called them "homicide bombers," a phrase that seemed redundant. In certain cases, the Israeli officials even suggested the term "genocide bomber," on the grounds that the ultimate goal was to kill all of the Jews.

Palestinians euphemized all attacks on Israelis, calling them "resistance operations." Some Palestinians called suicide bombers "F-11s," a name that played off the Palestinian position that they didn't have high-tech firepower such as Israel's F-16 warplanes. "We have F-11s," a Palestinian would say, drawing a perplexed look from a listener. Then the Palestinian would explain by wiggling his index and middle fingers simultaneously to approximate the legs of a suicide bomber walking toward a target. "This is an F-11," he would say.

At one point, Israel decided that Palestinians in the West Bank who were suspected of assisting in attacks would be forcibly moved to Gaza, where they would be cut off from family and friends. The Palestinians denounced these "forced deportations." The Israeli military defended the policy, which it described as an "order limiting the place of residency."

The military's armored bulldozers frequently flattened Palestinian olive groves that were used for cover by militants. After one particularly large operation in Gaza, the army's statement described it in the usual way: "engineering work." The words "olive," "grove," and "tree," were not mentioned.

When called on to break up mobs of Palestinian stone throwers, the Israeli security forces did not load up with tear gas, rubber bullets, and other riot-control gear. They took "dispersing tools." And when a Palestinian killed himself accidentally with a bomb that exploded prematurely in a workshop—a regular occurrence—Israelis sarcastically called it a "work accident."

The term that always proved most contentious was "terrorist." Israel had a very broad definition, applying it to almost anyone who had even an indirect connection to violence. In addition, many Israelis rejected "militant" as a euphemism that whitewashed Palestinian actions. Palestinians, in contrast, were allergic to the word "terrorism."

Because the definition of "terrorism" was so contested, news organizations had lengthy internal debates about how and when to use it, but it was impossible to come up with hard-and-fast rules. In some cases, it was clearly appropriate, if not mandatory. The most obvious example was when a suicide bomber struck at civilians.

Yet there were many gray areas. Israeli troops staged almost daily raids in the West Bank and Gaza, and the armed Palestinians they faced were a mixed lot. They ranged from those responsible for terror attacks against Israeli civilians to uniformed members of the Palestinian security forces who felt it was their duty to defend their town against Israeli troops.

When speaking to Western reporters in English, Israeli government officials often described all Palestinians taking part in the

shooting as "terrorists." Yet Israeli military spokesmen would sometimes say that the same shooting was carried out by "militants."

Even the most prominent Palestinian leaders were difficult to
categorize. In the eyes of most Israelis, Yasser Arafat had been an
archterrorist for decades. Then the Israeli government set aside
that label when it made him a negotiating partner during the 1990s.
After the Palestinian uprising began in 2000, the Israeli government dropped the diplomacy and described Arafat as the "head of
a terrorist regime."

Ariel Sharon's government refused to deal with Arafat, but
Sharon and his successors have not hesitated to deal with Mahmoud
Abbas and other senior members of Arafat's Fatah movement. Even
though Abbas had been a senior lieutenant to Arafat for decades,
the Israelis said he did not "have blood on his hands," and therefore he was not a terrorist.

We would wrestle with these questions to the point of absurdity. Take this common scenario: A Palestinian with an AK-47 rifle
hides alongside a West Bank road. When an Israeli army jeep drives
past, he opens fire. Is he a terrorist? Most American journalists
covering the conflict would refrain from using the term, because
the Palestinian was shooting at a military target.

What if the same gunman waited for the army jeep to pass and
shot at the next car, carrying an Israeli family? Did it matter that
the attack took place in the occupied West Bank, as opposed to
inside the borders of Israel proper? Many Palestinians would make
this distinction; most Israelis would not. Perhaps it would be appropriate to describe the Palestinian gunman as a "militant" when he
was firing on an Israeli army jeep and a "terrorist" when he fired on
the civilian car, but such compromises satisfied no one.

Often the critics were blinded by their passion. Some supporters
of Israel claimed that the *New York Times* had a policy of never using
"terrorism" and "Palestinian" in the same article. Yet a quick computer search revealed that during the worst years of the fighting,
the words "terror," "terrorism," or "terrorist" appeared in roughly
a third of our stories.

Not all Western journalists were treated alike. When we introduced
ourselves and our respective organizations, we would get an instant

reaction. Often it was a chuckle, followed by a question: "How can you two remain married while working for Fox News and the *New York Times?*"

Sometimes, Israelis would gush over Fox News, saying that it was the only place where Israelis got a fair shake in the international media. At this point, I knew I was likely to spend the evening being ostracized, if I was lucky, or being attacked, if I was not. At other gatherings, the reverse was true. Longtime *New York Times* loyalists would wistfully recall the first time they began reading the paper, as if they were recounting the first time they fell in love. At such events, these folks would look at Jennifer as if she had two heads.

In many foreign countries, residents have a limited knowledge of U.S. news organizations. In Israel and the Palestinian areas, however, both sides seemed obsessed with Western news reporting. The governor of the Palestinian Monetary Authority, George Abed, first started reading the *New York Times* decades earlier when he was a student at the University of California at Berkeley. He had a copy of the paper faxed to his office every morning, which he proudly displayed to me when I interviewed him. "It's just not the same reading it online," he said.

Jennifer and I both had devoted e-mail pals, although they shared little in common. My correspondents tended to be Jewish Americans who thought that the *Times* existed primarily as a vehicle to slander Israel. One man sent me a note virtually every time my stories appeared, highlighting what he perceived as anti-Israel bias. One day, he stunned me by writing, "I couldn't find anything in today's report that I would disagree with." Then he went on to suggest several stories I should write about Palestinian perfidy. Jennifer, meanwhile, received a steady flow of supportive letters from Jewish Americans, Christian evangelicals, and rock-ribbed American conservatives, many of whom said they were praying for her safety in such a dangerous environment.

We found this rather amusing. The news of the day was often obvious, and therefore we frequently covered the same event. Even on days when there was no breaking news, we sometimes came home to find that we had been independently reporting the same or similar stories and often had spoken to the same people. We chased stories because they were good ones, and the editorials in the *Times* and the commentary on Fox News were of no concern to us.

. . .

Israelis were so convinced that the world misunderstood them that they created a reality television show to address the matter. *The Ambassador* featured fourteen young Israelis competing in the United States, Europe, and at home to win a job spreading a pro-Israel message around the globe. The first episode of the highly publicized show aired in November 2004 on Israel's Channel Two television and focused on the country's preoccupation with *hasbara*, a Hebrew word that literally means "explanation," although it is best translated as "advocacy."

In the first episode, the contestants were divided into two teams, men and women, with each side delivering a speech and answering questions from skeptical students at Cambridge University in Britain. "The only aim is to make them more sympathetic to Israel, to modify their opinions if just by a millimeter," said Nachman Shai, one of the show's three judges and a former military spokesman who is regarded as a skilled practitioner of *hasbara*.

The speaker for the men's team, Tzvika Deutsch, asked audience members how they would feel if a British soccer match was canceled due to the threat of a rocket attack. Such dangers were an everyday concern in Sderot, the southern Israeli town that came under rocket fire for years from nearby Gaza. "I have a simple dream," Deutsch said. "I want to wake up every morning to a boring life. To just turn on the telly and watch a match between Arsenal and Manchester United."

The women's team presented a more formal recitation of Middle East events, including the collapse of Israeli-Palestinian negotiations and the start of the Palestinian uprising. Responding to a question, Ofra Bin Nun, of the women's team, said, "Let me make it clear that Israel has not taken anything from anyone." Her comment drew snickers from the British audience, which ultimately favored the men's presentation overwhelmingly.

While the men's team celebrated with champagne, the women were flown back to Israel and debriefed by the judges. Bin Nun was the first contestant dismissed under a format similar to *The Apprentice*, the American show where Donald Trump does the firing. "*Hasbara* means knowing you are speaking to a hostile audience and knowing how to win their ears," said Rina Matzliah, a judge who was a prominent television journalist.

The show played out over eleven episodes, and the winner, Eytan Schwartz, received a job in New York with Israel at Heart, an advocacy group established by Joey Low, a New York businessman. When approached by *The Ambassador*, Low initially had reservations but decided to take part because "I was very upset with the way Israel was being perceived. I felt Israel was not delivering its message in the best way." Low's group recruited Israelis in their early twenties who had just completed mandatory military service and sent them to universities in the United States, Europe, and Latin America to speak on behalf of Israel.

Gideon Meir, a senior official in the Foreign Ministry, said he was not bothered by the show's premise that amateur diplomats could perhaps be more effective than the professionals. "Israelis feel if we could only do a better job explaining, the world would understand us," Meir said. "But it's much more complicated than that. I hope this will show that public diplomacy is not easy."

Shai, the judge, had been a military spokesman during the 1991 Gulf War, offering assurances that everything was under control even as the country came under repeated missile attacks from Iraq. He said that Israel's representatives had a greater challenge today. In 1991, as well as in the 1967 and 1973 wars with Arabs, Israel faced actual or imminent attack. Yet in recent years, the country has often been portrayed as the aggressor in the fighting with the Palestinians, particularly in the European media.

"The David and Goliath roles have been reversed, and it's more difficult to explain what we're doing today," Shai told me. "I meet often with American Jews, and there's a strong feeling that Israel is right, but the world doesn't understand we are right. I think we're doing a pretty good job, but we're always critical of ourselves. I think it's fair to say that we are obsessed with *hasbara*."

9

A BATTLE IN JENIN

I could see the Israeli helicopters firing missiles as they hovered over the Jenin Refugee Camp for what seemed like an hour at a time. I could hear the staccato of automatic gunfire echo off the hills surrounding the camp. I could almost smell the thick plumes of black smoke that curled high into the clear sky. What I could not manage to do was finagle a way into the camp.

The Israeli military and Palestinian militants were waging the most intense and sustained battle they had ever fought, and there was no way to witness it. The Israeli troops that surged into the West Bank in March 2002 as part of Operation Defensive Shield easily overwhelmed the Palestinian militants almost everywhere. This was no surprise in an asymmetrical fight that featured the most powerful army in the Middle East against bands of militants. In Jenin and Nablus, however, two towns only fifteen miles apart in the northern West Bank, the Palestinian factions had banded together and slugged it out with the Israeli military in brutal urban combat.

The Israeli-Palestinian feud is waged in such a small theater that access was rarely an issue. Journalists could often plant themselves between the combatants and watch the bullets fly in both directions if they so wished. Yet this important and widely disputed battle was impossible to cover firsthand because the Israeli military had blocked the few available routes into the tiny, congested Jenin Refugee Camp, which was less than one square mile and set at the base of a hillside.

Jenin had a tradition of Palestinian militancy dating back decades and was the launching pad for many of the suicide bombings in the second intifada. The Jenin Refugee Camp was attached to the town, and the camp probably had more armed Palestinians per square block than any other place in the West Bank. The Israelis preferred to fight from inside their tanks and armored personnel carriers, but the massive vehicles were too wide to make it down the narrow streets in the camp, and the Palestinian militants had booby-trapped every place that soldiers might venture on foot. Doorways, roadside sewers, and boxes all contained explosive surprises. Israeli troops advanced block by block toward the center of the camp, bulldozing entire apartment buildings along the way. As the Israelis made their way forward, the first rumors of large-scale Palestinian civilian deaths began to emerge. Yet it was impossible to confirm them or knock them down without entering the camp.

For more than a week, I tried every possible approach to the camp. I traveled in an armored car and on foot, but Israeli troops were always waiting. They blocked off the main roads, the back roads, the dirt roads, and places where there were no roads. From the military's perspective, the quarantine of the camp was essential. One of the army's toughest challenges was separating combatants from civilians, and the last thing it wanted was pesky journalists running through the streets, further complicating the mission.

For several days, the closest I could get was the rooftop of a three-story Palestinian home about a half-mile outside Jenin. Virtually all Palestinian civilians had fled the camp, making it impossible to get firsthand Palestinian accounts of what was happening inside. The Israeli military offered general reports on the fighting but few details. One afternoon, Prime Minister Ariel Sharon visited a hilltop military outpost overlooking the battered camp. He vowed to break the back of the Palestinian uprising in Jenin and Nablus. The Bush administration issued a rare criticism of Sharon's tactics, expressing concern over the ferocity of the fighting and the reports of heavy civilian casualties. "Jenin and [Nablus] are at the center of terror," Sharon told the assembled journalists.

The slivers of information emerging from Jenin described street-to-street and even house-to-house fighting. In the worst single

episode for the Israelis, Palestinian gunmen lured a reserve unit
into the courtyard of an apartment building and ambushed them.
Israel lost thirteen soldiers, its heaviest single-day toll in years.

The Palestinian resistance proved much tougher to break than
the Israelis expected, but, as promised, Sharon kept up the siege.
After nine days of heavy fighting, Israel declared on the morning of
April 11 that the final Palestinian holdouts, thirty-six gunmen who
had exhausted their bullets and food, had surrendered. Israel said
that the camp was still off limits, but I prepared to make another
push. I piled into the Associated Press's armored car with three
supremely talented photographers, the AP's Jerome Delay, American James Nachtwey, and Frenchwoman Alexandra Boulat.

Jerome, a highly skilled operator in war zones, decided this
would be an ideal time to test the manufacturer's specifications
on the AP's vehicle. He asked everyone to get out and then drove
the lumbering, top-heavy armored car down a ridiculously steep
embankment just outside Jenin. It looked as if he were performing a movie stunt, with the intent of sending the car somersaulting
down a hill until it landed in a mangled heap at the bottom. I could
hardly bear to watch, yet somehow Jerome made it down and kept
the car upright. We scampered down on foot behind him, having
found a crack in the Israeli blockade.

Reaching the first intersection at the edge of the refugee camp,
we were immediately struck by both the destruction and the silence.
As we looked around, the first person we saw was a most unlikely
survivor: an elderly Palestinian woman, alone in her wheelchair.
She was weeping uncontrollably as she sat in the middle of the
intersection, where the pavement had been reduced to chunks of
tar and piles of sand by Israeli tank treads. We could not fathom
how she had reached that particular spot. We approached her to
help, but she could not speak coherently.

We were still trying to figure out where we could take the woman
for assistance when we drew the unwanted attention of several very
angry Israeli soldiers. The soldiers drove up in their armored vehicles and jumped out without bothering to close the doors behind
them. They wasted no time on introductions and demanded to
know what we were doing in the camp. The soldiers then saw the
Palestinian woman and paused for a moment to take her into their
care. They soon revisited their wrath on us, though, seizing our
press cards and passports and calling their commanding officers.

A half-hour later, the order came down. We were told to disappear immediately, if not sooner.

Yet the stealthy and relentless Jerome Delay had not come this far to be turned back. As we were driving out of the camp, we reached a paved road. Jerome was supposed to go left and head out. Instead he turned right, and the soldiers, several hundred yards behind us and seemingly preoccupied, failed to notice. Instantly, we vanished into a warren of ramshackle buildings in the camp, most of them pocked with bullets, some scorched by fire, and others completely demolished. We quickly made our way to the center of the devastated camp and began looking for Palestinians, dead or alive.

Eventually, we found several of the living. None were hurt, but all seemed mentally adrift. Virtually all of the camp's residents had fled at some point to the adjacent town of Jenin, which was just a short sprint away. Some of the physically and mentally disabled had been left behind to fend for themselves, however. Dazed and disoriented, they wandered amid the rubble. Ali Damaj, a camp resident who stayed, said that the Palestinian gunmen had shot from buildings and alleys near his home, attacks that drew fire from the Israelis. As many as fifty people had huddled inside his three-room apartment for days. "Keep on the floor. Keep quiet. Don't look out the windows," Damaj had told the kids. Eventually, the other Palestinians left, but for reasons he could not articulate, he alone stayed behind.

The Palestinians in the camp claimed that the Israelis had killed hundreds of Palestinian civilians. But where were the bodies? The photographers searched through the rubble and entered badly damaged apartment buildings, despite the possibility that they were booby-trapped. On the streets, the Israeli incursion had knocked down the camp's electrical poles and phone lines. In this tangled spaghetti of wires crisscrossing the streets, it would have been easy for a Palestinian militant to add one more wire to the mix, then attach it to a hidden explosive.

We searched out the most devastated parts of the camp, climbing over mounds of rubble. During the fighting, the military had relied heavily on bulldozers, known as D-9s. They are huge, powerful machines built by the U.S. manufacturer Caterpillar and modified by the Israelis, who covered them with armor and bulletproof glass so they can operate in combat zones. The bulldozers could not squeeze through Jenin's narrow streets, but the soldiers driving the bulldozers pressed ahead anyway, shaving the front walls off entire apartment blocks throughout the camp. Walking past these four-story apartment blocks was like looking into a doll house. The living room furniture was untouched. Clocks, plates, and diplomas hung on the wall, a bit dusty but unscratched.

We spent two hours in the camp, talking to survivors and searching through the debris. The fighting had been extensive, as advertised, yet the Palestinian claim of hundreds of dead was not holding up. The residents gave confusing stories, with some saying the Israelis had dug a huge grave in the camp and buried the bodies. This made no sense, because the bodies could easily be uncovered after the Israelis left. One Palestinian claimed that the Israeli military had removed all of the bodies in refrigerated trucks. This, too, seemed implausible.

Israeli military patrols continued to move through the camp. We stayed out of sight, but as they passed closer and closer, we decided not to push our luck and left. We went to Jenin's hospital, to see if we could piece together the Palestinian claims. Dr. Mohammed Abu Ghali said that he received eight Palestinian bodies during the first two days of the fighting, but none after that because the army sealed off the camp, keeping Palestinian ambulances and rescue workers out.

We were still struggling to put this story in perspective. We were the first journalists to see the camp, and, as far as we knew, the only ones to tour it extensively that day. Yet it was far from clear what had happened in Jenin. Senior Palestinian officials claimed that up to five hundred Palestinians had been killed, many of them civilians. Palestinians were already calling it the "Jenin Massacre."

Shortly after leaving Jenin, I called an Israeli military spokesman, Lieutenant Colonel Olivier Rafowicz, and pressed him for his best estimate of the Palestinian death toll. He said he did not have precise figures, but perhaps one hundred Palestinians were killed, most of them militants.

The only thing that was clear was that the story would be a Rorschach test for the larger conflict. The facts were murky. The claims were contradictory. Both sides would see what they wanted to see.

The Arab media reported the Palestinian massacre claims at face value. Many European journalists also played up the Palestinian account. "We are talking here of massacre, and a cover-up, of genocide," said a report in Britain's *Evening Standard*, one of several in a similar vein. The American media were far more circumspect. They reported the Palestinian allegations but stressed that these were not proven and gave at least equal weight to the Israeli version.

In my story, I noted the wild discrepancies and did not claim to have all of the answers:

"The army says it killed about 100 Palestinians, mostly militants. However, the location of the Palestinian dead remains a mystery. Palestinian officials, including Information Minister Yasser Abed Rabbo, have talked about mass killings of civilians, without providing evidence. In a first comprehensive look at the devastation in the camp, Associated Press journalists found widespread destruction but no bodies on the streets. Several Palestinian men gave journalists a tour of the wreckage and said they had heard rumors that bodies were buried in mass graves but didn't know where. Palestinian Cabinet minister Saeb Erekat said he received reports of 500 Palestinians killed in the offensive but said he could not confirm the figure. 'We did not touch the Palestinian bodies, we did not remove them,' army spokesman Lt. Col. Olivier Rafowicz said. 'This is Palestinian propaganda.'"

For the next several weeks, the two sides waged a furious public relations campaign. The AP kept reporters in Jenin full-time and sought to document every Palestinian death. Eventually, the picture became clear. About fifty-five Palestinians had been killed, most of them combatants, although some were civilians. Israel had lost twenty-three soldiers. The fighting was brutal and the destruction widespread. The battle did not produce heroes. One Israeli soldier later told Israel's *Haaretz* newspaper of his drunken rampage in a military bulldozer. He said he tore down as many buildings as he could during the course of several days, but there was no massacre. The Palestinian leadership was eventually forced to retract its claims.

Yet years afterward, some Palestinians still clung to the myth. "I think five hundred Palestinians were killed in the battle, and most of them were civilians," Maya Awad, a resident of the Jenin Refugee Camp and a mother of three teenage boys, said in 2008. One of her sons, Kamal, was quick to add, "I think Israel lost."

He disputed Israel's own casualty figures of twenty-three soldiers killed. "Resistance fighters wrote on their hands how many soldiers they killed," he said. "My cousin had thirteen on his hand, another killed ten and so on, so it was more than forty soldiers."

As the battle for Jenin illustrated, the Israelis and the Palestinians tell their stories in very different ways. The Israeli military has an information desk staffed around the clock. When a battle erupts, the spokesperson's office often takes the initiative and starts calling journalists. Even when the shooting is still under way, the Israelis are busy putting out their story. As far as the Israeli military is concerned, it is never too late at night or too early in the morning to call with an update. The goal is to provide as much information as quickly as possible, even if the information is often premature and incomplete. The biggest shortcoming is that the Israeli military is often not aware of how much damage it has inflicted on Palestinian civilians. Still, the military regularly puts journalists in touch with senior Israeli military officers fresh from the battlefield. There are regular background briefings for journalists at the military headquarters in Tel Aviv. There are tours of military facilities. Journalists often do not get the information they want, but "no comment" is not part of the military's lexicon.

When comparing Israel's well-oiled military information machinery to the Palestinian system, the first important point is that the Palestinians have no system. Despite the daily fighting for years, the Palestinians never developed an organized way to tell their side of the story. For journalists, getting information from the Palestinians inevitably involved scrambling to find witnesses and checking with Palestinian hospitals and security force members, as well as with the armed factions.

At the beginning of the uprising, the Palestinian accounts were often imprecise and contradictory, and no one on the Palestinian side was in charge of verifying them. The Palestinians almost always described their casualties as civilians, even when it was clear that militants were involved.

Yet fairly quickly, the Palestinians caught on. They became much more precise about casualty numbers and their affiliations. The battle in Jenin was the most glaring example of wildly inaccurate Palestinian information, but it was very much the exception after the early days of the fighting. In many cases, the Palestinians provided more detailed and accurate accounts when the facts were in dispute. Jennifer was witness to one such case.

One bloody day in the fall of 2003, Israeli warplanes and helicopter gunships carried out a series of strikes in Gaza. Israel said the attacks included a targeted nighttime bombing in the Nuseirat Refugee Camp that killed several Hamas militants traveling in a sedan on an otherwise empty street. But the Palestinians offered a different version, saying that the militants were among seven people killed and more than seventy injured, most of them civilians. I was in Gaza that day and went to the hospital that night after the final air strike. The Palestinian evidence was unassailable. The dead and the wounded were on full display.

Yet the Israeli military immediately challenged the Palestinian account, insisting that the Hamas men were the only casualties. The military was so adamant that the following day, it took the unusual step of inviting a small group of journalists, including Greg, to military headquarters in Tel Aviv to show a videotape taken by a drone flying above the street.

Greg watched the grainy black-and-white images, which the drone had transmitted live to commanders. The footage showed the first missile striking the hood of a car traveling on an empty street. The car had the Hamas men inside but managed to carry on in its damaged state for about fifty yards until it bumped into the curb. Then the vehicle backed up slowly, and, about a minute after the first missile, a second one scored a direct hit on the car, destroying it.

The videotape appeared to support the military's account that both missiles were fired at a single car on an empty street, with no civilians nearby. "We would not allow any munitions to be launched on a massive gathering of people," the military officer said. "To fire into a crowd is not professional, it is not ethical, and it's not moral."

We were stumped. Both sides had presented compelling evidence. The dead and the wounded Palestinians were real—I saw them with my own eyes, as did Greg's New York Times *colleague James Bennet, who was in Gaza that day as well. Yet the Israeli military was so sure of its counterclaim that it distributed its videotape to journalists.*

The Fox News bureau chief, Eli Fastman, was determined to solve this discrepancy. A former cameraman with a keen eye for detail, Eli put the tape in his video machine and scrutinized it frame by frame. Slowly, he replayed it over and over. After multiple viewings, Eli noticed something the Israeli military had missed.

After the first missile struck, the Palestinians in the neighborhood did something strange. Instead of remaining inside, where they would have been relatively safe, they came running out of their homes into the narrow alleys in the direction of the explosion. They were barely visible on the videotape. It had to be replayed repeatedly to detect the slightest blurry movement in the corners of the screen. Many disappeared entirely under awnings and balconies. It would have been extremely difficult, if not impossible, to notice such peripheral details when viewing the video in real time and focusing on the car in the middle of the street.

The tape also raised the question of why the Palestinians ran toward a missile strike, rather than away from it. It was, however, a fairly consistent response in Palestinian areas, where young people in particular were drawn to explosions. The Palestinians say they do it in part because they want to help the wounded, and in part because they want to see what happened. Almost every incident produced an instant crowd, and the Palestinians showed little regard for their own safety.

Muhammad Abu Amuna, an eighteen-year-old high school student, told James Bennet that after the first blast, he raced to his apartment balcony. "I saw smoke, and then I ran downstairs. I wanted to save people." He was just a few yards from the blast site when the second missile hit, piercing an arm and a leg with shrapnel. Dr. Zain al-Abedin Shaheen ran down the street from his medical clinic to help. He was killed.

As was often the case, the Israelis and the Palestinians came away with completely different interpretations of the same event. The Israeli military was sure it had taken every possible precaution and was hugely offended by the Palestinian claims of civilian casualties. But I had seen them—the hospital staff had opened the refrigerators in the morgue to show me the evidence.

Eli asked the Israeli military officials to come to the Fox bureau and view the tape in slow motion and then give their response as our camera rolled. The officials declined but acknowledged they had not seen the Palestinians in the shadows. "It seems to me there may be people in the alleyway," an Israeli military official conceded. "It's possible this is the cause for all the casualties."

10

"WE'LL TAKE THE AMBULANCE, IT'S FREE"

About a month into the uprising, Fares Odeh literally became the poster boy for the intifada. One of my AP colleagues, Laurent Rebours, took a stunning photo of fourteen-year-old Fares, with his right arm cocked as he was about to hurl a stone directly at an Israeli tank that had its cannon pointed in his direction. The photo appeared in newspapers worldwide. Among Palestinians, it instantly became an iconic poster. It was plastered on bedroom walls and featured on calendars. For Palestinians, it defined their David versus Goliath struggle.

Fares became an overnight celebrity, although he was already a veteran rock-chucker. He loved being the bravest boy in the pack, out in front of all of the other kids at the Karni Crossing, east of Gaza City, where Palestinian youths and gunmen battled daily with the Israeli troops. He was one of nine kids, which was not unusual for a Gaza household. His parents thoroughly disapproved of his hobby but had trouble keeping track of him. "I would go three times a day to find [Fares] and bring him home," his mother, Enaam Udah, told me. "But he would always go back."

Her dilemma was shared by countless Palestinian parents: how do you keep teenage boys from throwing stones at Israeli army vehicles? "Sometimes I'd sit down to lunch, and before I could put the first bite in my mouth, some kids would come by and tell me Fares was at Karni again, throwing stones," she said. "I'd drop my fork and rush out to find him." Her husband, Fayek, "beat him black and blue for throwing stones," she added.[1]

The peer pressure was overwhelming. The Israeli soldiers were a constant presence. All of the other teenage boys were doing it. Even if a parent trusted a child not to throw stones, all sorts of terrible accidents happened when the Israeli troops were sharing the streets with civilians. Every day presented a choice: do you let your kids go to school, or do you keep them home?

The following scenario also played out thousands of times: The Israeli military declared a nighttime curfew, and no Palestinians were supposed to be on the streets after dark. But what was a Palestinian man to do if his child got sick or his pregnant wife went into labor? In principle, Israeli soldiers allowed medical emergencies to pass checkpoints and travel to hospitals. Yet there were many documented cases in which Palestinians with urgent medical needs were delayed for hours or denied permission to pass. Many times, Palestinian babies were born in cars at checkpoints. Most often, the Palestinian women were attempting to reach the closest Palestinian hospital and were not trying to go into Israel.

None of this concerned young Fares Odeh. Just three days after the famous photograph was taken, however, a cousin of his, who also happened to be a Palestinian police officer, was killed in clashes with the Israelis. When Fares received the news, "he crossed his heart and promised to fight the Israelis every day," his mother recounted. And he did. Nine days later, Fares was shot in the neck and killed while throwing stones at Israeli troops. Thousands attended his funeral. Iraqi President Saddam Hussein sent the family a $10,000 check.

In the early days of the Palestinian uprising, the fighting was so ritualistic and grimly predictable that you could almost set your watch by its daily rhythms. I was in Gaza City on the morning of November 10, 2000, barely a month after the intifada began, and

I sketched out my day in advance in order to cover the trauma that was inevitable. As I set out from my hotel at daybreak, the only unknown was which Palestinian families would receive the wrenching news that one of their young men had fallen.

I headed first to the simple whitewashed mortuary at Shifa Hospital, Gaza City's main health-care facility, where the dead and the wounded were delivered. On this morning, about a thousand young men had descended on the mortuary, behind the main hospital building, to collect the bodies of three Palestinians who had died from Israeli gunfire in clashes a day earlier. "Every day I see the men come here, and I feel very bad," said Abdulrazaq al-Masri, who ran the mortuary. "I know there will probably be more dead soon."

As soon as the three bodies were collected by relatives, the impromptu funeral march began. The bodies were placed on wooden stretchers and carried back to their family homes in the slums of Gaza City. One of the three, eighteen-year-old Khalil Abu Saad, had died overnight from a bullet wound to the chest.

As the men carried the bodies through the streets, the crowd grew bigger as women, children, and older men joined in the procession. Women in black wailed as Abu Saad's thin body, wrapped in the red, white, green, and black Palestinian flag, was carried through the Beach Refugee Camp along Gaza's Mediterranean coast. Two of Abu Saad's friends raced a block ahead of the procession, clutching a tub of glue and the "martyr posters" of Abu Saad that had been hastily produced at a local print shop.

His friends plastered posters on every building they passed, adding to an already large public gallery of martyrs. Abu Saad's poster was simple and standard—it included a head shot of him, surrounded by images of the Dome of the Rock shrine in Jerusalem and AK-47 automatic rifles. Other youths, anticipating their own deaths, carried their favorite photos in their chest pockets so that their friends would know which images to use. Some left nothing to chance. They went to photo studios and had pictures taken while holding an assault rifle, with a bandolier of bullets draped over a shoulder and a headband from the faction they represented.

As the crowd marched past, young boys, wide-eyed and barefoot, emerged from rundown apartments and stared in fascination. Their older brothers joined in, many carrying Palestinian flags. Gunmen in civilian clothes fired bursts of automatic gunfire skyward.

"Death to our enemies," shouted a man with a microphone, riding in an old, beat-up Peugeot that led the procession. "Paradise for martyrs," shouted another. An Israeli flag was torched. From a truck, an Arabic song blared a pulsating message to the Israelis: "We are coming."

By late morning, the three separate funeral marches, now made up of perhaps ten thousand men and a small number of women, converged on the ancient Omari mosque in the center of Gaza City. The crowd sat shoulder to shoulder and spilled out into the equally crowded street. "There will be paradise for these men because they were defending Al Aksa," cried the sheik leading the service, in reference to the seventh-century mosque in Jerusalem.

After a short service, a roar rose from the crowd as the bodies were taken from the mosque. The day was still young, but already there was word of more deaths. "Do you think we can make these kids stop the intifada?" asked Sam Nasser, thirty-four, a neighbor of one of those killed a day earlier. He then answered his own question. "I have kids, and I can't keep them away."

Young Palestinians had no other options as exciting and appealing as taking part in the intifada. Even those who might have been hesitant about joining were swept along by the crowd. Young men and boys crammed onto pickup trucks, wedged into minivans, and even attached themselves spread-eagle to the roofs of cars as the procession flocked to a large cemetery on the eastern edge of Gaza, near the border with Israel. There, the mourners encircled three adjacent burial plots. A brother of one of the dead collapsed in grief. With little ceremony, the three were interred in Gaza's sandy soil, their graves topped with wreaths of pink and red carnations.

Many of the mourners headed home, but for a few hundred teenage boys, the action was just beginning. Some had managed to scrape together five shekels, a little more than a dollar, for a taxi ride to the Karni Crossing, where Israeli soldiers were always waiting at the border. I asked a group of boys whether they had enough money for a taxi home. "We'll take the ambulance, it's free," one joked.

Several hundred teenagers crept through an olive grove, which provided enough cover to allow them within a hundred yards of the Israeli soldiers. No one questioned the wisdom of confronting heavily armed Israeli troops with nothing more than stones and bottles of gasoline.

All of their projectiles fell far short of the soldiers in their armored vehicles. The troops responded sporadically, mostly with tear gas. But then came a blast of rubber bullets, and one youth was hit in the jaw and seriously wounded. He was one of seven hurt that day at the Karni Crossing, a mercifully mild clash compared to most days.

Back at Shifa Hospital that evening, casualties were coming from several places in Gaza. Dr. Mouaweya Hassanein commanded the emergency room from a tiny office that he rarely left. He came every day at 8 a.m. and stayed until midnight. "Sometimes I'm very angry, other times I'm just very sad," Dr. Hassanein told me in a weary voice.

Journalists and relatives of the wounded streamed into his office throughout the day, but most of those wandering in and out of the emergency room were stone throwers checking on injured comrades. The youngsters, collectively known as *shabab*, the Arabic word for "youth," roamed the halls and mingled freely with doctors and nurses on the blood-slicked floors of the emergency room. With his booming, scratchy voice, Dr. Hassanein periodically lost patience. "*Shabab, shabab*," he shouted, shooing them out of a crowded room with his arms flapping furiously. "You must leave, we can't work like this."

As night fell, the day's toll throughout the Palestinian territories was four dead and dozens wounded. In Gaza and the West Bank, families mourned. The printers were already working on the next batch of martyr posters. More funerals were planned for the next day.

Israel also had its own grim rituals, and they often played out at the National Center for Forensic Medicine, a modest, three-story, tan stucco building set along a busy roadway in Jaffa, just outside Tel Aviv. It was an old Arab family compound and is still commonly known as Abu Kabir, the name of the family that lived there prior to the 1948 war between Arabs and Jews at Israel's independence. For the uninitiated, it would be easy to drive past without taking notice, let alone grasping the remarkable stories that unfold inside. Israel's home-grown system for responding to terror attacks has many extraordinary components, but perhaps none is so unique as the country's lone forensic institute.

The center was run for nearly two decades by Dr. Jehuda Hiss, a bespectacled, mild-mannered man with a professorial mien who witnessed the carnage caused by almost every major attack in Israel during his long tenure. Every person who dies an unnatural death in Israel is taken to the center, which made it the gathering point for the anguished relatives of the victims after every suicide bombing. Even if an attack occurred in a distant part of the country, all of the bodies and the scraps of flesh were delivered to the forensic center. Facing intense time pressure and overwrought families, Dr. Hiss had to simultaneously piece together the broken bodies of the dead and minister to the raw emotions of the living.

In February 2004, he and his team had just made a grisly discovery following a suicide bombing on a Jerusalem bus a day earlier. Police said that seven people were killed, plus the bomber, on the charred and crumpled bus. Yet when Dr. Hiss and his team developed genetic profiles on the scores of body parts brought to the institute, they discovered that one set of remains did not match any other. All of the small bits and pieces constituted an eighth victim, an immigrant woman from Ethiopia whose body had disintegrated so completely in the blast that rescue workers did not recognize any of her body parts as belonging to another person. "This person must have been sitting next to the bomber," Dr. Hiss said. "We could not have identified her without DNA tests."

Dr. Hiss's office walls were mostly bare, except for a slate of black wood featuring twenty-four types of bullets. The most prominent book on his desk was *Gunshot Wounds*. Within arm's reach was a plastic container of ball bearings that had been packed inside one bomb to make it more lethal. From the time the second Palestinian uprising began in 2000 until Dr. Hiss left his post four years later, he was intimately involved in more than a hundred suicide bombings, missing only one while traveling in the United States. In his dry manner, Dr. Hiss rattled off the disturbing realities he encountered.

"After so many attacks, I can recognize in an instant which one is the bomber," said Dr. Hiss. A bomber often had twenty or more pounds of powerful explosives strapped to his waist, and his torso all but disintegrated. "All that remains of the terrorist is the head, the feet, and the hands," Dr. Hiss explained. Even bodies that are largely intact can be difficult to identify because the power of the blast so distorts facial features. One time, two young Israeli women with similar features were killed. When the husband of one woman arrived at the morgue, he tearfully embraced the one who was not his wife for several minutes before he realized his mistake.

Every bombing meant an all-nighter for Dr. Hiss and his staff as they rushed to identify the dead. Jewish religious law demands that the work be both swift and thorough. It calls for the whole body to be buried as soon as possible, preferably within twenty-four hours. Yet in most Western countries it can take two or three days, sometimes longer, to work up a DNA profile. Dr. Hiss's lab shaved the time to as few as twelve hours. Still, a major bombing produced hundreds of small pieces of flesh that could not easily be traced to their original owners. Performing DNA tests on every last sliver could take weeks, if not months. "Although we have the technology to identify all of the parts, we simply don't have the time," said Dr. Hiss. With no easy solution, the lab bundled together all of the smallest remains—which likely included parts of the Palestinian bomber, as well as of the Israeli dead—and carried out an uncomfortable compromise of burying them in one common, unmarked grave.

After dealing with the dead, Dr. Hiss's job became even more difficult. While he and his team were in the lab, relatives packed the small waiting area. In most cases, the relatives had already been to hospitals near the bomb site. When they were unable to locate loved ones among the wounded, they traveled to the forensic center, expecting the worst. Dr. Hiss took it upon himself to inform family members, who could be angry and irrational in their grief. "Someone leaves home at 8 a.m. and is killed a half-hour later," Dr. Hiss said. "The families want to know if they suffered. They want to know exactly how they died. I'm always surprised that they ask so many detailed questions."

The families often waited through the night at the center, which was not built for the crowds of two hundred or more that descended after major attacks and sometimes spilled out onto the grounds. As the bombings mounted, a center for the families was built next to the morgue, easing the crowding, if not the trauma. The most awkward moment came when a family asked to see the victim. "I say, 'It's better to remember them when they were living,'" Dr. Hiss said. But about a quarter of the families insisted. "I explain it's only part of the body. Still, they will hug a foot if that is all there is." For many years he rejected such requests, but psychologists recommended otherwise. "The families want to touch the body one last time to prepare for the separation," he said. "If they don't see them, it is like a virtual death. They are right to ask for this."

On a sweltering morning in the summer of 2002, Dr. Hiss and his team were bleary-eyed after working until 1 a.m. the previous night, handling the bodies of seven Israelis killed in a shooting ambush on a bus. Three bloodied corpses were on gurneys in the morgue. Bloodstained medical gowns filled a laundry bag. The piercing smell of death hung in the humid air. The lab had temporarily become an open-air facility due to renovations. A hole large enough to drive a car through had been punched through a wall. The renovations were regularly interrupted by bombing attacks elsewhere in Israel, and when the dead were brought in, the squeamish construction workers would step aside. Some workers were so spooked by the delivery of the dead that they never came back. Faced with this relentless stream of death, Dr. Hiss said that he coped without any special means. "As soon as I leave the premises, I really don't think about it. I keep myself busy, and I never discuss my work with my family," he said. "I've been asked many times if I need psychological support, but I don't."[2]

11

SOLDIERS TO THE LEFT OF US, MILITANTS TO THE RIGHT

We never seriously considered leaving Jerusalem because of the violence. We were not trying to prove a point. It was a simple calculation that this was an important story we wanted to cover, and we felt we could minimize the dangers. Having covered most of the bombings, Greg and I believed that we could predict the locations of attacks with roughly the same accuracy that you could plot the murders in a major U.S. city by reviewing the annual homicide statistics. We didn't ride buses. We avoided cafés on busy streets and steered clear of pedestrian malls, the places most likely to be hit. We did not take the kids to the grocery store—partly because we did not want to fight with them in the candy aisle, and partly because the stores could attract a bomber. As a result, we felt that the risk to our kids was minimal. They lived in a small world that consisted almost entirely of home, school, and the neighborhood park, none of which were targets.

In covering wars and conflicts, we were often struck by how few people chose to leave the danger zone. People made small adjustments and adaptations, hoping this would somehow bring them a measure of safety, although it often seemed as if they were deluding themselves. Yet here we were, doing exactly the same thing.

Israelis, who had dealt with terror attacks in one form or another for decades, had long ago reached a collective decision to go about their day-to-day lives in as normal a fashion as possible, no matter how dire the circumstances. In many ways, it was not rational, but it was perhaps the only way to stay sane. We could not have imagined getting on a bus at the height of the bombings. In Israel, however, cars were prohibitively expensive for some people, and gasoline cost more than five dollars a gallon. Many Israelis had no choice but to take buses to work or school.

For parents with teenage children, every weekend was a source of nail-biting anxiety. Even in Jerusalem, where the Jewish Sabbath was widely observed from sundown Friday to sundown Saturday, a few clubs and restaurants remained open, drawing large numbers of young Israelis who were determined to have a good time. In more secular places such as Tel Aviv, the restaurants were full and the clubs were packed. The more popular the hangout, the longer the line out front—and the more likely a Palestinian bomber would target it. Despite the obvious danger, many Israeli parents simply resigned themselves to the reality that their kids were going to find a way to their favorite spots. The best the parents could do was stay in cell phone contact with their kids throughout the night. Time and again, we heard a familiar tale from bleary-eyed parents who stayed up until 2 or 3 a.m. in a haze of apprehension and sleep deprivation, desperately waiting for a call from their teenager needing a ride home.

In our circumstances, we felt we could make largely rational decisions because we followed the bombings so obsessively. We knew it was virtually impossible for a Palestinian with a bomb to get out of the fenced-in Gaza Strip. Almost every bomber came from the West Bank, and the main breeding ground was the northern part of the territory, particularly Nablus and Jenin. When leaving their homes, bombers would often head south, passing near or through Ramallah and entering the northern part of Jerusalem. Jaffa Street, the main commercial strip in the northern part of the city, was the most obvious target. As a result, we tried to avoid Jaffa and its cross streets.

There was one small problem. My Fox office and Greg's AP office were in the same building, Jerusalem Capital Studios, at 206 Jaffa Street. The building also happened to be right across from the Central Bus Station, which was considered a prime target in the early days of the intifada. Police cordoned off the area around the bus station at least a couple of times a month to destroy a suspicious-looking package with a controlled explosion. The police never found a bomb, but they frequently blew up brown-bag lunches carelessly left behind by passengers. Countless falafels were sacrificed in these fireballs.

Although we never hesitated to go into the thick of the fighting in the Palestinian areas, we held extended debates about which places in Jerusalem were reasonably safe. We were consistently amazed at how quickly Israelis returned to places that had been bombed. The police, the rescue teams, and the cleanup crews restored a bomb site to an outward semblance of normality within hours of an attack. Debris was swept out. Hoses washed away blood from the sidewalk. Shattered windows were replaced overnight. The yellow police tape came down. The next day, Israelis placed flowers and candles at the scene. By the time those flowers wilted, the street tended to be as busy as ever.

During the two-year period when the bombings were at their worst, from the summer of 2001 to the summer of 2003, Jaffa Street and its cross streets were the scene of nine suicide bombings, a suicidal shooting attack, and several car bombs. All of the attacks took place inside a grid less than a mile long and a few hundred yards wide. Commerce plummeted, and middle-class Jerusalemites who had cars and other shopping options avoided downtown. Yet Jaffa Street was still busy during the day, and many people shopped and ate lunch on Jaffa as a personal act of defiance.

"I can understand that people who are far away think the Israelis and the Palestinians should just sit down and make peace," said Yona Assaf, a special education teacher and a former New Yorker who had moved to Israel a decade earlier. "But if you're here, you can't run away from the truth. And I think the truth is that there isn't going to be peace."

Despite her assessment, Ms. Assaf was not taking any special precautions and, in fact, seemed to be courting danger. She was at the corner of Jaffa and King George V streets, a major intersection that was perhaps the most likely place in the country to be bombed. She had just emerged from lunch at Sbarro pizzeria, the site of a devastating 2001 bombing that killed fifteen people. And a hundred yards up Jaffa Street, a bus bombing had recently killed seventeen Israelis. Yet there was a long line of passengers at the bus stop.

"We are staying here," said Rina Daniel, who was behind the counter of a family-owned bookstore that has been at the same spot on Jaffa Street since 1959. She said business was down 40 percent since the Palestinian intifada began, but she was committed to weathering the crisis. "This is our city, our country. Why should I move?" Unlike many other stores on

Jaffa Street, no guard was at the door. Her only security upgrade since the intifada began was to visually scrutinize Arab customers for hints that they might have a bomb. But, she acknowledged, "this probably won't stop an attack."

One bombing in this area took place just outside the apartment building where our babysitter Rose lived. She was, however, at our home when the bomber, Muhammad Hashaika, detonated his explosive on a crowded sidewalk, killing three Israelis and splattering himself all over the front of Rose's building. Pieces of his flesh landed on her second-floor balcony.

Rose and her roommates had their laundry hanging out to dry, and the clothes were speckled with the blood of Hashaika and his victims. As we had done many times before, we urged Rose and her Filipina roommates to move out. Rose finally relocated later that year, when we moved to a larger place and insisted that she live with us. Even though our place was only a short distance away, residential streets were much safer than her downtown neighborhood, where apartments occupied the floors above the commercial strip at street level and where so many buses passed.

If Jaffa Street was the most dangerous place in all of Israel, conditions near our home in the southern part of Jerusalem were nearly as bad. We lived close to Emek Refaim Street, which is part of the German Colony neighborhood that is lined with trendy stores. It was the most convenient place for us to shop, yet we generally avoided it because it was a likely target for Palestinian bombers coming from the southern West Bank. Palestinian attackers passed through Bethlehem on their way to Jerusalem, and Emek Refaim Street was one of the first busy commercial strips they reached.

Everyone performed his or her own calculus, and we knew our approach was not bomb-proof, but we felt that it was guided by facts and driven by logic. Many Israelis, however, seemed to act on the quirkiest of notions. Some thought it was perfectly fine to go back to a place that had already been bombed, on the theory that lightning never strikes twice. Others insisted on sitting at the back of a restaurant, as far away from the glass windows as possible. The thinking was that a bomber usually blew up at the entrance, and shards of glass from the windows could be nearly as dangerous as the bomb's shrapnel.

A competing theory was that it was less risky to sit outdoors at a café. Enclosed spaces, such as restaurants and buses, magnify the force of an explosion, while blasts dissipate in open space. Any high school physics student could appreciate this reasoning. As a rule, the bombings in contained spaces were much deadlier than those outside. The weakness in this line of thinking was that bombers tended to be in a hurry to reach "paradise." They often blew themselves up at the first sign of a public gathering. As a result, they were more likely to detonate at the entrance to a restaurant or a shop or next to the sidewalk tables, rather than trying to get inside, where a security guard might block their path.

One seemingly sound plan was to patronize only places that had security guards at the front door. In exchange for long, lousy hours and a minimum-wage paycheck, thousands of Israelis were willing to work as security guards, risking and sometimes sacrificing their lives to keep bombers out. In performing their jobs conscientiously, however, security guards had to inspect every purse, bag, and briefcase, and this often created long lines on the sidewalk. On multiple occasions, bombers went for the long lines at shopping mall entrances and made no attempt to get inside the buildings.

A day of routine errands raised an endless series of life-and-death security questions, and if you thought about it too hard, you would never make it out the front door. But it was equally impossible not to think about it. During this time, we regularly spent the week working in the most volatile battle zones in the West Bank and Gaza. Yet when we returned home to Jerusalem for the weekend, we would refuse to meet friends at restaurants in the more bomb-prone parts of the city. This logic simply did not compute with Israelis, who assessed danger with a different algorithm. For Israelis, a trip to Gaza was a death wish fulfilled. Going for coffee at a favorite café in Jerusalem was something they had done for years, and they were not going to stop because a Palestinian bomber might interrupt.

The one place we knew to be a Palestinian target, yet still chose to frequent, was the Jerusalem Mall on the southern edge of the city. It was the largest and busiest mall in Jerusalem and, more crucially, had the only real range of movies. The mall was close to Jerusalem's border with Bethlehem and the West Bank. The place was always packed, and many Palestinians had shopped there and knew it well. On two occasions, the Israeli security forces thwarted Palestinian bombers only a short distance from the mall. Yet we went because we needed a mental break from the carnage and felt that the security at the mall was good enough.

What was "good enough"? Well, to take a seat at a movie, you had to pass three separate security checks. First, security guards inspected cars, looking in the trunks and the glove compartments and searching any bags at the entrance to the parking lot. After parking, patrons walked through an airport-style metal detector at the entrance to the mall. And finally, a security guard at the movie complex waved his electronic wand over your contours before you entered the theater.

On a busy day, you could easily be subjected to a dozen security checks, some of them quite absurd. Our favorite was watching Israelis, both soldiers and civilians, carry their automatic rifles into banks. The dutiful bank security guard had no interest in a customer's weapon that was on full display. The guard would conduct a cursory body search to make sure the gun-toting Israeli was not hiding a bomb. Having found none, the guard would direct the armed person to the nearest teller. For these guards, a bank heist was the least of their concerns.

On our frequent visits to the Palestinian areas, the dangers were equally real. This was particularly true when the Israelis carried out a major military incursion, such as Operation Defensive Shield in the spring of 2002. During this time, I learned a crucial survival skill: how to talk to tanks.

I traveled from one battered West Bank town to the next in a hulking, four-wheel-drive, armored Land Rover. Finding the day's story often involved random cruising through these towns, where the Israelis had retaken the streets. With regularity, my colleagues and I would turn a corner onto a narrow lane and find ourselves staring directly into the 120-millimeter cannon of a sixty-ton Israeli Merkava tank. No matter how many times this happened, it was always a rude surprise.

The Israeli military was not targeting journalists, but it had declared the West Bank cities "closed military zones," and anyone traveling on the otherwise deserted streets was sure to draw the interest, if not the aim, of Israeli soldiers. We had a sign inside the front windshield that read "Press" and gaffer tape on the doors that said "TV." Next to a tank, our armored vehicle looked like a toy car. The bulletproof windshield could withstand a couple of rounds of automatic rifle fire, but it was not going to hold up to a tank shell. And any rash move could make the soldiers edgy in areas where they constantly came under Palestinian fire.

Out of these regular encounters, an informal etiquette quickly developed. When facing a tank, we immediately brought our armored car to a stop. The driver and the front-seat passenger pressed the palms of both hands on the front windshield to show we meant no harm. Within seconds, we generally received a clear message from the tank. Most often, the driver revved the engine, sending up a puff of diesel fumes. This smoke signal could roughly be translated as, "We're very busy hunting terrorists. It is in your interest to leave immediately." Other tank gunners were no more obliging, but at least they had a sense of humor. On multiple occasions, the gunner wiggled the tank cannon from side to side, like a mother wagging a forefinger at her misbehaving child. The gesture cut the tension, even if it prevented us from passing. Sometimes, tank units displayed tolerance and, dare I say, respect for the press. In several instances, the gunner swiveled his cannon 90 degrees to the side, indicating that we were welcome to drive past. Which we did. Slowly.

Our Israeli friends often asked us whether we felt threatened when working among armed Palestinian groups. The short answer was "no." Even during the most intense bouts of fighting, Palestinians, including the gunmen, were generally hospitable to foreign journalists. We told the Israelis that our repeated forays into the West Bank and Gaza had nothing to do with bravery. We never hesitated to flee if we sensed menace. For us, the equation was simple: how do you get the story and not get shot? Cowardice, we often said, was a highly underrated virtue and always an acceptable option. Then we would explain that when we did feel threatened, the source was almost always the Israel Defense Forces.

For most Israelis, this was impossible to accept. The majority of Israelis served in the military and had great respect for the institution. Israelis were fond of describing their armed forces as "the most moral army in the world." They believed that Palestinian civilian casualties were a rare and unintended by-product of the fight Israel was forced to wage. The Israelis had great difficulty acknowledging the risks faced by noncombatants, whether they were Palestinian civilians, foreign journalists, or international aid workers. Yet in such a messy, volatile, and unpredictable environment, bad things happened. Often they were accidents. Sometimes they were the result of poor judgment. Occasionally, there was no excuse.

One Saturday morning in 2001, a young female photographer, Yola Monakhov, was sent on assignment by the AP to Bethlehem to photograph a feature story on how Palestinian bakeries were coping during the fighting. "It was eerily quiet that day,"

Yola wrote later in the *Columbia Journalism Review*. Though she was not looking for trouble, Bethlehem had been tense. Yola, a petite woman, donned an oversized bulletproof vest that had been loaned to her by a much larger male photographer. After taking photos at a bakery, Yola saw a group of Palestinian youths throwing stones over the top of a house toward an Israeli military outpost on the other side. Yola hung around to take a few shots. Her oversized vest proved too cumbersome, however, and she took it off. "I walked back to the car to put it in the trunk and saw a small group of Israeli soldiers. We exchanged wary 'shaloms.'" What she did not know was that a Palestinian sniper had killed an Israeli soldier at that outpost a day earlier, and his comrades were in a foul mood.

The Palestinian boys eventually gave up on the stone throwing, and Yola was ready to leave. "Suddenly, a cry went up," she recounted. "An Israeli soldier had appeared at the end of the street and was aiming his M-16 at us." The Palestinian boys immediately fled. Yola could see the soldier clearly and thought she was easily identifiable as a photographer with her two cameras. Still, she tried to take cover in a doorway along the street—but a single shot rang out, hitting her in the pelvis. "It was a slow and deliberate error and not at all something done in the chaos of battle," she declared. "I also wonder why there was not a single rubber bullet or warning shot or anything proportional to match the threat posed by the incompetent Palestinian boys with stones."

"I crumpled in pain and surrender but retained the presence of mind to release a loud, shrill feminine wail," she said. "I wanted the soldier to know: What have you done? You have shot a civilian, a woman, a photographer."

Moments later, the Palestinian youths returned and carried Yola to a Palestinian ambulance. She was taken to the nearby Palestinian hospital, but its facilities were limited and her injuries were serious. She needed to get to an Israeli hospital quickly. Yet the Israeli military checkpoints made it difficult for anyone in a Palestinian vehicle to enter Israel. Yola needed to travel only a few miles from Bethlehem to the nearby Hadassah Ein Kerem Hospital in Jerusalem, but this required tense negotiations between the AP office in Jerusalem and the Israeli military, which initially insisted that its soldiers had not shot anyone.

Eventually, Yola was allowed into Jerusalem. She underwent emergency surgery in the skilled hands of Dr. Avi Rivkind, the doctor who had tried unsuccessfully to save the Israeli soldier a day earlier. "I couldn't save the soldier, but I will try to save her," he told journalists outside the operating room. The doctor immediately made the link between the two shootings, even if the Israeli military did not.

Yola suffered a number of internal injuries, but Dr. Rivkind saved her. As she began her long recovery, which required multiple surgeries and months of rehabilitation, the AP bureau chief in Jerusalem, Jocelyn Noveck, began pushing the Israeli military to investigate the shooting. After protracted negotiations, a senior military commander agreed to visit the hospital to meet with Yola and Jocelyn. During the conversation, the commander kept referring to the "Palestinian boy" who had been shot and taken away in an ambulance. Finally, Yola blurted out, "There was no Palestinian boy. I am that Palestinian boy."

The commander had clearly received a less-than-accurate account from his subordinates, according to Jocelyn. As the commander left a few minutes later, Jocelyn heard him telling another officer who accompanied him, "This doesn't make any sense to me."

Ultimately, the Israeli military acknowledged that one of its soldiers had shot Yola. That soldier was sentenced to twenty-eight days in jail, and his commanding officer demoted. The Israeli military described Yola's shooting as an aberration that was prosecuted. Palestinians said that such episodes were all too common and that the military would not have investigated if the victim had been an anonymous Palestinian youth, rather than a Western photographer backed by a major American news organization.[1]

THE FIRST MAN AT
THE SCENE

Long before the era of suicide bombings, Dr. David Applebaum had made a name for himself in emergency medicine. A man of boundless energy, Dr. Applebaum was a native of Cleveland who graduated from Roosevelt University in Chicago in 1972, before reaching his twentieth birthday. He was ordained as a rabbi two years later and graduated from the Medical College of Ohio in Toledo in 1978. A few years after that, he moved to Israel, where he earned acclaim for pioneering thrombolysis, a procedure that helps dissolve blood clots in heart attack victims during the first critical moments. He also worked to establish private clinics that greatly reduced the burden on emergency rooms at government-run hospitals. During one episode in 1984, Dr. Applebaum came to the aid of a man who had been shot in a clothing shop and began to operate on him while the shooting was still going on outside.

Dr. Applebaum worked for years with the Israeli counterpart to the Red Cross, Magen David Adom. He would race to accidents or terror attacks and became known as "the first man on the scene." He eventually made his professional home at Shaare Tzedek Hospital, a large facility in western Jerusalem affiliated with Hebrew

University. He directed an emergency room that often received the victims of suicide bombings and other violence. In August 2003, Dr. Applebaum hosted New York City mayor Michael Bloomberg, who visited to express solidarity with Israelis at a time of frequent bombings.

A few weeks later, on September 9, 2003, Dr. Applebaum was in Lower Manhattan, speaking at a conference linked to the second anniversary of the World Trade Center attacks. The conference was held at the investment bank Goldman Sachs, a short distance from where the Twin Towers once stood. Dr. Applebaum gave a step-by-step presentation on how his hospital responded to attacks that produced mass casualties. He concluded his remarks by saying, "From one moment to the next, we never know what will happen in the ER." Shortly after speaking, he had to rush home for a major event in his own life. With some of his U.S. relatives joining him, he boarded a flight for Israel that landed on September 10, the day before the wedding of his twenty-year-old daughter, Nava.

Around the time that Dr. Applebaum and his relatives were landing at Ben-Gurion International Airport, a Palestinian suicide bomber struck at a bus stop packed with soldiers only a few miles away on the edge of Tel Aviv. The bomber struck at the height of rush hour with a bomb hidden in a leather bag, killing seven Israelis and wounding more than a dozen.

Craig Nelson, a good friend of ours and a reporter for Cox newspapers, raced to the scene, where the bomber's head was wedged between beams on the bus stop's overhang. In the gruesome physics of suicide bombings, the force of the blast usually decapitates the bomber, and this memorable image stuck in Craig's mind as he reported the story and then headed back home to Jerusalem. He knew it would be a long night of writing, and on his way home he stopped to pick up dinner at Pizza Meter, on Emek Refaim Street, the commercial drag near his home and just a few blocks from ours. "After seeing the dead bodies and the head of the bomber, a lot of people might go throw up in a field and would really be shaken. They would want to think about a whole range of important and profound things in life," Craig said. "But here, you just have to get on with life. I was just thinking, 'I'm going to call for a pizza because we're not going to have time to cook tonight.' It's not just me, the whole country thinks this way. Israelis just get on with it. They will not be intimidated, and you have to respect it. But I think it does come back to haunt all of us over time."

Meanwhile, Dr. Applebaum, a father of six, arrived at his home in Jerusalem. With additional relatives on hand, the place was buzzing with excitement in advance of the wedding planned for the following day at a nearby kibbutz. To escape the commotion, Dr. Applebaum took Nava for coffee and a quiet father-daughter talk at the Café Hillel restaurant, which was next door to Pizza Meter. Large family dinners at home were the tradition for the Applebaums, not trendy restaurants. "He was not a café goer," said Dr. Jonathan Halevy, the director general of Shaare Tzedek Hospital.

Next door to the café, Craig Nelson sipped a soft drink while waiting for his pizza. He heard a commotion at the entrance to Pizza Meter, just a few feet behind him. After a long, stressful day, and in a city where disturbances were commonplace, he did not bother to turn around. If he had, he would have seen Itzik Meir, a fifty-three-year-old security guard, scuffling with a suicide bomber who wanted to blow up Pizza Meter. "He had some big package on his back," Meir said afterward. "I stopped him, and he ran into Café Hillel."

The café was just steps away, and only seconds after the bomber was rebuffed at the doorstep of Pizza Meter, he turned himself into a fireball at the entrance of the café. The bomb produced a deafening blast, followed by the crashing of broken glass. Then came the strange stillness, amounting to an almost total silence, that lasts for a few fleeting seconds after an explosion. Witnesses to suicide bombings often describe this phenomenon, saying that it is as if the sound and the air have simply been sucked out of the entire neighborhood. After this brief pause, the silence is broken by the jagged cries of the maimed, desperate cell phone calls for help, and the wailing of a hundred car alarms, all set off by shock waves emanating from the blast.

Craig emerged from the pizzeria and could scarcely believe the sight that confronted him. For the second time in the space of hours, he found himself staring at the severed head of a suicide bomber. This one had rolled onto the asphalt and came to a stop in an upright position in the middle of Emek Refaim Street. The bomber's horribly singed face was pointed directly at Craig.

Craig turned and went to the entrance of Café Hillel, then dropped to his knees to assist a young woman who was badly burned and gushing blood from the neck. He held her in his arms and tried to stop the blood loss with his hand. Craig felt helpless but continued to embrace the young woman for several minutes, waiting for rescuers to arrive.

Another reporter and friend of ours, Michael Matza of the *Philadelphia Inquirer*, lived just three blocks from the bombing and ran to the scene. He arrived when the air was still thick with smoke and dust. He immediately noticed one of those details peculiar to suicide bombings in Israel: the police were stopping ambulances as they approached. The police briefly checked the identities of the ambulance crews to make sure they were Israelis—and not Palestinian impostors attempting to follow up with a second bomb. Once vetted, the rescue crews were allowed to the bomb site. Yet there was nothing they could do for the young woman in Craig Nelson's arms—Nava Applebaum was one of seven people who died in the attack.

At Shaare Tzedek hospital, the director, Dr. Halevy, needed eight minutes to travel from his home to the emergency room when there was a bombing. Yet Dr. Applebaum almost always beat him there. In one instance, a 2 a.m. explosion in Jerusalem roused Dr. Applebaum from his slumber, and he instinctively raced to the hospital. On his arrival, the staff told him that the blast had been caused by a car tire that overheated and exploded, a regular occurrence during the city's blistering summers. On the night of the Café Hillel bombing, Dr. Halevy was surprised when he reached the hospital and found that Dr. Applebaum was not already treating the wounded. Dr. Halevy called Dr. Applebaum's cell phone. There was no answer. Dr. Halevy instantly suspected the worst.

Dr. Applebaum died next to his daughter at the entrance of the café. His body was identified by ambulance workers who had been his partners in many rescue missions over the years.

The following day, instead of giving his daughter away at a large celebration, Dr. Applebaum was buried alongside Nava in an even larger funeral at the stony hilltop cemetery of Giv'at Sha'ul, on the western edge of Jerusalem. Hundreds had planned to spend that evening dancing with the Applebaums. Instead, thousands mourned, many with red eyes and rubbery knees, as they recalled

Dr. Applebaum's good works. "He was a great combination of spirituality and humanity," said Aviva Cayam, who had known Dr. Applebaum since he was a teenager in Cleveland. "When people think of him, they use the Hebrew word *tzaddik*. That's a very special person who has both a human and a godly touch."

Three years passed, and a small item appeared in the *Jerusalem Post*. It said that one of Dr. Applebaum's surviving daughters, Shira, was riding in ambulances as she trained to be a paramedic. One of his sons, Yitzhak, was already a medical student.

13

MEN OF GOODWILL

George Saadeh, a Palestinian Christian from Bethlehem, is exactly the kind of person who inspires hope that there will be peace someday. Like many bright Palestinians, he went abroad for college and graduated from the University of Southern California with a degree in aerospace engineering. He returned to Bethlehem to teach and eventually became the principal of the Shepherd's School, a private Greek Orthodox institution with more than five hundred students. He had an extensive network of Israeli friends and was deeply saddened when the fighting led to travel restrictions that made it impossible for him to get together with them. Still, he continued to deliver a message of Israeli-Palestinian coexistence at his highly regarded school.

On a blustery, rain-soaked night in March 2003, Saadeh headed to the grocery store in his beige Peugeot 305 sedan with his wife and two daughters. They had traveled only a few blocks in their middle-class neighborhood when they approached two Israeli military jeeps parked on the side of the road. Troops were a common sight at this time, and Saadeh thought it prudent to slow down but felt no imminent danger. He had no way of knowing that his timing was so bad, it defied the laws of probability.

Moments earlier, those same Israeli troops had exchanged fire with Hamas gunmen in a seemingly identical beige Peugeot 305 sedan in the same neighborhood. The militants had managed to lose the Israeli soldiers on Bethlehem's hilly, winding streets. The tense Israeli soldiers believed that Saadeh's car was the one carrying the gunmen. As Saadeh neared the jeeps, the Israeli troops opened fire with automatic rifles and pumped at least thirty bullets into the car.

"We were stunned," Saadeh said the next day at Hadassah Ein Kerem Hospital in Jerusalem. He had received gunshot wounds to the abdomen and the back. His wife, Najwa, suffered minor injuries. Their fifteen-year-old daughter was hit in the knee. Their twelve-year-old girl, Christine, was killed.

"We couldn't believe they were shooting at us," Saadeh told me. "I screamed that we were civilians. I looked behind me, and I saw Christine had fallen to the floor." Saadeh said that no one in his family had heard any shooting, and they were not aware of any trouble in the area when they got in their car and set out for the supermarket. After their car came under fire, Saadeh turned the corner and came to a stop. Ten yards in front of their car was the other beige Peugeot 305. It, too, was riddled with bullets, and three men in the car, including two Hamas gunmen, died of their wounds.

As the Saadehs emerged from their pockmarked Peugeot, bloodied and screaming for help, the soldiers came around the corner. When they reached the Saadehs, they realized their mistake. "The soldiers were shocked when they saw the girls," Najwa Saadeh said from her hospital bed. "They told us, 'We are very sorry. We didn't mean to shoot you.' They came with us to the hospital. But what does sorry mean to me? I lost my daughter." Najwa Saadeh was still in the clothes she was wearing when she was shot. She pointed to the bloodstains on her sleeve and sobbed, "Look, Christine's blood is still with me."

When asked about the fighting, George Saadeh did not respond with venom or bitterness, as many victims of violence did. He spoke softly and with sadness about the inability of the two sides to live together. "We teach our kids peace and love and about democracy," he said. "But people are just getting crazy nowadays. It's really a shame what's going on."

· · ·

Some six thousand Palestinians have been killed since their uprising began in 2000. The two sides disagree on how many were civilians and how many were combatants. Israel says the vast majority were fighters, while Palestinians claim that most of the dead were civilians. Neither the Israeli nor the Palestinian government has offered detailed figures. Human rights groups and news organizations have tried to make the distinctions, and the most thorough ones found that roughly two-thirds of the Palestinians killed were combatants and the other one-third were not. That equates to about four thousand Palestinian combatants killed and two thousand civilian deaths. The number is far from precise and open to debate, but it is a reasonable figure for anyone who has followed the fighting. On the Israeli side, close to twelve hundred Israelis have been killed, and the breakdown is much clearer: about nine hundred of the dead were civilians, and about three hundred belonged to the security forces.

In short, the Israeli security forces have killed many more civilians unintentionally than Palestinian terrorists have killed on purpose. Most Palestinians find this statement so obvious that it need not be stated, while many Israelis view it as slander against their protectors. Yet it cuts to the heart of the conflict. Both sides see the other as the aggressor and their side as the victim. Each has stories of civilian deaths to prove their claims. The Israeli civilians tended to be killed in suicide bombings that attracted widespread coverage because of the spectacular nature of the attacks. Palestinian civilians often died in ones and twos. They were killed in places that were harder to get to, and the circumstances were often murky and disputed. Palestinian officials complained that many of these deaths received little attention, although the Palestinian leadership made no real effort to provide details.

Many Israelis argued passionately that there was no moral equivalence between a Palestinian terrorist who intentionally killed as many Israeli civilians as possible and an Israeli soldier, who, during an exchange of fire with armed Palestinians, accidentally killed a Palestinian civilian. Every country makes a moral and legal distinction between premeditated murder and accidental death. Yet the sheer firepower of the Israeli army guaranteed that the civilian toll would be high when it operated in urban areas.

. . .

When Israeli troops entered Palestinian towns in either the West Bank or Gaza, most Palestinian civilians refused to leave. In some cases, poor families had no options; they simply had no place to go. Yet even families that could move out during Israeli incursions tended to stay put. Palestinians called this *sumud* or "steadfast-ness," and regarded it as a form of resistance. In addition, some Palestinians felt that the Israelis were more likely to destroy homes that were empty. Some older Palestinians recalled the 1948 Israeli-Arab war, when hundreds of thousands of Palestinians fled or were expelled. They believed that the Israelis would claim any land that the Palestinians vacated, never to return it. The Palestinian motives for remaining planted in their homes varied from family to family. Collectively, however, they contributed to a remarkable scene when the Israelis invaded: intense fighting and routine daily life playing out side by side. Gun battles raged in one neighborhood, while an outdoor market carried on undisturbed just a few blocks away.

One of the more vivid examples was in October 2004, when Israel made a major push to damp down Palestinian rocket fire that was coming out of northern Gaza and tormenting the southern Israeli town of Sderot. The Israelis sent a large armored force to the edge of the Jabaliya Refugee Camp, the sprawling slum next to Gaza City that is home to many Palestinian militants. Israeli helicopters and unmanned drones circled overhead for days, while tanks parked on the southern and eastern fringes of the camp. Israeli snipers tried to pick off the elusive masked militants darting through the narrow streets. Yet civilians were everywhere. There are few playgrounds in Gaza. Kids play in the streets, all day, every day, even when tanks are literally a stone's throw away. Indeed, for many Palestinian kids, the presence of Israeli troops in town is an irresistible lure. Two Palestinian youths sought to emulate the militants, setting up a hollow piece of pipe as if it were a rocket launcher. The imitation worked all too well: an Israeli helicopter spotted the faux launcher and, believing it was real, fired a missile that killed the two boys.

Just a few blocks from the front line, pedestrians clogged the streets, making it difficult to maneuver a car. Policemen casually watched over street corners, and men sat on the front steps of shops, sipping tea as if it were a most ordinary day. The Israeli drones buzzing overhead were just white noise in a place where cacophony was the norm.

In the nearby town of Beit Lahiya, where the Israeli military was also active, all eleven members of the prosperous Filfil family were huddled in their living room one night during a firefight. The Israelis said they believed that the home was a source of Palestinian fire. At 1 a.m., an Israeli shell crashed into their five-story, stand-alone home. Everyone in the Filfil family was sprayed with shrapnel. When I caught up with them in the hospital, Sumaya Filfil was sharing a room with several of her wounded children. All of their faces were cut and reddened from shell fragments.

The family could have moved out of Beit Lahiya until the danger passed. Gaza City was just a few miles away and was largely unaffected. Yet Mrs. Filfil was defiant, saying that no one in her family was involved in the fighting, nor had militants used the house to shoot at Israeli forces. "Why should I run? This is our house," she declared. Where would the family go when they recovered, if the Israelis were still in the neighborhood? "I would go straight home and take my kids."

Dr. Mahmoud al-Asali, the head of the Kamal Adwan Hospital, told me that the sentiment was common among his many patients. "We say, 'We will die here, but we will not leave here.'"

Bassim Aramin thought he was leaving the conflict behind.

As a teenager in the 1980s, Aramin had a brief career as a wannabe militant. "We played cops and robbers among ourselves. Our problems started when we raised a Palestinian flag in a tree near our school," said Aramin, who grew up in a village near Hebron. "It was a game for us. We did it because it provoked the Israeli soldiers. We collected old clothes so we could keep making flags and putting them up, and the soldiers kept cutting the trees down. Eventually, the soldiers cut down every tree at our school."

The trees were gone, but the soldiers kept coming, and the Palestinian boys escalated to stone throwing. Then one day, Aramin and his friends found an old rifle and two grenades in a cave. The next time the soldiers visited, Aramin's friends threw the grenades and fired the ancient rifle. No one was hurt, but the soldiers arrested six youths, including Aramin, who was seventeen. He acknowledged he was part of the group but insisted he did not handle any weapons. "I wanted to, but I had polio when I was a child and couldn't run. So my friends wouldn't let me," said Aramin, who has a pronounced limp.

Aramin was sentenced to seven years in jail in 1986 and became politically active behind bars. He joined Fatah and spent his days in political discussions with his fellow prisoners and, when he could, with his jailers. "Prisoners used to have three meetings every day. We discussed whether armed struggle was useful," Aramin said. "Some argued we could only pursue armed struggle, but most said there had to be negotiations."

Like many Palestinian prisoners, he learned to speak Hebrew while in jail by watching Israeli television, and this allowed him to converse with the prison guards. "I had an argument with a jailer who was a settler in the West Bank," Aramin told me. "He said Palestinians were the settlers, and the Jews came back to liberate the land. He said they came and provided us with food and gave us a decent life, and we rejected them. He did not understand why we fought. We agreed to continue our discussion when he was on duty near my cell. So I prepared myself as if I was preparing for an exam. After seven months, he came to believe the two-state solution was the right solution. I thought that if this person could change his mind after a dialogue, then this was the way to go. Our cause was strong, even if we were weak."

Aramin was released from prison in 1992, but it would still be more than a decade before he would act on the lessons learned in prison. "I didn't wake up one day and decide to follow the path of nonviolence. It's a long process. It's a long journey," he said. "Both sides have decided that the other only understands the language of force. But still, it's illogical to continue for another forty years if you think that force is not the right solution."

Aramin decided that it was time to speak out when he learned about a group called Combatants for Peace. It was founded in 2005 and is made up of former Israeli soldiers and ex-Palestinian militants. Aramin joined and was frequently paired with Zohar Shapira, a former member of an elite Israeli commando unit. Together, they spoke often to students and community groups in Israel and the West Bank about the futility of fighting. "I address all sectors of Israeli society," Aramin said. "I think most Israelis don't know the Palestinian reality. I'm convinced we could make peace if they understood."

His belief was put to the ultimate test on January 13, 2007. On that day, Aramin's ten-year-old daughter, Abir, was in an upbeat mood after completing a math exam at the Anata Girls School, on the edge of Jerusalem. She walked out the front gate and crossed the dusty street, to a shop where she bought a small gift for her mother, who had helped her study.

As Abir emerged from the store, a clash suddenly erupted between stone-throwing Palestinian boys and Israeli border police who rumbled down the street in a jeep. When Abir stepped into the street, she was hit in the back of the head, a blow that threw her headlong onto the road, according to her sister Areen, twelve, who was with her. Abir was rushed to Hadassah Hospital in Jerusalem. After three days, she died without ever regaining consciousness.

Israel's West Bank barrier was just a few yards away from her school in Anata, and the area was the scene of frequent confrontations. Abir's sister Areen, along with other Palestinian witnesses, said they had no doubt that Abir had been hit by the Israelis. Michael Sfard, a prominent Israeli lawyer representing the Aramin family, said that he received a rubber-coated steel bullet that witnesses said they found at the scene. He presented it to the Israeli police. Abir's wound suggested that she was hit by a blunt object, consistent with the mark left by a rubber bullet, which generally does not enter a person's body because it is so large, but which can cause serious injuries and even death. The Israeli police, however, said they suspected that Abir might have been hit by a rock that one of the Palestinians threw at the police.

"This is the strange thing. I have to prove that the police are responsible for the killing of my daughter," Aramin said. He agreed to meet me in Anata in May 2007, four months after Abir's death, but he insisted that we talk at a small restaurant. "I didn't want to meet at home, because it would reopen this wound for my wife."

He said he drew strength from the support he received from many Israelis, particularly those in Combatants for Peace. "They were at the hospital with me the entire time," said Aramin, who worked at the Palestinian National Archives in Ramallah. "I received phone calls from tens of Israelis expressing their sympathy for my family and condemning the killing of my daughter."

Killings often bring calls for revenge, yet Aramin expressed understanding. "I want my daughter to be the last victim," he said, adding, "There are partners on the other side who believe what I believe." Aramin did not miss a single speaking engagement after Abir's death. He made it the centerpiece of his remarks and frequently spoke to Israelis, addressing them in Hebrew.

"I live with my dream. I'm convinced Abir is alive in heaven," said Aramin, who had five surviving kids. He spoke almost exclusively in Arabic during our interview, but at the end of our discussion, he broke into English to recite a poem that an American woman had sent to him after hearing about Abir's death.

> Don't stand at my grave and weep.
> I am not there, I am not asleep.
> Don't stand at my grave and cry,
> I am not there, I did not die.

In August 2010, more than three years after Abir's death, an Israeli court ruled that she was killed by a rubber bullet fired by Israel's border police.

14

A REVOLUTION OR A STATE: WHAT DO THE PALESTINIANS WANT?

When I first met Hitler, he was a fugitive and looked the part. The Israeli security forces were pursuing him, and he had been sleeping in his rumpled clothes. He had dark circles under his bloodshot eyes, several days' worth of stubble on his cheeks, and no recent access to a comb. Everyone called him Hitler, although his real name was Jamal Abu Roub, and he was a leader of the militant Al Aksa Martyrs Brigade in the northern West Bank town of Qabatiya. He was in his late thirties but looked much older. For two decades, he had answered to the nickname his friends pinned on him as a teenager because he was so adamant in his opinions.

Aside from his moniker, Abu Roub was best known for dragging a suspected Palestinian collaborator into the main square of his hometown and executing him with an automatic rifle as a large crowd looked on. The episode, which was captured on video, only seemed to enhance Abu Roub's reputation as one of the toughest guys in the roughest part of the West Bank. When I arranged a meeting with Abu Roub in January 2006 in the town of Jenin, he was hiding from the Israelis, while simultaneously running for a seat in the Palestinian parliament. His underground campaign was an attempt to refashion his image, but his entire persona still screamed "militant," rather than "legislator." Supporters plastered posters on the streets of Jenin, but they just as easily could have served as wanted posters put up by the Israelis.

He joked that our meeting was his "one and only campaign appearance." As we finished our discussion in an office building and began to walk out, we passed a group of women in the hall who were on a break from their own meeting. One woman blurted out, "Look, it's Hitler," followed by another, and then another. The entire hallway started buzzing with his nickname, and in an instant, more than a dozen women surrounded him. They insisted that he address their group of fifty, who immediately reconstituted themselves in their meeting room. Abu Roub hesitated for a moment, pondering the wisdom of such a public appearance, but he quickly decided that he wanted to be a politician, rather than a fugitive, at least on this day.

A week later, he easily won a parliamentary seat. Although his Fatah party lost the election to Hamas, Abu Roub's personal triumph was in keeping with an election that rewarded more radical Palestinians at the expense of moderates.

I sat down with Abu Roub again a little more than a year later, in April 2007, and he was a man transformed. He was dressed in a well-tailored tan suit. His hair was coiffed, and he was clean-shaven. Instead of a semisecretive meeting in gritty Jenin, we met openly at the headquarters of the Fatah movement in Ramallah, a modern building where he drove up in a shiny new Skoda sedan. He was a gracious host, ushering me into the main suite on the top floor. He asked an aide to bring us tea and then launched into a speech on international politics and the need to negotiate a settlement with Israel. The only sign of his violent past was the absence of a pinky finger. When he was a teenager, Abu Roub explained, he got his hands on an Israeli military explosive, and in his curiosity, he accidentally detonated it.

Abu Roub's makeover was worthy of a cable TV reality show. Marveling at his rebranding, I asked whether his politics had changed as much as his fashion sense. "What I'm doing now is part of the same struggle," he said of his nascent legislative career. "But the Israelis are not giving me the chance to do what I should be doing." Abu Roub said it was too risky to travel back and forth between his hometown and Ramallah, the de facto Palestinian capital in the West Bank. They are just a couple of hours apart by road, but with so many military checkpoints along the way, he could easily be seized. Abu Roub said that he had pushed his luck just to come to Ramallah after his election triumph, although, as a result, he felt cut off from his constituents. "We have much better security in Ramallah, so I stay here because it's a little more difficult for the Israelis to come and get me."

At that time, Israel was detaining about forty members of the Palestinian parliament. Most were Hamas members who had been elected along with Abu Roub in 2006. Yet several detainees belonged to Fatah and other parties, and Abu Roub was still on the Israeli wanted list. I asked whether he was concerned about his safety. "I am worried about it all the time," he said.

Many of Abu Roub's comrades in the Al Aksa Martyrs Brigades opposed negotiations with Israel as proposed by Palestinian Authority president Mahmoud Abbas. What was Abu Roub telling his comrades, who were still waging regular shootouts with the Israeli troops? "My message to Al Aksa is that they have to be committed to the negotiations on a Palestinian state," he said. "I tell Al Aksa that they have to accept this, but the obstacle is the daily attacks carried out by the Israelis." Now that Abu Roub was a member of parliament, I wondered whether he was still a member of Al Aksa. "As long as I am still considered wanted by Israel and on the run, I still consider myself a member of Al Aksa," he told me. "I consider myself a brother."

So, which Abu Roub was the real one? The radical who was willing to put a bullet into the head of a fellow Palestinian in the name of politics, or the articulate politician urging peace talks with Israel?

His split personality was an extreme case, but it spoke to the conflicted nature of many individual Palestinians, as well as of Palestinian society. For the last two decades, the Palestinians have not been able to make a clear choice about whether they want to wage an endless fight with Israel or make the compromises that will be part of any negotiation. Not only do the various Palestinian factions hold widely divergent stances, individual Palestinians such as Abu Roub often seemed to be walking contradictions—militants one day, moderates the next. All too often, radicals have carried the day and defined the Palestinians and their cause.

There are more than ten million Palestinians, and they are scattered in every corner of the globe. The ones who tend to get the most attention account for about half of that population: the roughly four million who live in the West Bank and the Gaza Strip, and the more than one million who are citizens in Israel. The other five million live throughout the broader Middle East, as well as in North America and Latin America.

They all share a desire for a Palestinian state, but beyond that, there are many different factions, and factions within the factions. Clans have quarreled for generations. There are differences between Palestinians living on the Mediterranean coast and those in the desert. There are the educated urban elite, the peasant farmers, and the nomadic Bedouin. There are Muslims, Christians, and Druze. In addition, the 1948 Arab-Israeli war added another complication by placing the Palestinians under the control of various ruling powers: Israel, Egypt, Jordan, Syria, and Lebanon.

Palestinians who have halfway decent lives, or at least a shot at improving their lot, are overwhelmingly moderate and not involved in radical politics or violence. They include the Palestinian Arabs who are citizens of Israel. In addition, there is a large Palestinian population in East Jerusalem, where they are legal residents of Israel, although they are not citizens. The Palestinians who live in Jordan, where they account for more than half of that country's population, also fall into the same broad category. The Palestinians living in the Americas probably are the most comfortable of all, at least in material terms.

In stark contrast to these Palestinians are their blood relatives who face much harsher conditions. This group includes the Palestinians in all of Gaza and much of the West Bank, as well as those who have been living for decades in refugee camps in Lebanon and Syria. These camps sprang up as Palestinians fled their homes or were driven out in the 1948 war. The camps have been the breeding ground for the vast majority of the Palestinian militants.

The most radical Palestinian elements tend to grab the headlines, although the reality is more complicated. As a group, the Palestinians are well educated. After years of dealing with the international community and negotiating with Israel, the Palestinians are politically sophisticated. The Palestinian media is full of lively debate. The Palestinians have held fair elections and at times have displayed a level of democratic development rarely seen in the Arab world.

Yet the Palestinians are also one of the most radicalized societies in the Middle East. Many Palestinians, particularly the young men, are besotted with the notion that they must wage ceaseless war with Israel to achieve Palestinian statehood, and they have ignored the great damage this has inflicted on their cause.

For decades, there was a broad Palestinian consensus that the only approach to Israel was confrontation. That position was not seriously reconsidered until Yasser Arafat signed the 1993 Oslo Accords and agreed to negotiate with Israel. Palestinians suddenly found themselves talking to Israel and officially embracing coexistence. Yet Arafat and many of his fellow Palestinians were still deeply conflicted by this process.

Arafat enjoyed a diplomatic process that put him in the international spotlight and made him a regular guest in world capitals. Yet even as he led the Palestinian Authority, Arafat preferred the role of revolutionary. He and other Palestinian leaders rarely, if ever, talked about the pedestrian tasks of nation building: forging institutions, shaping the educational system, collecting the trash, or accounting for the billions of dollars that the international community gave to the Palestinian Authority. Arafat never abandoned his trademark military-style uniform. He liked to refer to himself in the third person as "Yasser Arafat, the only undefeated Arab general." Aside from his exaggerated claims of military prowess, he neglected to mention that he was also the only Arab general without a state. In his speeches, he riled up Palestinian youths and never spoke of the compromises that would be the inevitable result of any negotiation.

This contradiction was particularly glaring when the second Palestinian uprising began. Arafat sought to pursue negotiations with Israel, while simultaneously embracing the intifada with a bear hug. For Arafat, there was no real dissonance. In his view, and in the view of many Palestinians, these dual policies were perfectly complementary. Arafat encouraged the uprising as a way to pressure Israel and win more concessions in the negotiations. Arafat appeared very much in sync with his people, who also backed the uprising even as the negotiations continued. The Palestinians did not debate this paradox until years later, long after the negotiations had collapsed and the uprising had brought only misery.

This disconnect reached the point of absurdity when the Al Aksa Martyrs Brigades, which were part of Arafat's Fatah movement, began to carry out suicide bombings. Arafat issued statements condemning the attacks shortly after they took place. Meanwhile, the Al Aksa Martyrs Brigades proudly claimed responsibility. When asked about this, the Al Aksa Martyrs Brigades declared themselves loyal to Arafat and his movement but insisted they were operating with autonomy. Israeli security officials said that Arafat was not relaying direct instructions to Al Aksa, but the Israelis were adamant that he was giving the militants a wink and a nod and doing nothing to rein them in. For years, Israelis had bristled at Arafat's mixed messages, and Ariel Sharon was determined to end this game.

15

ARAFAT'S FINAL DAYS

Yasser Arafat faced a moment of truth at the end of 2001. His fortunes had been spiraling downward since the second intifada began more than a year earlier. He was no longer courted as a negotiating partner after Prime Minister Ehud Barak and President Bill Clinton left office at the beginning of the year. Instead, Arafat was dealing with Ariel Sharon and George W. Bush, neither of whom had any interest in talking to him. Sharon sought to squeeze Arafat in every possible way. The Israeli leader made it increasingly difficult for Arafat to travel abroad, dropping hints that he might not be allowed back into the Palestinian territories.

After several major Palestinian attacks against Israel in December 2001, Sharon tightened the screws again. Sharon parked Israeli tanks a few hundred yards outside of Arafat's compound in Ramallah, known as the Muqata, which put the Palestinian leader under virtual house arrest. Taking measure of his predicament, Arafat went on Palestinian television on December 16. He put on his oversize black reading glasses and made his most direct call for Palestinians to stop attacking Israel. He told the Palestinians to "completely halt any [violent] activities, especially suicide attacks, which we have condemned." The Israelis were deeply skeptical, suspecting that Arafat's remarks were an attempt to get out of his immediate bind, rather than a sincere and enduring commitment. Yet during the next two weeks, the violence dropped dramatically. It appeared as if

Arafat might be looking to wind down an uprising that had brought the Palestinians misery and jeopardized his own standing.

On the night of January 3, 2002, however, Israeli navy commandos carried out a predawn raid, storming aboard the Karine-A, a cargo ship traveling in the Red Sea some three hundred miles from the southern tip of Israel. The Israelis seized the Palestinian crew and then went through the cargo, uncovering some fifty tons of weapons that the Israelis said had been purchased from Iran.

The Israeli military laid out the tons of confiscated weapons in neat rows on a dock the size of a football field in the Red Sea resort town of Eilat. The shipment included hundreds of rockets, as well as mortars, sniper rifles, and ammunition. The weapons were packed in dozens of wooden crates that contained flotation devices. The Israelis said the crates were to be dropped in the Mediterranean waters off Gaza, where small boats would pick them up and deliver them to shore. The captain of the Karine-A, Omar Akawi, was an officer in the Palestinian Naval Police. Just days after the Israelis snatched him and his ship, I was given permission to interview Akawi at the Ashkelon prison, in southern Israel.

Akawi was dressed in a brown prison jumpsuit. Paunchy and middle-aged, he raised his arms as if celebrating victory when he walked into the interview room, escorted by Israel's Shin Bet officers. His legs were still shackled. Akawi matter-of-factly explained his role to me. He knew he had been caught red-handed and appeared to have little to hide.

"I'm an employee in the Palestinian Authority," he told me, as we sat in what looked like a classroom. Akawi then went on to explain that he received his orders from a ranking figure in the Palestinian Authority and had picked up the weapons off the coast of Iran. He was directed to take them off the coast of Egypt, where small vessels would come alongside his ship, the Karine-A, to pick up the arms. "They have to go to Palestine," he said. I asked the jowly, mustachioed sea captain whether the operation could have taken place without the knowledge of Arafat and the Palestinian leadership. Without hesitation, he shook his head and said, "No, I don't think so."

Akawi told me that when he heard about Arafat's call for a halt to attacks on December 16, he thought his mission would be canceled. "I expected to receive an order. 'OK. Stop it,'" Akawi said. Yet no such order ever came. During the interview, he seemed resigned to spending many years in an Israeli prison. Before he was taken back to his cell, he wiped the tears from his eyes and asked whether I would explain his situation to his young daughter, who lived with his wife in Tunisia. He gave me

*his wife's cell phone number and asked me to tell her what had happened.
"I'm a soldier," he said. "I have to obey the orders."*

*The Israelis trumpeted the case as evidence of Arafat's duplicity. The
Bush administration, which had been looking for reasons not to deal with
Arafat, effectively wrote him off. A few months later, as the fighting intensified, the Israeli forces took up semipermanent positions on the edges of
Arafat's fortress. For two and a half years, from the spring of 2002 to the
fall of 2004, Arafat never left his compound. For the restless Arafat to be so
confined was a form of torture, and he seemed to wither away.*

*No one had done so much to bring the Palestinian cause into the inter-
national spotlight and keep it there. Yet Arafat seemed incapable of taking the Palestinians the final mile and helping them build the institutions
needed for statehood. Arafat still appeared regularly from the front steps
of his compound, with sandbags piled high to guard against sniper fire.
But his rants against Israel sounded increasingly dated and out of touch.
He assumed a ghostly pallor from a lack of sunlight. The trembling in his
hands and his lips became more pronounced. Palestinians joked bitterly that
Sharon's vision of a future Palestinian state consisted of the wall that surrounded Arafat's compound, which covered one city block.*

*Arafat became seriously ill in the fall of 2004 with a mysterious stom-
ach ailment. As his condition worsened, Israel allowed a helicopter to pick
up Arafat on the first leg of a journey that took him to a French military
hospital outside Paris. Arafat's last days were filled with drama, turmoil,
and confusion, an apt summary of much of his career. As the French doctors tried to save his life, the information leaking out of the hospital was
sparse and often contradictory. One source would say Arafat was in a coma
and near death; another would say he had just sat up in bed and enjoyed
a bowl of cereal. Arafat's wife, Suha, began feuding publicly with Arafat's
closest aides. Suha had never gotten along with Arafat's associates, and
she left the Palestinian territories with the couple's young daughter early
in the uprising. They spent much of their time in Paris. The arrangement
kept her out of public view, but her sudden return unleashed all of the old
tensions and rivalries.*

*After a week in the hospital and multiple premature reports of his death,
Arafat passed away in the early hours of November 11, 2004. There was
never any definitive information released on the exact nature of his illness
or the cause of death. This only encouraged speculation and conspiracy,
and the rumors ranged from AIDS to poisoning at the hands of Israel.*

The following day, the man without a state was given a state funeral in Cairo, as the world watched. With many Arab leaders in attendance, a horse-drawn carriage pulled Arafat's coffin, draped in a Palestinian flag, through the Egyptian capital. The formal, dignified ceremony was in utter contrast to the chaos that would erupt when Arafat's body was flown back to his compound in Ramallah, where I was waiting with my crew.

Kids filled the parking lot inside the compound, and those who could not fit climbed onto every tree branch and balanced atop the cinderblock walls that surrounded the Muqata. My crew and I joined the young Palestinian men who swarmed to the rooftops of apartment buildings overlooking the compound. When Arafat's body arrived from Cairo, there was barely enough room for the two military helicopters to touch down. The Palestinian security forces had no prospect of maintaining order. The best they could hope for was to keep the frenzied crowd away from the coffin. They fired shots in the air in a futile attempt to impose some discipline on the proceedings. As Arafat's coffin was removed from the helicopter, the crowd surged forward and called out for their leader as if it were a rock concert. The pallbearers were jostled as the mourners pressed tighter and tighter, their arms outstretched, in an attempt to touch the passing coffin, which seemed to be floating on this turbulent sea of humanity. The plan was to let Arafat lie in state in his office one last time, but the pallbearers soon realized they could not get there and switched course suddenly to make a direct line for the grave. There was no attempt at ceremony; it was all the pallbearers could do to take the coffin one hundred yards from the helicopter to the hastily prepared grave site that had been dug out of the parking lot. We wondered aloud on air whether the crowd would seize the coffin and try to march toward Jerusalem, only a few miles away.

Arafat's wish was to be buried in Jerusalem, but Sharon rejected the request. The best the Palestinians could do was to dig up soil from the Noble Sanctuary in Jerusalem and toss it in the grave of their deceased leader. It was as close to Jerusalem as Arafat would ever get.

16

AFTER ARAFAT

When the Palestinians held their 2005 election to replace Yasser Arafat, only one name generated any real enthusiasm: Marwan Barghouti. Yet there was a small problem. Barghouti was in an Israeli jail, serving a life sentence.

Arafat's death could have cleared the way for a new generation of Palestinian leaders, such as Barghouti, who was in his forties at the time. Instead, Arafat's longtime associates clung to power. Mahmoud Abbas, who was about to turn seventy, easily won the Palestinian presidential balloting to succeed Arafat. Other Arafat aides in their sixties and seventies, who had been by his side during his extended exile, retained their positions. There was no emotional connection between this older generation that had spent so many years abroad and the young Palestinians who grew up clashing with Israeli soldiers in the streets. Fatah leaders in their thirties and forties were openly frustrated as they found their path to advancement blocked by gray-haired elders who had passed retirement age. The Fatah revolution had become a gerontocracy, while the promise of statehood was still somewhere over the horizon.

I first met Barghouti in the summer of 2000, a couple of months before the uprising, and even at a routine meeting on a sleepy afternoon, he made a strong impression. He is not an imposing figure, at just a bit over five feet tall, with cherubic features. He was wearing his standard outfit consisting of blue jeans and a flannel shirt. Yet he was a charismatic speaker who filled a room with his presence and reveled in confrontation with friends and foes alike. At that meeting, he went on at length about the failings of the Palestinian Authority. He was particularly critical of the way Palestinian prisoners were being treated in Palestinian jails, volunteering that several had been tortured to death. He sounded more like a crusading human rights lawyer than a senior member of Arafat's ruling party.

Barghouti had been a prominent student activist at Bir Zeit University in Ramallah in the 1980s, and Israel later arrested him and deported him to Jordan during the first Palestinian uprising that began in 1987. Barghouti was allowed to return to the West Bank in 1994 after the peace negotiations began, and he quickly developed many contacts with Israeli officials. He learned Hebrew during his time in Israeli jails, was an avid reader of Hebrew-language newspapers, and impressed the Israelis with his detailed knowledge of their politics. Israeli political and military officials did not trust Barghouti; however, they recognized his leadership skills and assumed he would be a top Palestinian figure for decades to come and perhaps even a successor to Arafat.

Yet when the second Palestinian uprising began, those cordial relations came to an abrupt end. Barghouti was one of the few senior Palestinian leaders who joined the stone-throwing youths in the streets. While Arafat and members of his generation chose to remain isolated in their offices, Barghouti was a regular at demonstrations, where he would rev up the crowd with a megaphone, urging them to confront the Israelis. The crowd needed little encouragement, and clashes inevitably followed.

Barghouti's standing soared as he became the symbolic leader of the intifada, winning the loyalty of young Palestinians and the enmity of Israel. When asked about his role in the uprising, Barghouti insisted that he was just a politician, not a militant. It was clear, however, that the gunmen of the Al Aksa Martyrs Brigades saw him as their leader. Each city had its own loosely organized branch of Al Aksa gunmen. Group members often wore ski masks on the streets and would not say who gave them money, guns, and orders, but when we engaged them as they sipped tea and smoked cigarettes, they eventually acknowledged that Barghouti was their guiding light. Another cup of tea and a few cigarettes later, they would usually recount an inspiring visit that Barghouti had made to their town.

Many Palestinians admired Barghouti because he was a skilled politician and orator who could represent the Palestinians in formal negotiations with Israel, yet he also spoke the language of the armed and angry young men in Palestinian cities who were always ready to fight Israel. For these very same reasons, the Israeli political and military leadership viewed him as duplicitous.

Israel accused Barghouti of masterminding roadside shootings in the West Bank against Jewish settlers, which were frequent events in the early days of the uprising. Barghouti denied any role but declared loudly that the Palestinians had a right to resist Israel's occupation in the West Bank and the Gaza Strip. This was the consensus position among Fatah supporters and the Palestinian mainstream. Barghouti said that he opposed attacks inside Israel, however, including the suicide bombings carried out by Hamas and other factions.

Yet in early 2002, Al Aksa began its own attacks inside Israel and resorted to suicide bombings in what was seen as an attempt to compete with Hamas. It was not clear whether Barghouti supported this change in tactics, and Israel was not interested in such distinctions. When the military launched its West Bank incursion in March 2002, Barghouti was at the top of its wanted list. The army captured him on April 15, after tracking him down in a house outside Ramallah.

He was charged with orchestrating the killings of twenty-six people, most of them Jewish settlers who had been shot in roadside attacks in the West Bank. Barghouti was tried in an Israeli civilian court, rather than in a West Bank military court, as was the case for most suspected militants. He turned the trial in Tel Aviv into a circus, with his frequent outbursts and his refusal to recognize the court's authority. "You don't have the right to try me," Barghouti, dressed in a brown prison uniform, shouted at the three-judge panel in Tel Aviv District Court. "This is a violation of international law and the Geneva Convention."

Judge Sara Sirota, the president of the panel, said, "We've heard you before, Mr. Barghouti." He continued to make unsolicited comments, and the judge had Barghouti removed from the courtroom several times as testimony proceeded without him.

The Israeli evidence against him was largely circumstantial. Israeli prosecutors put several Palestinians on the witness stand to testify against Barghouti, but they were so full of praise that they sounded more like his character references. By any commonsense standard, Barghouti was a leader of the Palestinian uprising, but the sketchy evidence in the court case made it difficult to assess whether he was behind the specific attacks he was charged with. He was eventually convicted of five killings—four Israelis and a Greek Orthodox monk—and sentenced to five life terms in prison.

Of the roughly ten thousand Palestinian prisoners held by Israel in recent years, Barghouti was by far the most prominent, and his name surfaced every time the sides discussed potential prisoner releases. Barghouti's many supporters often compared him to Nelson Mandela, but this greatly inflated Barghouti. We were present when Mandela walked to freedom in 1990, and we covered the final years of apartheid in South Africa. Barghouti lacks Mandela's statesmanship, his gravitas, and his moral authority. Mandela was revered by the vast majority of black South Africans and also won over the country's whites, while Barghouti's popularity was much more limited and concentrated among secular West Bank Palestinians.

Barghouti's release would still be a significant event, however, and could potentially breathe new life into the sclerotic Fatah movement. Barghouti sends out occasional messages from prison, and he has not been forgotten by the younger members of Fatah, who continue to clamor for new leaders. If Barghouti is freed, it could go a long way toward shaking up Palestinian politics. What is less clear is whether Barghouti and a younger generation would make those politics more moderate or more radical.

When it comes to politics, the Palestinians, like many in the Arab world, seem to instinctively resist change. To even suggest change is to hint at an unseemly compromise with Israel and an abandonment of core Palestinian values. Instead, the Palestinians consider steadfastness, or *sumud*, one of their highest virtues. For many years, this kept them united in their opposition to Israel and in their determination to achieve statehood. Yet the flip side is that it made them very rigid and reluctant to adapt to an evolving global landscape. The Palestinians often see only two options: all or nothing, and often end up with the latter.

The reluctance to discuss compromises has been harmful on many fronts, and created almost total paralysis on one critical issue: the fate of Palestinian refugees. It has been the Palestinian mantra that all refugees have the right to return to their original homes. It is sacrilege for a Palestinian to suggest anything less. The Palestinians have never had a full, open, and honest public debate on this question since the first wave of refugees more than six decades ago. Yet the Palestinians will ultimately have to make difficult choices and accept painful compromises to resolve the refugee question.

An estimated 750,000 Palestinians fled or were driven from their homes in the 1948 Arab-Israeli war. In December 1948, the United Nations General Assembly passed Resolution 194, which said that "the refugees wishing to return to their homes and live at peace with their neighbors should be permitted to do so at the earliest practicable date." The resolution added that Palestinians who chose not to return would be compensated.

Ever since, the Palestinians have clung tenaciously to this lone paragraph on refugees.

The world, however, has changed a great deal since then. Today, the surviving Palestinian refugees and their descendants number more than four million. The largest numbers are in Gaza, the West Bank, Lebanon, Syria, and Jordan. Whenever the refugee issue is raised, Palestinians instinctively cite the UN resolution, saying that they have a "right of return" to their land, although many of those old homes were destroyed decades ago.

The term "refugee" conjures up an image of dispossessed families living in rows of tents, cooking meals on fires made from sticks, drinking water stored in jerricans, and sharing a communal trench latrine. After sixty years, though, the Palestinians have become the world's most permanent refugees. A United Nations agency, the UN Relief and Works Agency, or UNRWA, is devoted entirely to their care, and Palestinians have passed down their refugee status from one generation to the next.

Refugee families still cling to the rusting keys and yellowed land deeds from their old homes. Time and again, we visited Palestinian families who kept those old keys hanging above the front doors of their current homes, a constant reminder of their loss. The refugees say that even if they do not return, they will pass their yearning to their offspring. The dream will continue to be nour-ished by their children and grandchildren, even as it becomes ever more remote.

Mustafa Ghwaleh has lived for more than a half-century in the same tidy house in the Al Amari Refugee Camp. The camp is in the West Bank, although it is just beyond the border of Jerusalem. Ghwaleh helped build and expand the cinder-block house with his own sweat to accommodate his large family, which included eight children and ten grandchildren, some of whom still lived at the home. Yet after all of these years, Ghwaleh, who was sixty-six when I visited him in 2004, still insisted he was a refugee.

His story began in al-Naani, a farming village that used to be southeast of Tel Aviv, adjacent to several Jewish communities. His family raised cows, chickens, and camels on its four acres, and, by his account, relations between Jews and Arabs were generally good. But Jewish fighters reached the village shortly after the 1948 war broke out, forcing residents to the nearby Arab town of Ramla, said Ghwaleh, who was ten at the time.

His father sought to slip back to their farm one night to har-vest wheat but was captured. He managed to get a glimpse of the village and saw that every house and structure had been torn down, except for the well. Several months later, the family of eight was taken to the West Bank town of Ramallah, in the hills just north of Jerusalem, where they spent the winter living in a school. After the war, they were placed in a tent in the Al Amari Refugee Camp.

By the time I met Ghwaleh, the tents were long gone. The camp had become a maze of alleys and a haphazard collection of homes. Because the camp was squeezed between Jerusalem and Ramallah, the most middle-class of Palestinian cities, its residents were a bit better off than those in many camps. Yet poverty was still the norm, and the residents still received assistance from UNRWA, which pro-vided an array of services, from health care to education, to feed-ing programs. Many Palestinians have been dependent on UNRWA for decades, particularly in Gaza, where roughly 70 percent of the Palestinians in the territory have refugee status. Israel has often been critical of the UN agency, saying that by maintaining the refugee status of residents for generations, it nurtures grievances, encourages extremism, and creates false hopes that the Palestinians will one day return to land in Israel.

Ghwaleh, like most refugees, placed no statute of limitations on his quest to return home. "The Jews say this is their land, and they came back after two thousand years," he said. "Me, my children, and my grandchildren will keep trying to get our land back, and some day we will."

The Palestinian attachment to the land is hard to overstate. The Palestinians have been ruled by foreigners for centuries— the Ottoman Turks, the British, the Egyptians, the Jordanians, and the Israelis. They have never had their own state. As a result, their loyalties are very much tied to their hometowns and their small, mostly rural villages, where they identified with their clan and their family. Many families lived on the same parcel of land for generations. When they lost their land, they lost everything. They lost their lone major asset, their community, and, to a large extent, their own identities and the one place where they fit into the world. Without their land, many Palestinians have been unable to figure out where they belong. It took me a while to fully grasp this, as a vagabond Westerner who has lived in fifteen cities and more than twenty homes on four continents. The Palestinian refugees will never feel that they have been made whole until they get their land back.

Whenever I met refugees like Ghwaleh, I had two distinct feelings. I had great empathy for people who had lost their land and spent their entire lives clinging to the dream that they would get it back. Yet I also wanted to hold a filibuster on the issue until they acknowledged that their homes had long since been torn down and that they had a better chance of winning the lottery than of returning to their land.

On most contentious issues, at least some segment of the Israeli population was sympathetic to Palestinian claims. But when it came to refugees, the Israelis were virtually unanimous in describing the Palestinian position as a fantasy that has stood in the way of resolving the conflict. Even the most liberal Israeli politicians said they would never allow an open-ended, mass return of refugees who would overwhelm Israel demographically, erasing the Jewish character of the state. In any peace agreement, the most likely scenario would allow Palestinian refugees to settle in a new Palestinian state consisting of the West Bank and Gaza. Perhaps a small number of

refugees would be able to return to their land in Israel. Nonetheless, Palestinian leaders have stuck to the absolutist position.

Once in a great while, hints emerged that the Palestinians have
a better grasp of reality than they were willing to admit publicly.
The leading Palestinian pollster, Dr. Khalil Shikaki, conducted
a survey in 2003 of forty-five hundred refugee families, and the
results indicated that many were open to compromises. Although
more than 95 percent insisted that Israel recognize the "right of
return" in principle, only 10 percent demanded permanent residence in Israel on their old land, and 54 percent said they would be
willing to accept compensation. For his troubles, a Palestinian mob
attacked Dr. Shikaki's office in Ramallah as he was preparing to
release the findings. They ransacked the office, shoved him around,
and pelted him with eggs. "They are trying to send a message that
the right of return is sacred, and that you who are negotiating are
on notice," said Dr. Shikaki, a refugee himself.[1]

The Temple Mount–Noble Sanctuary in Jerusalem's Old City is the most disputed piece of real estate in the conflict and a symbol of the irreconcilable differences. In 2000, the Palestinian uprising, or intifada, began at this spot. Here, Jewish worshippers hold a prayer service at the Western Wall. *(AP Photo/Dan Balilty)*

The stone-throwing clashes, like this one in Jerusalem, soon escalated into the most violent and sustained confrontation ever between the two sides. Palestinian suicide bombings and Israeli air strikes became common. *(Rina Castlenuovo/New York Times)*

This photo was taken on the first day of the uprising, September 29, 2000, and incorrectly identified the bloodied young man as a Palestinian. He was a Jewish American, Tuvia Grossman, who was beaten by Palestinians. The mistake was corrected, but Israelis saw it as bias, and it became a symbol of the propaganda war. *(Zoom 77)*

Fares Odeh, age fourteen, became an instant Palestinian hero after this photo was taken on October 29, 2000. Less than two weeks later, an Israeli soldier shot and killed him in a similar clash near the same site in the Gaza. *(AP Photo/ Laurent Rebours)*

This Palestinian suicide bombing on a bus in northern Israel in 2002 was one of many such attacks that ravaged Israelis for several years. Israel responded with a tough crackdown on Palestinian movements. *(AP Photo/Ronen Lidor)*

Sheik Ahmed Yassin, a quadriplegic, was the leader of the radical Islamic group Hamas, which carried out the deadliest attacks against Israel. The sheik was killed in an Israeli air strike in 2004, but his group continued to grow more powerful and took control of the Gaza Strip. *(Rina Castlenuovo/New York Times)*

In response to Palestinian attacks, Israel built a separation barrier, including this stretch in East Jerusalem. The barrier reduced attacks, but is highly controversial because much of it runs through the West Bank. It also symbolized the way Israel cut itself off, physically and psychologically, from the Palestinians. *(Rina Castlenuovo/New York Times)*

Our daughters, Annalise and Amelia, were born in Jerusalem during the worst of the fighting. Hospitals often seemed the only place where Jews and Arabs could interact without tension, before we checked out, we were offered an air-tight tent to protect our children against chemical weapons attacks. *(Malcom James)*

Yasser Arafat's chaotic funeral in November 2004 in the West Bank city of Ramallah seemed an apt summation of his life. He brought international attention to the Palestinian cause, but left his people in disarray. *(Rina Castlenuovo/New York Times)*

Israel's withdrawal of its settlers from Gaza in 2005 was a wrenching process that demonstrated how difficult it was for either side to relinquish territory. In the Jewish settlement of Kfar Darom, youths barricaded themselves on a synagogue rooftop and battled the security forces. *(Rina Castlenuovo/New York Times)*

Jennifer meets with gunmen from the Al Aksa Martyrs Brigades in the West Bank city of Nablus. The Palestinian authority largely collapsed, and the gunmen effectively controlled the streets in many Palestinian cities. *(Fox News)*

Jennifer conducts one of several interviews she had with Prime Minister Ariel Sharon. Israelis and Palestinians consider the public relations battle as important as the actual fighting. Foreign correspondents had great access to leaders on both sides. *(Fox News)*

An Israeli woman settler tries to keep Israeli troops from tearing down an unauthorized settler outpost in the West Bank in 2006. Such action by Israeli authorities is rare. For decades, successive governments have been reluctant to confront the increasingly powerful settler movement. *(AP Photo/Oded Balilty)*

Israeli soldiers carry a comrade who was wounded in the fighting against Hezbollah in Lebanon in 2006. The brief war ended in a stalemate. Many Israelis were disappointed that their country failed to win decisively. *(Rina Castlenuovo/New York Times)*

Israel unleashed a major offensive in December 2008 to stop rocket fire coming out of Gaza. The Israeli operation reduced the rocket fire, but Hamas remained in full control of the territory. *(AP Photo/Khalil Hamra)*

After decades of conflict, Israelis and Palestinians still have not found a way to see eye-to-eye. *(Rina Castlenuovo/New York Times)*

17

UNINTENDED CONSEQUENCES

For Israeli intelligence officers, no Palestinian was more dangerous than Salah Shehadeh, the veteran leader of Hamas's armed wing. This clandestine corps operated in small cells and was known as the Izzedine al-Qassam Brigades. While many Hamas leaders courted publicity, Shehadeh, a middle-age grandfatherly figure, was invisible. Even his name was not well known. He rarely spent more than one night sleeping in the same place. From his ever-changing hideouts, he orchestrated bombings and shooting attacks against Israeli soldiers and settlers in the Gaza Strip. He masterminded the weapons smuggling from Egypt and the rocket fire into southern Israel. He was a very busy man as the Palestinian uprising reached its peak in 2002 and was very good at what he did. Hamas demonstrated time and again that it had become the most potent Palestinian armed faction. And for his efforts, Shehadeh earned a high-ranking spot on Israel's most wanted list.

Though I did not know it at the time, Israel was hot on Shehadeh's trail when I headed to Gaza in July 2002 to investigate rumors of a possible cease-fire. As our crew was having a late-night dinner at a seafront restaurant, we heard the buzzing of Israeli drones over Gaza City. The unmanned aircraft had long since become background noise that few

*noticed. Yet we all looked up from our meals when we heard the purpose-
ful roar of an F-16 fighter jet. As the warplane came screaming over
Gaza City, it fired a one-ton, laser-guided, American-made bomb into
Shehadeh's apartment building in the congested Gaza City neighborhood
of Daraj. My mobile phone rang almost immediately afterward. It was
Abu Askar, a Palestinian who ran a media center in Gaza and served as
our eyes and ears in the territory. His instructions were simple: "Yalla."
Go. We piled into our van and made our way toward Daraj. The streets
were dark and crowded. The thunderous explosion had brought residents
out of their homes and cut electricity in the area. The people on the streets
were covered in a fine, gray dust.*

*Normally, the target of an Israeli attack was known within minutes,
but it quickly became apparent that this time was different. When we
arrived on the scene, even Palestinians in the neighborhood did not know
who had attracted such special attention from the Israelis, who usually
fired much smaller weapons when going after Palestinians in civilian
areas. The Israelis normally announced the results shortly after a raid,
but on this night they were uncharacteristically coy, saying only that it was
a "precision strike." The Israeli language was at odds with the evidence
in front of me. The bomb was so powerful, it collapsed the entire building
and badly damaged two neighboring apartment blocks, completely shaving
the front wall off one of them.*

*Amid this chaos, I needed a phone to report what I had seen, but the
mobile phone network was jammed. My Gaza colleagues found a helpful
family and guided me up a dark, narrow stairway to an apartment where
several family members were huddled in a living room lit only by candles.
Even in such moments, Palestinian hospitality never wavered—the family
offered me tea and fresh dates as I dialed an old-fashioned rotary phone to
call the Fox office in Washington and provide a preliminary account.*

*It took hours before we could confirm that Shehadeh was the target
and that he had been killed. Red Crescent workers picked through the
rubble all night and into the morning. The rescuers ultimately recovered
fifteen bodies, including Shehadeh, his wife, their fifteen-year-old daughter, and a bodyguard. Eleven neighbors were also killed, nine of them
children. "This is the Israeli peace. These are American weapons," said
the graffiti on the wall of an apartment belonging to a family that lost
several members.*

*Ariel Sharon initially declared the operation "one of our greatest suc-
cesses"; however, the civilian toll resulted in blistering international criticism, including a rare rebuke from the United States. A few days later,*

Sharon was quoted as saying that "had I known the outcome, I would have postponed the assassination." In killing Shehadeh and other Hamas leaders, Israel bumped up against the limits of its military power. Many top Hamas figures were eliminated, and the Hamas attacks declined, but the radical Islamic group only seemed to gain new recruits and grow more popular.

18

HAMAS RISING

Prior to the second Palestinian uprising, Hamas was known for its radical positions, the social services it provided for the poor, and the occasional suicide bombing that was intended to undermine peace negotiations. Yet the group had largely been a sideshow compared to Yasser Arafat and his Fatah movement. The intifada changed all of that.

Times of great violence often enhance the appeal and the standing of extremist groups, and this was particularly true for Hamas. The Palestinian uprising was a disaster for Arafat, Fatah, and the Palestinian people, but Hamas rose in stature almost from the day the uprising began. The group carried out the deadliest Palestinian attacks against Israel. These bombings won the group more followers on the Palestinian street. This public support encouraged Hamas to start participating in a political system it had previously shunned. And when Israel moved forcefully against Hamas, it only seemed to give the group an additional boost.

Hamas, which means "zeal" in Arabic, is an acronym for the Islamic Resistance Movement. The group grew out of Egypt's Muslim Brotherhood, which was founded in 1929 and spread, in some form or another, to many Arab and Muslim states. While Gaza was under Egyptian rule from 1949 to 1967, many Gazans went to universities in Egypt, where they were introduced to the Brotherhood and its teachings. Even after Israel captured Gaza in the 1967 war, many Gazans continued to study in Egypt. When the Gazans returned across the Sinai Desert, they brought with them the Brotherhood's vision of a single Islamic society governed by the teachings of the Koran. Over the years, many Gaza clerics were also influenced by the Brotherhood, with its appeals to help the downtrodden. The Brotherhood gained a foothold in Gaza with a message of strict adherence to Islam and its increasingly broad network of social services, including schools, medical clinics, and charity operations. For a time, Israel even encouraged such activity, viewing it as a religious counterweight to Arafat and Fatah. What Israel failed to envision was that Fatah, the main component of the Palestine Liberation Organization, would become willing to engage in negotiations, while the Brotherhood would morph into Hamas and become the most dangerous Palestinian faction confronting Israel.

Hamas was formally established in 1987 at the beginning of the first Palestinian intifada. The group stated flatly that there could be no compromise with Israel and decreed that the "Zionist entity" should be eliminated and all of the land between the Mediterranean Sea and the Jordan River should become an Islamic state. Hamas was the most strident opponent of the Oslo Accords of 1993, which led to the creation of the Palestinian Authority the following year. Most Israelis and Palestinians supported the peace process, but Hamas refused to join the Palestinian Authority on the grounds that it was the illegitimate offspring of negotiations with Israel. While peace talks waxed and waned in the 1990s, Hamas stayed on the sidelines and talked about its long-term goal of an Islamic state, which critics sometimes mocked as the "one-thousand-year plan."

Israel pressured Arafat to crack down on Hamas. The Palestinian leader, who wanted to keep the group in check lest it challenge his rule, did so with great vigor. In the mid-1990s, Arafat's security forces moved against Hamas and arrested many of its leaders. Many Hamas members said they were beaten while in Palestinian prisons. For good measure, Arafat's security forces, made up mostly of secular men, humiliated the Hamas prisoners by forcibly shaving off their bushy beards, which the Hamas men had maintained as a symbol of religious piety.

By the time the second Palestinian uprising began, most Hamas leaders had been freed from Palestinian prisons. Hamas quickly took the lead in attacks against Israel. In response, Israel went to great lengths to capture or kill Hamas militants who were deep in hiding, many of them mid-level or even low-level. Yet in a self-imposed restriction, Israel did not target the senior political leaders of Hamas for the first few years of the uprising.

These Hamas political leaders led very public lives and were not hard to track down. During the early years of the uprising, we found it easier to make an appointment with a senior Hamas leader in Gaza City than with our dentist in Jerusalem. Our dentist worked out of an apartment one floor beneath ours. Most mornings, we could hear him rev up his drill while we were eating breakfast, but he always seemed to be booked for weeks into the future. We could, however, find a notable Hamas figure almost any day of the week. In Jennifer's case, one regularly tracked her down.

Sheik Abdel Majid Atta was not a senior Hamas leader, but he did host a popular religious call-in show on Nativity TV, a Christian television station in Bethlehem. He could have passed for Santa Claus with his full white beard, an easy smile, and a gentle demeanor. When I paid him a visit just before Christmas in 2001, a Palestinian Christian dressed up as Santa had just finished his program at the station, when Sheik Atta arrived on the set to start his show. The two look-alikes exchanged fraternal greetings as the technicians replaced the Christmas-tree background that had been superimposed on the screen, in favor of the Dome of the Rock, the Muslim shrine in Jerusalem.

I stayed to watch Sheik Atta's show, and afterward he invited me to his home for the evening feast that broke the dawn-to-dusk fast during the Muslim holy month of Ramadan. He was not one of the fire-and-brimstone preachers whom we often found in Gaza. He wanted to explain Islam to people and answer their questions. I could feel a real warmth from his family. Of course, there was also a poster on a wall in his home that showed a Hamas bomber with a bandolier of bullets over one shoulder. Such were the contradictions of the Middle East.

A while later, I spent a long day covering a Hamas suicide bombing in Jerusalem. When I returned home late that night, the phone rang. It was Sheik Atta. "I just wanted to see if your family was all right," the sheik said. Yes, I told him, I was all right, but there would be no need to call if Hamas was not bombing Jerusalem.

I never had any indication that the sheik was part of Hamas's armed wing. Still, it was mind-twisting to come back from all of that carnage and receive well wishes from a Hamas sheik. He continued to call periodically. Even when the Israelis later detained him and sent him to a West Bank prison, he rang me up. He was never charged with any offense and was released several months later. When he returned home, he received a hero's welcome in Bethlehem.

Palestinian factions had a long history of bitter internal disputes. For the most part, however, they kept these in check and managed to channel their anger toward their common enemy, Israel. Yet as the uprising wore on, Hamas in particular became increasingly vitriolic toward Arafat and his Palestinian Authority.

One Hamas leader, Dr. Mahmoud Zahar, was a particularly abrasive, argumentative man who enjoyed playing the provocateur, regardless of whether he was talking about Israel or his fellow Palestinians. During a chat in 2003, he was utterly dismissive of Arafat and spoke as if Hamas had all but taken over. "Where is the Palestinian Authority?" Dr. Zahar said with an air of contempt. "People have lost hope in them. They don't offer protection from the Israelis. And people see massive corruption at a time when they are looking for one hundred shekels [twenty-five dollars] to send their kids to school." Dr. Zahar said that the increased Israeli military presence in Gaza highlighted both the weakness of the Palestinian Authority and Hamas's ability to fight back. "Israel is simply facilitating our role by coming to Gaza," he said confidently.

In addition to being a Hamas leader and a surgeon, Dr. Zahar was a novelist who also wrote a screenplay for a movie about a famous Palestinian militant. He was a dour man, and the only time I ever saw him smile was at the end of a lengthy interview in the living room of his Gaza City home. I asked him what his medical specialty was. "Thyroids. I'm very good at cutting throats," Dr. Zahar said, drawing his forefinger across his neck as a grin spread across his face.

As with other Hamas political leaders, Zahar was a featured speaker at the group's rallies. He was always ready to offer a public comment on a Hamas attack and often answered his cell phone on the first ring. Yet in the summer of 2003, with Hamas's popularity surging, Ariel Sharon decided to end Israel's hands-off policy toward the group's political leadership.

The Israeli military was beginning to get the upper hand in the West Bank, where Operation Defensive Shield had been launched a year earlier. Now Sharon was looking at Gaza, and he gave the military the go-ahead to kill the top echelon of Hamas. For Sharon, the move carried potential risks and rewards. The risk was that Hamas would respond by escalating its suicide bombings. The reward was that Hamas would be weakened by the loss of its leaders. It took the Hamas leaders a surprisingly long time to figure out that Sharon was playing by new rules.

In August 2003, I took my visiting *New York Times* colleague Ethan Bronner to Gaza City to see Ismail Abu Shanab, a top Hamas figure. A fluent English speaker with a master's degree in civil engineering from Colorado State University, the affable Abu Shanab was considered the least radical Hamas leader and therefore was often wheeled out to speak to Western journalists. Given the imminent danger facing Hamas leaders, we expected gun-toting security guards to greet us with suspicion when we knocked on the front gate of Abu Shanab's home in a modest Gaza City neighborhood. Instead, one of Abu Shanab's eleven children, a son who looked to be no older than ten, welcomed us and sat us down in the living room while he went to fetch his father.

Abu Shanab gave us the predictable speech about the illegitimacy of Israel and the international Jewish cabal that allegedly controlled everything from the global economy to our newspaper. Yet after several cups of tea, Abu Shanab loosened up. Having spent almost all of his life on the tiny spit of flat, sandy land that is Gaza, he waxed on about the majesty of the Rocky Mountains and the free and open spirits of the Americans he knew as a student. Then he began to speak heresies, confiding that the Palestinians had actually benefited in many ways from their contact with Israelis.

Abu Shanab said that many in the Palestinian political class were avid students of the Israeli parliament and marveled at the freewheeling debate in the Knesset. The Palestinians learned from this, and it made them more democratic. Abu Shanab appreciated the Israeli work ethic and thought that the Palestinians had much to emulate here as well. To top it off, he acknowledged that Israel's economic strength and technological prowess had trickled down to the Palestinians, making them more advanced than many of their Arab neighbors. Abu Shanab pointed proudly to a new computer on a desk across the room. "You know what's inside?" Abu Shanab asked rhetorically. "A Pentium Four. What do you think they have in Cairo and Damascus? Maybe a Pentium One. If they're lucky."

Ethan and I walked out of his house and into the dusty streets of Gaza City, shaking our heads as we tried to make sense of the contradictions. Abu Shanab was a full-throated supporter of Hamas's suicide bombings and its mission to wipe out Israel. Yet he also understood the benefits of living an hour's drive from a huge Intel plant in southern Israel, where some of the world's most advanced microprocessors were fabricated by technicians in moon suits.

I was looking forward to future discussions with Abu Shanab. Two weeks later, however, Israeli military helicopters fired several missiles that incinerated a station wagon carrying Abu Shanab, killing him near the house where we met.

The strike that killed Abu Shanab and other bombardments that wounded several more Hamas leaders around that time did have an impact. In December 2003, Hamas unilaterally suspended its bombing campaign in what was seen as an attempt by the Hamas leadership to save itself. That bought them some time, but not much. The Israelis were intent on keeping Hamas off balance. All Hamas leaders were considered targets, and that included Sheik Ahmed Yassin, the quadriplegic who had cofounded the group. Yassin, who was described as Hamas's spiritual leader, was an unusual figure. His family hailed from a fishing village in what would become southern Israel. During the 1948 war when Israel gained independence, the family became refugees and moved to nearby Gaza. A sports accident as a boy caused his injuries but did not keep him from becoming one of Gaza's most prominent preachers. He was always known for his absolutist views. "I believe completely that Israel will vanish, and that we Palestinians will recover the lands and homes that were stolen from us in 1948," he told my *Times* colleague John Burns shortly before the second Palestinian uprising began.

Sheik Yassin was instantly recognizable in his white robe and headdress, with a long white beard. He rarely spoke at length, and his high-pitched rasp was difficult to hear, even in a small, quiet room. He suffered frequent illnesses and had poor eyesight and hearing that deteriorated during years in Israeli prisons, he said. Despite his infirmities, he was still revered as the group's leader, although it was difficult to gauge how much he guided the group's day-to-day actions. Aside from daily trips to a mosque in his neighborhood, he rarely ventured out from his simple Gaza City home.

He was being pushed home from the mosque in his wheelchair on March 22, 2004, when Israeli helicopters tracked him down, fired several missiles, and killed him instantly. "I could not recognize the sheik, only his wheelchair," said one witness, Maher al-Beek.

Only days after Sheik Yassin's death, Hamas named Dr. Abdel Aziz Rantisi as the new Hamas leader in Gaza. A pediatrician who was a generation younger than Sheik Yassin, he was as fiery and bombastic as the sheik had been soft-spoken. Dr. Rantisi had narrowly survived an Israeli missile strike the previous year, but less than a month after Yassin's death, the Israelis struck again, and this time they killed Dr. Rantisi.

Both killings sent outraged Hamas supporters flooding into the streets of Gaza City for mass funerals. Hamas leaders declared that they would strike back hard. "All of us will be martyrs," said Ismail Haniya, who subsequently became the new Hamas leader in Gaza. My editors at the *New York Times* asked whether they should send additional reporters to the region to deal with possible surge in violence.

The Israeli bombing campaign against the Hamas leadership did indeed have consequences, but not the kind that my editors and many other people had forecast. The Israeli military continued its comprehensive crackdown on Palestinian militants, and all of the factions found it increasingly difficult to hit at Israel. Hamas, meanwhile, had always stressed its collective leadership and did not depend on a single dominant leader, as was the case with Arafat and his Fatah movement. Hamas replaced its slain leaders without much fuss, and although Hamas still carried out additional attacks, the group started to play a much more active role in Palestinian politics. Arafat and Fatah appeared weak and corrupt, and their support was waning. In contrast, the Hamas leaders were willing to give their lives for the Palestinian cause. Every time Israel's security forces tracked down and killed a Hamas leader, they created a new "martyr" who only added to the group's appeal.

19

"WE FAILED ENTIRELY"

One spring day in 2005, Gandhi came to the Palestinian territories—at least in the form of British actor Ben Kingsley, who won an Oscar for his role in the 1982 biopic of the Indian resistance leader. Kingsley was the guest of President Mahmoud Abbas and was visiting to publicize the first Arabic-dubbed version of the movie *Gandhi*. Kingsley said that the movie's theme was still timely and relevant. "The force of truth is irreducible, and this is the center of the message," he told the audience at the Palestinian Palace of Culture in Ramallah. Kingsley stressed that his message was nonpolitical, and that he and the other organizers were not trying to take positions in the Israeli-Palestinian conflict.

Decades of head-on confrontation with Israel had brought only heartache for the Palestinians, and the notion of nonviolent resistance rarely cropped up as a possible alternative. Jeff Skoll, the former president of eBay, was the driving force behind the Gandhi project. When the movie was originally released, it included a version with Arabic subtitles, but not one with Arabic voices.

The new version did manage to ignite a debate at the theater, where Palestinians differed over whether Gandhi's philosophy of peaceful protest against British colonial rule of India could be translated to the Israeli-Palestinian dispute. "I wanted to see how he confronted occupation," said Abla Afanah, a teacher in Ramallah. "I think it may be possible to implement this here."

Sudki Safat, a friend of Afanah's and an official in the Ministry of Education, disagreed. "It's not possible," he said. "I know Gandhi and his principles. But I also know my enemy very well. Gandhi would fail if he faced the Israelis."

The film was shown throughout the West Bank and Gaza and was later presented to Palestinian refugees in Jordan, Syria, and Lebanon. Many were intrigued with tactics such as economic self-reliance and the Indian boycott of British products, but the film did not exactly catch fire. "We have studied revolutions all around the world and try to learn from them," said Rajai al-Biss, eighteen, a college student. "But I don't think we have the means to boycott Israeli products. We have a different reality here."

Some Palestinians argued that they had tried nonviolent protests, to no avail. They noted that unarmed Palestinians had staged weekly demonstrations against Israel's separation barrier in the West Bank village of Bilin and elsewhere. Yet these persistent efforts attracted only limited attention and did not keep the barrier from going up. The Israelis regularly broke up these demonstrations with tear gas and sometimes with arrests.

Still, the Gandhi project was part of a sustained effort by Arafat's successor, Mahmoud Abbas, to retool the Palestinian approach to the conflict with Israel. With the Palestinian uprising still going full throttle back in the fall of 2002, Abbas caused a minor stir by becoming the first senior Palestinian leader to criticize the intifada. At that time, Abbas was best known as Arafat's longtime associate, a soft-spoken, behind-the-scenes negotiator who had played a central role in the peace talks of the 1990s but rarely spoke publicly. Abbas's standard dress was a suit and a tie, and you could find him in an office behind a stack of papers, but you would never see him on the street when the rocks and the tear gas were flying.

He made his point about the shortcomings of the intifada in his own understated way. Abbas's office leaked a speech from a closed-door meeting that said taking up arms against Israel was a mistake that had cost the Palestinians dearly. "Many people diverted the uprising from its natural path and embarked on a path we can't handle, with the use of weapons," Abbas said in the speech to fellow Fatah leaders. "What happened in these two years, as we see it now, is a complete destruction of everything we built."

Abbas was a very lonely voice at that stage. Two years later, when he took over as the Palestinian Authority president following Arafat's death, he became much more direct. He repeated his remarks about the misguided approach of the intifada. He tried to curb the incitement in the Palestinian media. He openly mocked Palestinian militants who fired inaccurate, short-range rockets into Israel, which rarely caused damage or casualties but often prompted a harsh Israeli response. He even sought to dial down the Muslim clerics who denounced the Israelis in vile terms.

"We are waging this cruel war with the brothers of monkeys and pigs, the Jews and the sons of Zion," Sheik Ibrahim Mahdi, a prominent Palestinian cleric, said on his weekly television program in 2004. Arafat, who was still alive at the time, did not interfere when it came to these outspoken clerics, even those appointed by his Palestinian Authority.

Yet Abbas saw the overheated sermons as harmful to his political efforts. Just weeks after Arafat's death, Abbas traveled from his West Bank headquarters to visit Gaza, where he attended a sermon by a more moderate cleric, Muhammad Abu Hunud. "We must respect the human mind, recognize the 'other,' respect his humanity, and show tolerance toward him," the preacher said in a speech televised in the Palestinian territories.[1]

In the first few years of the uprising, Palestinian television repeatedly played video clips of young Palestinian men who were killed and maimed in fighting, accompanied by wailing mothers and patriotic music. News broadcasters routinely called Israeli troops "the savage occupation forces." After several years of this fare, some Palestinians began to complain that they could no longer stomach the endless stream of gory images. When Abbas came to power, the archival scenes of violence appeared much less frequently.

Palestinian propaganda was often directed at children. One kids' show on Palestinian television featured a talking yellow bird that responded to questions from youngsters in the audience. A little girl asked the bird what it would do if someone cut down the olive trees in front of her house. The bird replied, "I'll call the whole world and make a riot. I'll bring AK-47s and commit a massacre in front of the house."

Radwan Abu Ayyash, the head of Palestinian broadcasting, acknowledged that the material was inappropriate, and he removed the show. Yet he said that Palestinian television was simply reflecting the mood of the Palestinian people. "I'd like to show more enter-tainment programs. My kids are upset that I've pulled *Sesame Street* off the air. But when Sharon launches a military operation, then I have to cancel our animal programs and show the bloodshed." With a sardonic smile, he added, "Sharon is our director of program-ming."

This was just one of the many challenges Abbas faced in his campaign for moderation, and initially he suffered more defeats than victories. He was a weak leader who lacked charisma. He was a shy man who did not enjoy being in front of the cameras, and he tended to sulk and retreat from public view altogether when he did not get his way. Neither the Israelis nor the United States took any real steps to enhance his stature, and hard-line Palestinians often ridiculed his calls for negotiations as a sign of impotence. He came to power as the Palestinians were splintering between Fatah and Hamas, and his greatest failure was in allowing Hamas to take full control of Gaza.

Out of that fiasco, however, came some successes. Abbas lost what little authority he had in Gaza, but it also prompted him to appoint his own government in the West Bank. He named as his prime minister Salam Fayyad, a former official at the World Bank and the International Monetary Fund who has a doctor-ate in economics from the University of Texas. The bespectacled Fayyad was as staid and as buttoned-down as Abbas. Both looked as if they would be more comfortable in the decorous atmosphere of the European Parliament than in the roiling politics of the Middle East.

Yet Fayyad has focused on building the institutions needed for statehood and has been the driving force behind an economic recov-ery in parts of the West Bank, including the main cities of Ramal-lah and Nablus. Shopping centers and car dealerships have begun to appear. Foreign aid is still critical, but private investment from abroad has also been coming to the West Bank. Fayyad has argued that the Palestinians have traditionally responded to the Israeli occu-pation in one of two ways—with a sense of defeatism that resulted in passivity, or with violent rage that was marked by the suicide bomb-ing campaign. There was another way, he said. Individual Palestin-ians must strive for self-reliance, and Palestinian leaders must offer sound economic management and administrative competence. It was not clear whether these notions would become entrenched, but in the West Bank, at least, Abbas and Fayyad improved living standards that had been in decline for years and offered a genuine alternative to decades of radicalism.

It has been a slow process, but some younger Palestinians have absorbed the painful lessons from the second intifada. They include Zakariya Zubeidi, who emerged as one of the most prominent Palestinian militants during the uprising. Before the fighting began, Zubeidi was, surprisingly, a thespian. He participated in a youth theater troupe in Jenin, the ragged town in the northern West Bank that was a hotbed for militants. Even more surprisingly, the theater group was run by an Israeli human rights activist, Arna Mer-Khamis. She ran the theater from a room in the apartment building where Zubeidi grew up, and this experience polished Zubeidi's natural charm and gave him a glimpse of the possibilities of coexistence between Israelis and Palestinians.

Yet community theater could not trump the harsh realities of the conflict. Zubeidi was already throwing stones at Israeli troops when he was thirteen and was shot in the leg by soldiers, an injury that required multiple operations and left him with a limp. His first of several stints in Israeli prisons came at age fourteen. When the second Palestinian uprising began, he was in his early twenties and joined the Al Aksa Martyrs Brigades. By the spring of 2002, Jenin was a madhouse. The town was one of the main launching pads for suicide bombers heading into Israel, and the Israelis staged regular raids on the town and the adjacent refugee camp. Zubeidi was at the center of the fighting, and his family paid a heavy price: his mother was shot dead during one Israeli raid, and his brother was killed in a separate Israeli incursion.

The Israelis staged their massive assault on Jenin in April 2002 and wiped out many of the militants, but Zubeidi survived and emerged as the Al Aksa leader. While other Al Aksa leaders spent their days in hiding and wore ski masks on the rare occasions when they emerged publicly, the actor in Zubeidi relished the limelight. The cocky young man wore tight-fitting T-shirts, kept a pistol tucked in his jeans, and chain-smoked cheap L&M cigarettes. He saw himself as the main source of authority in the lawless refugee camp. He could not resist appearing before the cameras and welcomed journalists who wanted to follow him through the streets of Jenin in broad daylight. This approach seemed certain to speed up his demise, and he had his share of close calls. Israeli troops tried to kill him on several occasions, and he almost did himself in when an explosive he was preparing went off prematurely, burning and permanently discoloring his face.

I met Zubeidi in April 2003, one year after the big battle in Jenin. Although the town was still a wreck, the militants saw the anniversary as a cause for celebration and paraded through the rubble of the refugee camp brandishing their AK-47s. As we interviewed Zubeidi on a roof overlooking the camp, the taping was interrupted by sporadic gunfire into the air. The lanky Zubeidi shouted down to his fellow gunmen to halt the shooting so he could be interviewed in peace. "Halas!" ("Enough!") he shouted in Arabic, and the shooting immediately stopped. He wore a black bandanna with Koranic verses written in white script. He remained defiant and expressed no interest in calling off the uprising. "I will agree to a cease-fire if I wake up in the morning and see Israeli military withdrawing from all corners of the West Bank," he said.

The Israelis were the main enemy, but Zubeidi and his men also saw themselves as crusaders against the rampant corruption in the Palestinian Authority. A few months after my interview, Zubeidi and his gunmen ransacked the office of Jenin's governor. They took a sledgehammer to his desk, doused the place in gasoline, and set it alight. They invited a cameraman from the Al Jazeera satellite channel along to film their efforts. "The people around Arafat are corrupt," Zubeidi said. Yet even as Zubeidi's reform-minded gunslingers took direct action against one of Arafat's hand-picked officials, they remained loyal to Arafat himself. Before torching the office, they took the trouble to remove a portrait of Arafat.

In 2007, several years after Jennifer's interview, I was in Jenin for a chat with Zubeidi. The town's refugee camp had been rebuilt, although the main room in Zubeidi's house was nearly empty, aside from a few plastic chairs, a sagging bed, and posters of his slain colleagues on the wall. Zubeidi said he was still being hunted by the Israelis. He pulled up his shirt to show me a fresh scar on his shoulder blade, courtesy of an Israeli bullet. Yet what I noticed most about Zubeidi was his new attitude. The swagger had been replaced with humility and introspection. The uprising was no longer a heroic cause; it was the cause of Palestinian infighting.

I had barely turned on my tape recorder when Zubeidi began to list the failures of the intifada and the Palestinian leadership. "It's unfortunate and sad to say, but the political result of the intifada was internal conflict, the beginning of the civil war among Palestinians," he said. I asked him to list any achievements in the intifada, expecting him to offer some defense of an uprising with which he was so closely associated. His response nearly made me fall from my chair. "There is nothing on the ground that was achieved for the Palestinians," he said matter-of-factly.

Zubeidi told me that the Palestinians were in total disarray, and his group, the Al Aksa Martyrs Brigades, had bad relations with its parent, the Fatah movement, as well as with the other Palestinian factions. As we drove out of Jenin, the scene was depressing. There were still posters celebrating Saddam Hussein, years after he had been ousted from power and executed. Angry graffiti covered the walls of the new apartments. Most Palestinians found it difficult, if not impossible, to leave the town, due to the Israeli soldiers surrounding it.

A year later, Zubeidi sounded even more disillusioned in an interview with Israel's *Haaretz* newspaper. "Today I can say explicitly: We failed entirely in the intifada," Zubeidi said. "We haven't seen any benefit or positive result from it. We achieved nothing. It's a crushing failure."

"Today there is no Palestinian identity," he told the newspaper. "Go up to anyone in the street and ask him, 'Who are you?' He'll answer you, 'I'm a Fatah activist,' 'I'm a Hamas activist,' or an activist of some other organization, but he won't say to you, 'I'm a Palestinian.' Every organization flies its own flag, but no one is raising the flag of Palestine."

Zubeidi said that he had returned to the theater as refuge from the bleak political reality. "We are marching in the direction of nowhere, toward total ruin. We, the activists, paid the heavy price. We've had family members killed, friends killed. They demolished our homes, and we have no way of earning a living. And what is the result? Zero. Simply zero."

20

SOUL SEARCHING

I was walking out the door of the *New York Times* office in downtown Jerusalem late one night when I received an urgent phone call from the Israeli military. If I acted immediately, I was welcome to witness a "very interesting" operation in Gaza. I pressed for details, to no avail. I was told only that I had two hours to reach a military base at the northern edge of Gaza and had just enough time to make it. "Bring your flak jacket," the young Israeli soldier told me.

The Palestinian uprising was in full swing in the spring of 2003, and many Israelis felt that they were being unfairly criticized for their crackdown in the Palestinian territories. In addition, the U.S. military had just launched its invasion of Iraq a few weeks earlier, and many journalists were embedded with the U.S. forces. At that early date, the U.S. operation in Iraq had gone relatively well, and media coverage was largely positive. The Israeli military wanted to experiment with a similar approach, and I would be one of their guinea pigs.

This little adventure also drove home the intimate nature of the Israeli-Palestinian conflict. In Iraq, American journalists traveled across oceans and deserts to get there. They lived with U.S. forces for days or even weeks at a time. After a month or two, most would leave the war zone and make the journey back home. I, on the other hand, was summoned when I was only a few minutes from home, where I had planned to spend the night in my own bed. The only drama I had anticipated was the nocturnal activity of our infant daughter, Amelia. Now, Jennifer would have to conduct Operation Lactation without my moral support. I was off to Gaza, where I would spend the night on the front lines.

Under a brilliant full moon, I arrived at the Israeli base shortly before midnight. Within minutes, I was standing next to a line of Israeli armored vehicles as I received a briefing on the mission from Lieutenant Colonel Ron (it was military policy not to divulge last names). He informed me that we would be making an uninvited visit to Beit Hanoun, a Palestinian farming community tucked in the northeast corner of Gaza. Militants used the lush citrus groves for cover as they fired short-range rockets over Gaza's border fence and into the nearby Israeli town of Sderot. The Israeli plan was to blow up the family homes of four Palestinians who were believed to be responsible for the rocket fire.

The Israeli troops did not expect to find the militants asleep in their beds. The aim was to destroy the houses and discourage additional rocket attacks, at least in the long term. Yet in the short term, this raid was virtually guaranteed to have the opposite effect. The militants could be counted on to have a knee-jerk reaction and fire a fresh round of rockets into Israel. And it was safe to assume that the next Palestinian rocket salvo would spawn yet another Israeli military response.

The lieutenant colonel took a final drag on his cigarette and flicked it into the sandy soil. He ordered his troops—and me—into the armored vehicles, which included tanks, bulldozers, and troop carriers. The lieutenant colonel, a slim, energetic man with a day's worth of stubble, was chatty as he prepared for the mission, but he grew silent and tense as his convoy started out along the narrow rutted roads in single file, with the lights out, navigating by moonlight and night-vision goggles.

In addition to the lieutenant colonel and me, four young soldiers were squeezed inside a specially designed armored personnel carrier, with thick bulletproof glass panels that allowed us to stand and take in a 360-degree view. Space was so tight that we constantly bumped shoulders and elbows as we bounced along the uneven path. The lieutenant colonel kept checking the positions of the other vehicles, and the radio that linked him to his officers rarely went silent. He frequently flipped on a small flashlight to check a map book with aerial photos of Beit Hanoun on a detailed grid.

The lieutenant colonel had received training at Fort Benning, Georgia, and, as commander of a Special Forces battalion, led some of the army's more sensitive missions in Gaza. Preparing for this one, he acknowledged the conflicting demands. "It's important just to hit the terrorists, not the civilians," he said before the raid. "Most of the time we succeed. But the terrorists sometimes use the women and children as human shields, and it makes our job very difficult."

After an hour on deserted roads, we reached Beit Hanoun, and the soldiers staked out positions in the dirt streets, many just wide enough to accommodate armored personnel carriers but not tanks. If not for the bulletproof glass, I felt as though I could have reached out and touched the houses on either side of the street. Spreading out over several blocks, the Israeli armored vehicles surrounded two houses thought to belong to Hamas members involved in the rocket fire.

Speaking in Arabic, an Israeli soldier on a megaphone told residents to get out of the two houses, as well as those nearby. The gunmen of Beit Hanoun responded with almost instantaneous bursts of fire, which set off intense shooting exchanges. The invisible Palestinian fighters also hurled grenades and detonated two roadside bombs. The shooting seemed to come from all directions as the bullets ricocheted off houses and armor. Both sides were firing furiously, but it was impossible, for me at least, to tell where the bullets were coming from or what was being targeted.

The sensation was strange. The battle generated an instant rush of adrenaline, but in the tightly sealed confines of the armored vehicle, there was nowhere to go and nothing to do except passively observe. All of my senses were on high alert. My eyes darted and my head swiveled as I tried to locate the gunfire. Yet I could make no sense of the random pops and bangs going off in the darkness all around me. It was all soundtrack and no pictures, like listening to a Rambo movie with your eyes closed. Were those noises outgoing blasts of automatic Israeli gunfire or incoming Palestinian fire? Where was the Palestinian fire coming from? Had anyone been hit?

After fifteen minutes, the gunfire died down. The Palestinian families in the two targeted homes emerged on the streets as ordered. Parents in pajamas carried frightened children in their arms as they scurried down the street to take shelter in the homes of neighbors. The Israelis shone spotlights on them to make sure they were unarmed. The wide-eyed children were terrified.

Small bands of Israeli soldiers then entered the two homes to confirm that they had been evacuated and to plant explosives. A few minutes later, a pair of blasts only minutes apart brought the two-story homes crashing down amid bright orange flashes and a shower of brilliant orange sparks. The concussive power of the blasts forced a hot gust of wind into the gun portals of our armored personnel carrier, carrying dust as fine as talcum powder.

The houses were destroyed, and job number one was finished. The Israeli convoy then rumbled on, traveling a short distance to another Beit Hanoun neighborhood. The scenario was repeated as if it were choreographed.

The Israeli convoy arrived, and the soldiers called out on the megaphone. The Palestinian gunmen opened fire; the Israelis returned fire. After a few minutes of furious exchanges, the guns fell silent. The two houses emptied out; the Israelis went in and planted explosives. The houses came tumbling down. The Israelis drove off. In the first episode, the action felt highly unpredictable. The second time, it felt bizarrely routine.

On this night, no Israeli troops were hurt. Neither I nor the Israeli soldiers had any immediate information about Palestinian casualties. As with so many shooting exchanges, particularly at night, it was impossible to know what was happening on the receiving end. One young Israeli soldier assured me that the Israeli troops were shooting only at the sources of the Palestinian fire. Yet there was no way of telling whether the Israelis were hitting gunmen, civilians, or no one at all. Only hours later, well after the shooting had stopped, did we hear from Palestinian hospitals that five Palestinians had been killed. Two of the dead were gunmen and three were youths, ages twelve, fourteen, and eighteen, who had not been involved in the fighting, according to the Palestinians.

As was so often the case, each side seemed to be delivering a message that was lost on its intended recipient. Israel wanted to show that it would not tolerate rocket fire and that all of Palestinian society would pay a heavy price if the militants continued to attack. Yet the Palestinians could only see Israeli troops tearing down houses and inflicting civilian casualties. Both sides were certain they were defending their own people against aggression by the enemy.

When the sun rose over Gaza, we left the crowded Palestinian neighborhoods, but the operation was not over. The lieutenant colonel directed his forces to a large citrus grove outside Beit Hanoun that was being used for rocket launches. The army's hulking, armored bulldozers, the D-9s, systematically flattened acres of orange groves. Five bulldozers took down hundreds of mature orange trees like huge lawn movers trimming an overgrown yard. The bulldozers were so powerful that as they pressed the trees forward to the ground, dozens of oranges were flung from their branches, as if they were being thrown by human hands. "With these trees gone, we now have a clear line of sight from our positions, and the terrorists can't hide," the lieutenant colonel said. The Israelis also had created a village of angry farmers who had just lost their livelihoods.

The Israeli troops remained in the area, and periodic clashes continued throughout the day. Young Palestinian men set up burning tire barricades in the streets and threw stones at the Israeli armor. Palestinian gunmen occasionally opened fire, but the Israeli presence kept most Palestinians inside their homes. "Until this moment, we feel like we are in jail," Sufian Hamad, a Beit Hanoun resident, told Taghreed El-Khodary, my *New York Times* colleague who was covering the Palestinian side of the incursion. "We are surrounded by tanks." He told his seven children to resist the temptation to peek out the window, reminding them of the twelve-year-old boy who had been killed the previous night.

When I told the Israeli lieutenant colonel about the Palestinian youths who were killed, he expressed remorse. "It's a terrible feeling," he told me. "It's the last thing I want to happen. I can only hope that we have made it difficult for the Palestinians to fire rockets from this area."

I was in the Israeli armored personnel carrier from about midnight until noon the next day. When I emerged, exhausted and coated in dust, one question kept rattling around in my head as I drove back to Jerusalem: do these operations help or hurt Israel's security?

From the generals in the military's high-rise headquarters in Tel Aviv to ordinary citizens sitting in coffee shops, virtually every Israeli has a pronounced opinion about how to deal with the Palestinians. There is no shortage of Israelis who favor the iron fist, and their numbers have increased during the last decade of fighting. Yet from afar, the conflict is too often cast in black-and-white terms and obscures Israel's incessant internal debate about security. Like any government, particularly one that is democratically elected and prone to collapse, Israel's leadership cannot sit by and allow suicide bombings and rocket attacks. Yet even in the worst days of the fighting, opinion polls showed that a majority of Israelis favored territorial concessions in exchange for a genuine peace deal with the Palestinians. Yitzhak Rabin summed it up nicely back in the 1990s: Israel should "pursue the peace process as if there is no terrorism, and fight terrorism as if there is no peace process."

From a purely military perspective, Israel's operations during the last decade have been broadly successful. Israel eventually snuffed out the Palestinian uprising and made itself much less vulnerable. Yet there are clear limits to military power, even when it is effective. Israel was not able to resolve the conflict or force a Palestinian surrender. Israel came under increased international criticism. The most radical Palestinian group, Hamas, grew stronger.

Israel has faced an evolving series of threats since its founding, and there has almost always been a range of opinions about where to draw the line between legitimate defense and excessive force. The best answer I heard had been delivered decades earlier from the German-Israeli philosopher Martin Buber: "What is necessary is allowed, but what is not necessary is forbidden."[1]

Buber's words are powerful. Reality is messy. And he never served at an Israeli military checkpoint.

Israel's many checkpoints are routinely manned by teenage soldiers just out of high school. They operate in Palestinian areas where the soldiers do not speak the language and must deal all day with a population that deeply resents their presence. The soldiers' behavior is much more casual than you might expect from a country where the army is often cast in mythic terms. The uniforms are scruffy, the attitude is informal, and no one ever salutes. Still, most

Israelis, both hawks and doves, would argue that at least some of the checkpoints are necessary to protect the country.

Yet the summer days are hot, dusty, and long. The winter nights are cold, rainy, and interminable. Teenagers have short attention spans. They get bored and lose their concentration. Their judgment is less than fully developed. The line of Palestinians seeking permission to pass is endless. Sooner or later, you will see the mistreatment of Palestinian civilians. The abuse may be the bad behavior of a single soldier or the outgrowth of an official policy. Either way, vast numbers of Palestinians have felt the sting of humiliation at the hands of an Israeli soldier. It may be that the soldier is just arbitrarily using his authority to prevent a Palestinian from passing. Or perhaps a soldier is genuinely concerned about an attack or is simply being overly cautious.

Whatever the reason, the long-term effect is the same. These daily encounters inflict hardships on Palestinian civilians and are corrosive to Israel's moral health. In the summer of 2004, a group called Breaking the Silence exhibited videotaped testimony from twenty-nine former soldiers who spoke about gratuitous harassment and the abuse of Palestinians in the West Bank town of Hebron. The soldiers, who had their faces and voices digitally altered so they could not be identified, had served in Hebron with the Nahal Brigade, where they guarded the small number of Jewish settlers whose homes were surrounded by the city's much larger Palestinian population.

The organizers held their first exhibit in Tel Aviv, where a studio featured dozens of car keys confiscated from Palestinian residents of Hebron, a punishment that was common and unauthorized, the soldiers said. In the videos, the soldiers described how some of their comrades experienced a rush in exercising power over those with no recourse. One soldier fired tear gas canisters "every time he climbed up to his post and came back from it," according to one testimony. "If he saw a group of people standing and talking, he would fire the tear gas just to see them run and cough. He got a big kick out of it."

The driving force behind Breaking the Silence was Yehuda Shaul, who recruited his former comrades for the project shortly after he completed his mandatory military service. "We feel like the army doesn't really want to deal with the serious issues," said Shaul. The group has continued to document improper actions by soldiers and has caused an uproar on several occasions with the testimony it has gathered from troops following major Israeli military operations.

Occasionally, the criticism came from the top. A senior Israeli military officer caused a stir in the fall of 2003 when he said that the country's hard-line security policies were working against Israel's strategic interest. Several leading Israeli newspapers reported the controversial comments, attributing them to an unidentified military official who had briefed reporters. Yet few things stay secret for long in Israel. Shortly after the newspapers came out the following morning, the official was identified as the military's chief of general staff, Lieutenant General Moshe Yaalon, the country's top soldier.

The travel restrictions and the curfews imposed on Palestinians "increase the hatred for Israel and strengthen the terror organizations," General Yaalon told the Israeli journalists with the expectation of anonymity. The Palestinians, he added, have "no hope, no expectations." Prime Minister Ariel Sharon was not amused; however, the comments did not ruin the career of Yaalon, who was considered a hard-liner. He remained chief of staff for two more years and later entered politics, then became deputy prime minister in 2009 under Prime Minister Benjamin Netanyahu.

Just a month after Yaalon made his remarks, four former heads of the Shin Bet security service delivered a blistering collective criticism of Sharon's tough military policies, saying that Israel was ignoring the possibility of a political solution. "We are taking sure, steady steps to a place where the state of Israel will no longer be a democracy and a home for the Jewish people," Ami Ayalon, the Shin Bet chief from 1996 to 2000, told the *Yedioth Ahronoth* newspaper. "Many Israelis thought we could defeat the Palestinians by military means, and this would solve our problems."

A lot of Israelis are prepared to give the security forces broad latitude in dealing with the Palestinians. Every so often, though, a slight twist in the story line casts events in an entirely different light.

In December 2003, Israeli troops clashed with demonstrators near the West Bank village of Masha, at the site where Israel was building its West Bank separation barrier. The barrier was intended to stop Palestinian attacks, but its construction inside the West Bank was a constant source of friction. On this day, about twenty protesters on the Palestinian side shook the chain-link fence, and some took out pliers to cut it. After calling out warnings and firing shots into the air, Israeli troops shot live ammunition at the legs of the protesters, according to both sides. One man was hit in both legs and seriously wounded. In a brief statement, the military said that soldiers shot at the man "who led the rioters" in the village, which is about twenty-five miles south of Jerusalem.

The episode passed unnoticed by most Israelis until one unusual fact emerged: the wounded man was Gil Naamati, a twenty-two-year-old Israeli who had just completed three years of military service as a combat soldier. The military did not realize that Naamati and other Israelis had been among the Palestinian demonstrators. The shooting instantly sparked national outrage. From President Moshe Katsav on down, Israelis wanted to know why soldiers had used live ammunition to shoot an unarmed Israeli who posed no threat. "I am in favor of building the fence," Katsav told Israel radio. "Israeli citizens are allowed to protest against the fence. But the reaction to this cannot be live fire."

Videotapes that aired on Israeli television showed soldiers standing next to a military vehicle. In a deliberate manner, one soldier went down on his stomach and pointed a rifle at the protesters. Shortly afterward, shots rang out, and one of the protesters shouted in Hebrew, "Don't shoot!"

General Yaalon, the military's chief of staff, visited Naamati in the hospital. Palestinians observed this urgent and earnest Israeli response and said that the entire episode supported their long-standing contention that Israeli troops were too quick on the trigger. "It shows how liberal the army is in using live ammunition against peaceful demonstrators," said Dr. Mustafa Barghouti, who headed a Palestinian group that monitored the violence. The protesters said they had no weapons and did not throw stones at the soldiers, who they said were twenty to forty yards away, on the far side of the fence.

"We didn't threaten soldiers," Naamati told Israel Army Radio from his hospital bed. "All we hurt was the fence. The fence does not threaten lives. We did not threaten anyone's life." Naamati acknowledged that he was among those shaking the fence and trying to cut through it. He added, "I am familiar with the rules of engagement, and what I did was not even close to something that I think would warrant opening fire."

Israel always refused to discuss the precise rules of engagement, but the basic principles were clear. Soldiers could use rubber bullets and tear gas when confronting Palestinians who did not threaten their lives, such as stone throwers. The soldiers could use live ammunition when faced with lethal force. The military said that soldiers were disciplined about obeying the rules, and that violations were rare exceptions. The Palestinians, in turn, said that the use of live fire was all too common.

Naamati's father, Uri, said his son supported the barrier, believing it would reduce Palestinian attacks. But his son opposed the route inside the West Bank, the father told me in a telephone interview from the hospital. Referring to his son by his nickname, Uri said that "Gilly is a sensitive kid and is not part of any extreme group." The father told me his son had been a willing soldier but was particularly critical of the way soldiers were operating at checkpoints. "He always said, 'Dad, we are doing terrible things to the people over there.'"

21

THE NEW JERUSALEM

On a brilliant fall day on the cusp of the millennium, I set out to explore Jerusalem's holy sites. At my initial stop inside the Old City, I was startled, in a good way, as I visited the Temple Mount–Noble Sanctuary and stepped inside the golden Dome of the Rock, the splendid seventh-century Islamic shrine with its ornate painted tiles of lemon and sky blue.

The Dome of the Rock, which rises above the Old City and is surrounded by soaring cypress trees, hosts a steady stream of worshippers all day long. In keeping with its traditions, I slipped off my shoes just outside the door. I stepped inside, where I expected to find devout Muslims. As I looked around, though, I did an immediate double take. Standing next to the massive stone at the center of the shrine were at least twenty young Israeli soldiers in their olive fatigues. They had left their boots outside and were padding around in their socks as part of a military field trip that focused on Islamic history and cultural sensitivity. Along the walls of the eight-sided structure, a few scattered Palestinian men and women, most of them elderly, sat cross-legged on the Oriental carpets with their heads buried in the Koran. They paid no attention to the soldiers, ignoring them as if they were an everyday sight, which at that time they were. There was no tension. In fact, quite the opposite. The

Dome of the Rock and the thirty-five-acre platform around it were an oasis of calm above the cacophony of the Old City.

I found a similar spirit when I visited the Western Wall down below. The Western Wall is the holiest place of Jewish prayer, and there is a constant flow of Jewish worshippers, many of them ultra-Orthodox, in the stone plaza. The men and the women pray in separate sections, although everyone writes prayers on slips of paper that are folded and squeezed into the crevices of the giant stones.

On I went, zigging and zagging through the Old City until I reached the Church of the Holy Sepulchre, the spot where Christians believe that Jesus was crucified and buried. As I made my way from one darkened chamber to the next, I was in the company of Christian pilgrims from Korea, Nigeria, Italy, and the United States.

It was impossible not to feel the power of Jerusalem's Old City and its holy sites. My pleasant excursion seemed to belie everything I had heard about Jerusalem. This place had the reputation of being the center of the world's most enduring conflict. Back in 1947, the United Nations partition plan called for Jerusalem to be a special international zone that would not be part of either Israel or Palestine. To this day, Israel claims all of the city as its own. The Palestinians demand the eastern part of Jerusalem, including all of the Old City and its religious shrines, for the capital of a future state.

Yet on that splendid fall day in October 1999, Jerusalem seemed to be doing just fine, thank you, in accommodating the faithful from all corners of the globe. The city was functioning as the seat of three major faiths, with the adherents bowing to God's sovereignty and going about their business largely disconnected from the worldly disputes of bickering politicians. According to the conventional wisdom, Jerusalem would be the hardest single problem to solve in the Israeli-Palestinian conflict because it is a zero-sum game. Both Israelis and Palestinians are unyielding when it comes to Jerusalem and, above all, the religious sites in the Old City. In the eyes of the faithful, there is no way to relinquish what God has given. Yet at that optimistic moment, it seemed that the politicians would be forced to acknowledge the way that life was actually being lived and make political compromises to accommodate that reality.

Tens of thousands of Muslims descended on the Noble Sanctuary to worship at the main midday prayers every Friday, many of them driving in from the West Bank, and some making the lengthy trip from Gaza. A similar number of Jews faced the Western Wall, coming and going at their own pace. Several years of relative calm, combined with the looming millennium, drew Christians in record numbers to Jerusalem. A visit by Pope John Paul II several months later, in March 2000, would spur even more pilgrims. For months afterward, it was difficult to walk down the narrow lanes of the Old City without getting stuck behind a slow-moving band of chanting pilgrims who were reenacting the drama of Christ on the cross as they trudged along the Via Dolorosa.

"You want to know what Jerusalem is?" asked Daniel Seidemann, an American Israeli lawyer who heads Ir Amim, or City of Nations, a group that advocates sharing the city. "It's not warm and fuzzy, it's not touchy-feely, there are no loudspeakers playing 'It's a Small World After All.' But Jerusalem has been doing this for thirteen hundred years."

Jerusalem, he predicted, could go one of two ways in the coming years. It could become the epicenter of the clash of civilizations—or the strongest argument against that theory.

"Jerusalem does not deserve the reputation of being nitroglycerine," he said. "Jerusalem can be the counter-paradigm to the clash of civilizations that shows in its very sober, pragmatic, sometimes irritable way that you can have, in God's little acre, the cohabitation of three mutually incompatible religious narratives and two mutually incompatible national narratives."

But, he cautioned, if this does not happen, "Jerusalem will become the embodiment of a clash of civilizations. I would suggest taking a hard look at the way the city already functions. Jerusalem is on our side; it knows how to do it. It requires the political leadership to listen to what this wise city is telling us and to put this into a political language that is not utopian but very, very sober."

During our more than seven-year stay, a blink of an eye in Jerusalem's long history, the city went from being a place that attracted the faithful from around the globe to becoming the suicide-bombing capital of the world, and then it transformed again into a security-obsessed town in which the rival communities were sharply segregated. For all of Jerusalem's timeless qualities, we witnessed what was the city's third major makeover in the last sixty years.

The first one came with the 1948 Arab-Israeli war that physically divided Jerusalem. A barbed-wire barricade split it into the Arab east and the Jewish west. Jordan annexed the West Bank, including East Jerusalem. Jews were driven from the eastern part of the city, which included the walled Old City, and could not pray at the Western Wall for nearly two decades. Palestinians, in turn, were ousted from some of the wealthiest and most prestigious neighborhoods in West Jerusalem.

This division remained until Jerusalem's next major transformation in the wake of the 1967 war, when Israel captured the eastern part of the city. In the tense days leading up to the war, Palestinians believed that the combined Arab armies would score a decisive victory over the Jewish state, which would include retaking all of the divided city. Nabil Feidy, an East Jerusalem businessman and a friend to many foreign journalists, was a boy in 1967. He recalled the heady atmosphere and the unbearable sense of anticipation among Palestinians. When the fighting began, news was scarce and accurate information virtually nonexistent. The official propaganda was particularly thick on the Arab side. Even after the fighting began, the Palestinians were full of optimism, bordering on euphoria, and had no way of knowing they were about to suffer a crushing defeat. When tanks entered East Jerusalem, many Palestinians assumed they were from Iraq, whose army was still remembered fondly for fighting alongside the Palestinians in the 1948 war. Young Palestinian men ran up to the tanks to shower their "Arab liberators" with flowers and candy. The Palestinians were stunned when the soldiers emerging from the turrets spoke Hebrew, Feidy said.

As Palestinians struggled with this new reality, Israelis saw it as a modern-day miracle. For the first time in nearly two thousand years, Jews once again ruled the entire city. This was not only a great moment in Israeli history, it was one of the great moments in Jewish history.

In the four decades since, Palestinians have never accepted Israeli rule over the eastern part of the city, while Israel has systematically imposed its identity on Jerusalem. Some two hundred thousand Israelis have moved into East Jerusalem, a figure approaching the Palestinian population in that part of the city. The western part of Jerusalem, meanwhile, remains nearly 100 percent Jewish. The

Palestinians have found it extremely difficult, if not impossible, to build new neighborhoods or even expand their existing homes in East Jerusalem, due to the web of Israeli bureaucratic restrictions. Palestinians have boycotted every proposal put forth by Israel, rejected offers of Israeli citizenship, and refused to participate in municipal elections. The Palestinians say that accepting any of these gestures would only serve to legitimize Israeli rule.

Linda Rivkind, a longtime Jerusalem resident who worked many years in the Israeli government press office, remembered the city's relatively relaxed atmosphere when she arrived in 1971 to study at the Hebrew University in East Jerusalem. Israel had recently reopened the campus on Mount Scopus, which had been closed from 1949 to 1967 and was surrounded by Arab neighborhoods. "We felt quite comfortable there," recalled Rivkind. "There were only a small number of students, and to get around, we took the Arab buses to go down to the Old City or to go to the West Bank and the Dead Sea. We didn't think anything of going to the Palestinian fish restaurants in East Jerusalem."

In most other cities, Jews and Arabs tended to have little contact with one another. In Jerusalem, however, mixing was inevitable in a city that was roughly two-thirds Jewish and one-third Palestinian. Even for those who preferred not to mix, a visit to a restaurant, a grocery store, a gas station, or a hospital meant you would be mingling. This interaction did not inspire a political solution, but it did necessitate Jewish-Arab coexistence, particularly in the cozy confines of Jerusalem's Old City. That interaction largely ground to a halt after the intifada began.

George Khoury was one of the rare individuals who embodied the possibilities of a Jerusalem that could absorb different cultures, religions, and languages and celebrate all of them. At age twenty, Khoury seemed destined to transcend the boundaries imposed by the conflict. He was an Arab and a Christian who was a resident of Jerusalem and a citizen of Israel. He was from a prominent family, the son of a well-known lawyer. The family lived in an expansive, three-story home in East Jerusalem. Khoury was a popular student of international relations at the Hebrew University in East Jerusalem. The university is primarily a Jewish institution but has a sizable

Arab minority. Khoury had a wide-ranging network of friends that included Jews, Arabs, and Americans. He was comfortable conversing in Hebrew, Arabic, and English. "George loved life, and he made friends with everyone," said his cousin Michael Zumot.

His ability to mix easily in such varied groups was his gift, and on a chilly Friday night in March 2004, he blended in all too well. An avid runner, Khoury asked his sister to join him for a jog, but she declined, citing the chilly weather. So Khoury went for a solo run in the East Jerusalem neighborhood of French Hill. Most residents are Jewish, but Arabs are also a common sight on the streets and in the stores. Khoury knew the area well. He often ran in French Hill, which was near both his home and the university campus. As he ran down a street, a Palestinian gunman was waiting in ambush. The gunman assumed that Khoury was a Jew and shot him in the head and the stomach, killing him.

Khoury did not have any identification on him when he was shot. Given the circumstances, Israeli police were initially as confused as the gunman had been. Here was a jogger in a Jewish neighborhood who had apparently been targeted as part of a politically motivated killing. At first, the police announced that the victim was a Jewish man. It took hours before the police were able to identify Khoury by locating his car and tracing the license plates to the Khoury family.

The Al Aksa Martyrs Brigades, the group that carried out the shooting, said shortly after the attack that it was in response to the "arrests and murders carried out by the Israeli Army." After learning that the victim was an Arab, not a Jew, however, the group revised its position. "The fighters thought he was a settler jogging in an area full of settlers," said one of the group's leaders. "It was a mistake and we extend our apology to his family."[1]

Fady Awwad, a cousin of Khoury's, said that the two used to hang out in downtown Jerusalem, but the frequent suicide bombings had made it too risky. "The last couple of years, he didn't go out a lot and stayed away from the center of the city." Khoury's shooting was not the first time his family had been hit unintentionally by Palestinian violence. In 1975, Khoury's grandfather was killed in a Palestinian bombing aimed at Israeli Jews in Jerusalem, which left fourteen people dead.

George Khoury was a graduate of the private Anglican International School in Jerusalem, where his class had fewer than twenty students but was remarkably diverse. It included Christians and Jews from the United States and other countries, Palestinian Muslims, and Israeli Arab Christians, such as Khoury. "That class represented the intercommunal bonds that are often so hard to develop here," said James Snyder, an American who was the director of the Israel Museum in Jerusalem and who had a daughter in the same class. "He was a wonderful kid from a very fine Jerusalem family."

Three years after George Khoury's death, I found myself at a dinner with his parents at the home of James Snyder. The father, Elias Khoury, said that being an Arab in Jerusalem had become much more difficult than when he first studied at Hebrew University in 1969. "My roommate was a Jewish student," he told me. "There were only about ninety Arab students on the whole campus, so we had to integrate to be part of the group. We made Jewish friends, we drank coffee together, we went to movies together, we ate in one another's homes."

Elias Khoury said that at that time, if an Arab accused an Israeli of discrimination, the Israeli would have been very offended. "They would have said, 'That's not true. That doesn't exist.' It mattered to them. The behavior has changed over the years. Today, it's very different. Both sides have become more and more extreme."

Elias Khoury said that his son George grew up at ease in diverse company. But when George got to Hebrew University, where there were some four thousand Arab students, he found Arabs and Jews very much segregated. "I made relationships there that have lasted all these years," said Elias Khoury. "But you don't see those kinds of relationships now. The two sides just keep to themselves."

Despite the clear divisions in the city, the thought of formally redividing Jerusalem still provokes a knee-jerk opposition from many Israelis. They reflexively recall the period from 1948 to 1967, when Jordan held East Jerusalem, including the Old City, and Jews were completely cut off. When Israel started to build its West Bank barrier in 2002, however, its official ideology collided head-on with reality when it came to Jerusalem. Israel began to erect the barrier along the eastern edge of the city to keep all of Jerusalem on the western, or Israeli, side of the barrier.

Yet when it came to setting the route in the northeast corner of the city, pragmatism won out. There are some fifty-five thousand Palestinians—and no Jews—bunched into this corner of Jerusalem. Keeping this area on the Israeli side of the barrier made little sense. The barrier was, after all, supposed to provide protection against Palestinian attacks, and the guiding principle was to have the maximum number of Israelis and the minimum number of Palestinians on the western side of the wall.

So Ariel Sharon's government made a very rational choice. Instead of following the eastern border of the city, the barrier sliced through the northeastern part of Jerusalem. The route put those fifty-five thousand Palestinians on the far side of the barrier, even though they are Jerusalem residents who account for about a quarter of the city's Palestinian population. The Sharon government did not advertise the move, although there was no way to hide the building of a twenty-five-foot-high concrete wall through Jerusalem. The move did not generate any real opposition among Israelis. Yet it did what decades of Palestinian protests could not do: it divided Jerusalem.

The northeast corner of Jerusalem remains part of the city in the formal, legal sense. Israel has not renounced its claim of sovereignty. For all practical purposes, however, this part of Jerusalem is cut off from the rest of the city. You will not find any Jewish Israelis setting foot there, aside from the members of the security forces. Palestinians who live in this enclave have retained their Jerusalem residence permits and can go to other parts of the city, but they must pass through the barrier to reach the rest of Jerusalem, which requires going through an Israeli checkpoint that resembles a border crossing.

There is no prospect of Israel reclaiming the northeast corner of Jerusalem in any meaningful way. Jerusalem has been divided by the Israeli government, and the only question is where the boundary will be when the division becomes formal and permanent. Yet Israeli leaders still pretend this has not happened. "United Jerusalem is Israel's capital," Prime Minister Benjamin Netanyahu declared on May 22, 2009, the day on the Hebrew calendar that marked the anniversary of Israel's 1967 takeover of the eastern part of the city. "Jerusalem was always ours and will always be ours. It will never again be partitioned and divided."

Jerusalem is not divided only by the barrier. The Israelis and the Palestinians have separate business districts, separate schools, and separate transportation systems. Daniel Seidemann, the lawyer who runs Ir Amim, the group that advocates sharing the city, said that dividing Jerusalem is not nearly as complicated as most people think. "You're not being called upon to create a new reality, but to recognize an existing one. You want to know where the border's going to be in Jerusalem? Watch the feet. In the places where Israelis walk today, that will be Israel. In the places where Palestinians walk today, that will be Palestine. That solves 95 percent of the border question in Jerusalem. In the 5 percent where they both walk, it will require one of three things: a special regime, special arrangements, or raw courage. This is not nuclear science. We know what a solution looks like, but we're scared stiff about how to get there."

You could spend a lifetime collecting stories about religious disputes in Jerusalem, but you only need to hear the tale of one family. Sari Nusseibeh, the president of Al Quds University in Jerusalem, is currently the most distinguished member of what has been one of the most prominent families in Jerusalem for well over a millennium. Nusseibeh said that his family history can be traced back to the time the Muslims first took Jerusalem in the seventh century. In his autobiography, *Once upon a Country*, he acknowledges that a few details have gone a bit fuzzy over the years, but the basic story goes like this:

Even before the Christian Crusaders arrived from Europe at the end of the eleventh century, control over the Church of the Holy Sepulchre was a contentious matter for the Muslims who ran the city and the Christians who sought to worship there. In a diplomatic compromise, the Muslim Nusseibeh family received the key to the church's massive front doors, made of solid oak. "And so, over the centuries, my family performed its duties: an ancestor opened up the door, the Christians filed in, at night they left again, and the door was locked until the next morning," Nusseibeh wrote.

The Nusseibeh family was chased out of town after the Crusaders captured Jerusalem in 1099. Shortly after the Crusaders were driven out in 1187, however, the Nusseibehs returned and prospered for several hundred years until the Ottoman Turks took over in 1517. The Nusseibeh family then unwisely participated in a failed guerrilla campaign against the Turks and ultimately "lost its lands and most of its rights," according to Nusseibeh. As part of its punishment, the Nusseibeh family was required to share the foot-long key to the church door with the Joudeh family, a Muslim clan that was on far better terms with the Turks. "And so it was. For the last half millennium, a Joudeh has brought the key to a Nusseibeh at 4:00 a.m., and the Nusseibeh has proceeded forthwith to the church," Nusseibeh wrote.

This arrangement lives, and not merely as tradition. It is still needed to preserve the peace. The six Christian denominations that share the Church of the Holy Sepulchre are so quarrelsome that none would trust the others to hold the key. The Israeli police are called in on occasion to break up fistfights between monks that usually center on who gets to use which space at a certain time.

During our time in Jerusalem, we witnessed only two moments when Jews, Muslims, and Christians came together. The first was in March 2000, when John Paul II became only the second pope in history to visit the Holy Land. John Paul succeeded in the enormously difficult task of winning over all sides. Even before he arrived, he was held in high esteem by Israelis. He had done more than any other pope to mend the tortured history of Catholic-Jewish relations. He won the hearts of Israelis by placing a written prayer between the giant stones that make up the Western Wall. The pope also traveled to Bethlehem and called for Palestinian statehood, instantly becoming a hero to the Muslim population. The blaze of publicity generated by his visit contributed to record levels of tourists, many of them Christian pilgrims. Of all of the world figures who have visited the Holy Land in recent decades, perhaps no one garnered such universal admiration and created such positive vibrations as Pope John Paul II.

The Catholic leadership was also part of the second moment of religious solidarity, which came five years later. Christian, Muslim, and Jewish clerics held a joint news conference at a Jerusalem hotel in March 2005 to denounce a planned international gay pride festival in the city. Gay and lesbian leaders from around the world had proposed a ten-day festival and parade in Jerusalem in August of that year, but five months before the event, the clerics joined forces to stop it. The clerics said that the event would desecrate the Holy City and convey the impression that homosexuality was acceptable.

"They are creating a deep and terrible sorrow that is unbearable," Shlomo Amar, Israel's Sephardic chief rabbi, said at the news conference. "It hurts all of the religions. We are all against it." He was joined by Israel's Ashkenazi chief rabbi; the patriarchs of the Roman Catholic, Greek Orthodox, and Armenian churches; and three senior Muslim prayer leaders, who were equally adamant. "We can't permit anybody to come and make the Holy City dirty," said Abdel Aziz Bukhar, a Sufi Muslim sheik. "This is very ugly and very nasty to have these people come to Jerusalem."

In liberal, secular Tel Aviv, gay pride parades are annual events that do not generate controversy, but it is a very different matter in Jerusalem. "That is something new I've never witnessed before, such an attempt to globalize bigotry," said Hagai El-Ad, the executive director of Jerusalem Open House, a gay and lesbian group that organized the festival. "It's quite sad and ironic that these religious figures are coming together around such a negative message."

Ultimately, the international festival was canceled in Jerusalem. Instead, a small local march was held in downtown Jerusalem, and an Orthodox Jew stabbed and wounded three participants. The following year, 2006, permission for the Jerusalem march was secured only after the Supreme Court turned down several attempts to ban it. There were also parliamentary debates launched by those opposed. The Vatican weighed in, saying the rally would "prove offensive to the great majority of Jews, Muslims, and Christians, given the sacred character of the city of Jerusalem." Ultra-Orthodox youths in Jerusalem's Mea Shearim community rioted for several nights leading up to the event by throwing stones at police and setting garbage on fire in the streets.

Organizers had planned a large march through the city center, but the venue was changed twice as police sought a secure area, well away from the ultra-Orthodox Jewish neighborhoods. The rally was confined to the sports stadium at the Hebrew University, which allowed police to seal off the surrounding area. The police contingent of three thousand was nearly as large as the crowd, and police blocked off streets for a half-mile in all directions. The marchers cheered speeches and danced to music from a stage draped in rainbow banners, but the controversy dampened the festivities. "I'm disappointed because I believe the religious people won this battle, and the people who believe in democracy and human rights lost," said Jonathan Oron, a graduate student at Tel Aviv University.

So, where is Jerusalem headed? The most eloquent description I heard came from Amos Oz, Israel's best-known writer. In the spring of 2007, as the fortieth anniversary of the 1967 war approached, Oz shared the stage at the YMCA in West Jerusalem with Sari Nusseibeh, of the famous Jerusalem Nusseibehs, in a discussion moderated by my *New York Times* colleague Steve Erlanger.

Speaking to Nusseibeh, Oz recounted his complicated and evolving relationship with the city, beginning when he was a passionate Zionist as a boy on the eve of the city's partition in the 1948 war. "What if we met in 1947?" Oz said to Nusseibeh. "I probably would have preached to you and tried to convert you to Zionism. Sari would have listened to me and smiled. It may have been that after the preaching and after the smiles, we would have become friends for a while. For a short while. Because in 1948, the wall came to divide Jerusalem into two prisons. I am aware how my own childhood in Jerusalem was amputated because we had no real contact with the other Jerusalem."

Within a few years, Oz was a restless teenager, and the city symbolized his father's life and all that the young Oz rejected. "When I was a boy of fourteen and a half, rebelling against my father's world, I decided to become everything he was not. At the time, he was right wing, and I decided to become left wing. He was a city dweller, and I decided to become a *kibbutznik*. He was an intellectual, and I decided to become a tractor driver. He was rather short, so I decided to become rather tall."

"I left Jerusalem in a state of rebellion," Oz said. "But Jerusalem never left me. In most of my books, Jerusalem is the setting and the background. In my dreams, I find myself in Jerusalem more often than not. I am strangely attracted to this city, and yet when I come here these days, I feel suffocated. Jerusalem has become a playground for Israeli Jews and Palestinian Arabs who compete for domination of Jerusalem."

Oz said that he despairs when it comes to the politicians and the games they play with the city, but that Jerusalem will outlast them all. "Everyone knows that at the end of the day, Jerusalem is going to be a capital city of both the Israelis and the Palestinians. There will be a Palestinian embassy in Israel and an Israeli embassy in Palestine, and those two embassies will be within walking distance from each other. One will be in West Jerusalem, and the other will be in East Jerusalem. The ambassadors will be able to walk to each other's embassy for coffee."

For Oz, the city is eternal, the conflict is not. "When a politician says 'forever,' I know the stones are laughing, saying, We've heard so many 'nevers' and 'forevers.' Leave the issue of sovereignty over the holy places unresolved. Maybe the Messiah will come and tell us we are all wrong."

22

THE BIG SQUEEZE

I first encountered the Karakis, the largest and most restless Palestinian family I had ever met, quite by accident. The Palestinian uprising was just a month old in the fall of 2000, and I was in the West Bank city of Hebron, about an hour's drive south of Jerusalem. There were always tensions and usually clashes in the winding streets and the narrow alleys of this city, which holds a special place in the hearts of Muslims, Jews, and Christians as the final resting place of the biblical patriarchs, including Abraham.

For decades, the Israeli military maintained a heavy presence in the center of Hebron to provide around-the-clock protection for the roughly 500 Jewish settlers who lived in tiny enclaves amid the city's estimated 150,000 Palestinians. It is an arrangement fraught with problems, and Hebron has perhaps generated more day-to-day friction than any other place in the Israeli-Palestinian conflict.

My guide in the city was the feisty and resourceful Nasser Shiyouki, the AP's Palestinian photographer in Hebron. The fighting in Hebron always seemed to have a nasty edge, and Nasser always seemed to be in the middle of it, clicking away. Over the years, he had been shot with Israeli rubber bullets three times, yet he still preferred to take his pictures while standing in the line of fire.

Nasser was leading me on foot around the corners and down the alleys, part of his endless quest for the perfect shot. We were working our way down one street when suddenly the combatants materialized at either end, leaving us caught in the middle. On one side, Palestinian kids were throwing stones and Molotov cocktails, and on the other were Israeli soldiers cutting loose with tear gas, rubber bullets, and deafening stun grenades.

By Hebron's standards, this was routine daily fare, yet we literally had our backs against a wall. The antagonists were no more than fifty yards apart, and we could not safely move either way on a street where the houses, some of them centuries old, were built right up to the curb. Nasser was thrilled with his good fortune. This was precisely where he wanted to be. He dropped into a baseball catcher's crouch and focused his Canon. He turned left to catch Palestinian kids when the stones flew out of their hands. He turned right to capture the muzzle flash as an Israeli soldier pulled the trigger on a canister of tear gas. Nasser's nonchalance was less than reassuring. Given that he seemed to be a human magnet for Israeli rubber bullets, I felt it prudent for both of our sakes to consider an exit strategy. I turned around and banged on the front door of the large stone house we were up against. A middle-age Palestinian man peeked out cautiously through the small grill in his front door. I did not wait for him to ask. I immediately invited us in.

The scene inside was nearly as unruly as the one in the street. The Karaki clan consisted of six brothers who had grown up in the house. All six had married, brought their wives into the household, and begun a fierce competition to see who could produce the largest number of offspring. At that time, more than seventy Karakis who were spread over four generations belonged to the household, including close to fifty children with atomic levels of pent-up energy. The family compound consisted of two large limestone houses, each three stories. There was an expansive blacktop area between the homes and a stone wall surrounding the entire property. The Karakis were truck drivers in the construction business, and by Palestinian standards, the homes were palatial—but there is no home in the West Bank that can comfortably accommodate fifty children.

The Israeli military had imposed a curfew a month earlier, shortly after the uprising began, and the entire Karaki clan had been confined to this compound for four weeks when we showed up. Every second or third day, the military lifted the curfew for a few hours to allow families in Hebron to head to the store and buy perishables, such as meat, milk, and vegetables. Then soldiers with loudspeakers drove through the streets announcing the reimposition of the curfew, which would last another two or three days. The Karaki adults went out on these brief shopping excursions, but none of the children had set foot beyond the front door for a month. How the Karakis were coping was beyond my comprehension.

The Karakis sat us down in their living room and brought us tea and cookies, paying little attention to the riot carrying on outside their front door. Out back, the Karaki adults were still rounding up the army of Karaki children and channeling them inside, lest they be struck by a stray projectile from the street.

"It's a miserable life," said Talib Karaki, forty-three, one of the six middle-age brothers. "We can't go to work. The kids are very restless. We aren't allowed to do anything but stay inside our big prison." With no other pressing business, the Karakis seemed happy enough to sit and chat with us until the dual uprisings, in the front and the back of the house, subsided. When the street clash ended, the Karaki kids returned to their blacktop playground. Yet it would be another couple of weeks before the curfew was lifted and they were allowed out on the street.

In quiet times, which were rare in Hebron, the Karakis felt blessed to live only a few hundred yards from the massive religious shrine that makes Hebron so important to three major faiths. Tradition holds that the biblical patriarchs were buried in Hebron's caves. Herod built most of the shrine above the caves in the first century BCE. The Jews call it the Tomb of the Patriarchs, and it is the second holiest site in Judaism, after the Temple Mount in Jerusalem. The Muslims call it the Ibrahimi Mosque, in honor of Abraham. The Christians are scarce these days, aside from a few brave pilgrims.

In tense times, which are much more common in Hebron, living near the holy site can be a curse. Back in 1929, during a bout of violence that spread across the region, Hebron's Arabs slaughtered sixty-seven Jews, trashed the synagogues, and forced out a Jewish community that had lived in the town for centuries. After Israel captured the West Bank in 1967, Hebron's religious significance made it the destination of the earliest Jewish settlers. Ever since, the town has attracted some of the most hard-core settlers. In 1994, Dr. Baruch Goldstein, a Brooklyn-born immigrant, shot to death twenty-nine Palestinian worshippers as they prayed at the Ibrahimi Mosque.

The neighborhood surrounding the shrine has always received special attention from the Israeli security forces, and the Palestinians living in this part of the city, known as H2, have faced the toughest restrictions in all of the West Bank. For the Karakis, it has often been a challenge to simply make it more than a few steps out the front door.

After my first chance encounter with the family, my visits to Hebron were never complete without at a visit to their compound. In part, I just wanted to get an updated census. Yet the plight of the Karakis and their neighborhood also seemed to be a gauge for the larger state of the conflict. I tried to imagine Hebron a decade into the future and wondered whether the Israelis would drive many Palestinians out of the center of the city and establish a larger presence of their own. Or would the Palestinians wait out the Israelis and, through a combination of patience and demographics, simply overwhelm the small Israeli settler community?

When I stopped by in 2003, the Karakis told me that the population in their compound was well over ninety, and that the family felt more confined than ever. "When will we be able to move around freely?" asked Abdel Wahab Karaki, who was then in his late fifties and was the eldest of the six brothers. "It's a constant headache with the kids stuck inside and the soldiers right outside. There is no amusement park, no green space to play. I don't think the kids have seen a park in almost three years."

The Karakis acknowledged a powerful dependency on a satellite dish that delivered 347 channels. "If we didn't have this, we would explode," said Abdel Wahab Karaki. The television was usually on Al Jazeera and other Arab news channels. "We have all become expert political analysts, but we are sick of the news."

The Israeli restrictions had also contributed to the population boomlet, the Karakis told me, because there was little to do besides make babies. But the compound was being strained to the limits. "We have reached the point where some people need to live outside," said Abdel Wahab Karaki, a father of ten and a grandfather of fourteen. "If someone wants to marry, we say, 'Look for a house elsewhere.'"

The compound remained shockingly neat, considering all of the kids. The children had few toys and darted around in clusters, entertaining themselves on the pavement between the homes. Small gardening plots just inside the walls produced grapes, figs, and lemons. Ayman Karaki, nineteen, rolled his eyes when I asked whether there was anywhere to go in the evenings. "I spend my life here with my cousins," he said. "I used to have friends in other parts of Hebron, and we played soccer or watched matches. Now I can't do anything like that."

When I stopped in Hebron in the fall of 2006, it was a virtual ghost town. The Israeli settlers and soldiers were still there, but for years, recurring Israeli curfews had kept Palestinian men from working, disrupted the schools, and shut down the main market. By this point, the vast majority of the thirty thousand Palestinians living in the center of the city had relocated to other parts of town or moved out of Hebron altogether.

The Karakis were one of the last families in the otherwise deserted neighborhood, but there was nothing deserted about their compound. The population surge had continued, pushing their numbers past one hundred, although the family could not agree on an exact count. The Karakis wanted to move out of the neighborhood but had no prospects. They were broke, and even if they had money, there were not a lot of rental options for families numbering in the triple digits.

In the latest security news, the Israelis had installed a bullet-proof guard post and an airport-style metal detector about fifty yards down the street. The Karakis had to pass through it every time they wanted to go to the center of Hebron. The city center used to be the focus of their lives, but now there was little reason to go. The schools were closed, the market was shuttered, and their friends were gone. "The whole area is completely dead," said Talib Karaki, the first member of the family I had met, six years earlier.

He told me that his three-year-old grandson, Walid, had recently picked up gravel and started tossing it in the general direction of a soldier who was manning the checkpoint well down the street. The soldier came to complain to Talib Karaki, and a shouting match ensued. "The whole thing was ridiculous," he said. "But it shows how crazy our life has become."

. . .

When I encountered the Karakis back in 2000, Israel's crackdown on the Palestinians was in its initial stage and tended to be informal and unpredictable. The Israeli military had just spent the 1990s pulling back from many Palestinian areas in Gaza and the West Bank, and neither the Israelis nor the Palestinians were quite sure whether the military's return was temporary or more permanent. During this period, the soldiers might make a show of force on the edge of a Palestinian town one day but pull out before nightfall. Israeli troops would appear at a major road junction to establish a checkpoint, but the following day they would be gone without a trace.

The Israeli military presence soon became much more formal. The many tentacles of Israel's military stretched into every dusty town and sun-baked village in the West Bank. To travel the territory as a Palestinian was to navigate an endless maze that often had no exit. Most of the time, it was not possible to go more than a few miles in any direction without encountering soldiers. There were military roadblocks, with rules for passage that often changed by the day. There were massive concrete cubes that suddenly appeared, blocking the road ahead. There were curfews and lockdowns of every description. As tough as the measures were, it still seemed as if they could be revoked with relative ease when the fighting subsided.

The turning point came in the summer of 2002. Prime Minister Ariel Sharon had decided to crush the Palestinian uprising several months earlier with Operation Defensive Shield. Sharon then sought a more permanent means for preventing Palestinian attacks. After overcoming his own reservations, he decided to build the separation barrier, some four hundred miles of concrete walls, chain-link fences, trenches, and watchtowers that zig and zag through the West Bank.

A couple of years earlier, some left-leaning Israeli politicians, including the previous prime minister, Ehud Barak, raised the prospect of a barrier. Yet liberals and moderates were conflicted, holding out the hope that Israelis and Palestinians could live side by side in peace. Conservatives, meanwhile, had their own reasons for opposing the barrier. They viewed it as an acknowledgment that Israel would eventually give up most or all of the West Bank land beyond the barrier, which included dozens of Israeli settlements. Sharon very much sided in principle with the security hawks but reluctantly accepted that the barrier was necessary to prevent attacks.

When I initially saw the barrier going up, it was such a massive undertaking that it seemed unlikely to be built in its entirety. I got my first glimpse on a sun-splashed morning in July 2002, when I drove to the Israeli town of Kfar Saba, northeast of Tel Aviv and on the border with the West Bank. Israelis in the town square were sipping coffee under giant green umbrellas at Starbucks. Barely two miles away, Palestinians in the West Bank town of Qalqilya were under curfew as Israeli soldiers patrolled the silent streets.

Two years earlier, before the Palestinian uprising, these two communities had mixed easily. Even though one town was in Israel and the other in the West Bank, you could drive between them without knowing it. There was not so much as a road sign to acknowledge the transition. Every weekday morning, Palestinian workers came into Kfar Saba for jobs in construction, in restaurants, and in the gardens of Israeli homes. On weekends, Israelis made the quick trip to Qalqilya to do a bit of bargain shopping and have a roasted chicken for lunch at a Palestinian cafe.

Those days were gone. Qalqilya became the launching pad for many Palestinian suicide bombings, and Kfar Saba was a frequent target. A Palestinian bomber needed less than five minutes by car to travel from Qalqilya to Kfar Saba, and even if the Israeli security forces were blocking the road, the bomber could simply walk across a farm field with little chance of being detected.

The Israeli answer was the barrier. On the day I visited, a construction crane groaned as it hoisted another giant slab of concrete into place, part of the twenty-five-foot-high wall that was rapidly formalizing the separation. "Before all the trouble, we didn't need a fence," said Ziva Schmidt, a Kfar Saba resident. "I thought there could be a peaceful solution. I used to go shopping in Palestinian areas, and I felt safe." The concrete wall was less than a mile long at Kfar Saba, and the construction was slow going. But once the Israelis began building, they never stopped.

23

THE FENCE IN JOHNNY ATIK'S BACKYARD

As the separation barrier started to rise in the summer of 2002, Johnny Atik, a prosperous Palestinian landowner in Bethlehem, awoke one morning to the shock of his life: Israeli army bulldozers were carving a wide path right through the middle of the olive grove in his sprawling backyard.

"We were never notified. They just started," said Atik, who did not look like the kind of man you would expect to be embroiled in a conflict with the Israeli military. A balding, mild-mannered fellow in his late fifties who wore thick glasses, Atik belonged to a Christian family that has lived for generations on sixteen acres of prime land at the northernmost edge of Bethlehem, where it abuts the southern side of Jerusalem.

The Atik family thrived by selling the olives, figs, almonds, grapes, peaches, and pomegranates that all grew in its orchards overlooking the valley that separates Jerusalem from Bethlehem. Anyone who has traveled the main road in and out of these two cities has probably gazed out on the Atik family's land, which includes a two-story stone home and several old, rusting tractors scattered around the rambling orchards.

When Atik was a boy, Jordanian soldiers were stationed on the next hilltop to the north, a few hundred yards away. There, they faced off against Israeli soldiers, separated only by a fence that marked the armistice line set down after the first Israeli-Arab war in 1948. For nearly two decades, this served as the boundary not only between Jerusalem and Bethlehem, but also separating Israel and the West Bank. The 1967 Arab-Israeli war changed all of that, as Israel drove the Jordanian army out of the West Bank in less than a week. In the aftermath, Israel hastily redrew the borders of Jerusalem, tripling the size of the city, and eventually declared all of it sovereign Israeli territory, a move that has never been recognized by the international community.

The 1967 war has defined the Israeli-Palestinian conflict to this day. Yet for decades, it had little practical impact on the daily routines of the Atik family. They kept tending their orchards and visited Jerusalem whenever they wanted, which was often. For thirty-five years, Atik simply assumed that Israel's unmarked boundary for Jerusalem began somewhere around the spot where his land ended. "I didn't know where they drew the border," Atik said. "I just got on my tractor and drove where I pleased."

When the Israeli bulldozers arrived in 2002, however, Atik discovered that he had been quite mistaken all of those years. It turned out that Israel's mapmakers had drawn Jerusalem's southern boundary directly through the middle of his property in 1967 without informing Atik, and Israel chose to follow this line in building its separation barrier.

The Israeli fence through Atik's property took two years to build, and it completely separated him from eight acres of mature olive trees, or roughly half of his land. The barrier consists of three parallel chain-link fences and a dirt patrol road on the Israeli side. Altogether, the barrier is about a hundred feet wide, and, worst of all, Atik cannot go to the other side. "How can you achieve peace at the same time you are confiscating the land?" Atik asked when I visited him.

One of the guiding principles for the barrier was to keep as many Jewish settlers on the Israeli side as possible. More than two hundred thousand of these settlers are protected by it, while an estimated seventy to eighty thousand Jewish settlers live beyond the barrier, deep inside the West Bank. The barrier's route keeps about 10 percent of the West Bank land on the Israeli side, although that figure greatly understates its impact. The West Bank land protected by the barrier includes some of the most desirable parts of the territory, particularly around Jerusalem. In addition, many Palestinian cities and towns rub up against the barrier, and this has greatly disrupted life in these areas.

Israel has claimed that the barrier's sole mission is to prevent Palestinian attacks, and that it was not intended to be a permanent political boundary. Of course, the Palestinians do not accept this. In their eyes, the route was chosen to keep the best parts of the West Bank in Israeli hands. The Palestinians have consistently said that Israel was free to build whatever it wanted on its internationally recognized boundaries, a reference to the so-called Green Line that separates Israel from the West Bank.

Yet most of the barrier is inside the West Bank, taking land that the Palestinians are demanding for a state and confiscating property that private Palestinian families have owned for generations. The fence running through Atik's backyard was a leading example of how the barrier's route has upended the lives of Palestinians.

From an Israeli security perspective, the fence did not need to cut through Atik's backyard. The Israeli government and the military often said that the entire route was carefully planned and revised many times to minimize the burdens on Palestinians. Yet in Atik's case, the fence could easily have been built a hundred yards to the north, leaving his property untouched without increasing the risk to Israel. There are no Israeli buildings within a half-mile of Atik's property, which has never been used to launch an attack.

The only way to understand the fence's route through Atik's land is to know that Israeli mapmakers drew the boundary in haste in 1967, and the bulldozers simply traced over that line when they were summoned in 2002, at the height of the Palestinian uprising. "I told the Israelis that if you want to build a fence for security, go and build it on the border of 1967, not on my land," said Atik.

Atik's grandfather acquired the land under the Ottoman Turks, who ruled Palestine for four centuries, until the aftermath of World War I. The Atik family held the land during the British Mandate, from 1922 to 1948, and under Jordanian rule from 1948 to 1967. "The land documents from the Ottomans were in my grandfather's name. In the British time, they were transferred to my father's name, and in the Jordanian period, the land was put in my name," said Atik. "I even have Israeli documents."

He waged a legal battle for several years to regain the right to visit his orchards. In 2006, the Israeli military granted him permission to go as often as he wanted for a period of three months, Atik said. Because there was no way through the fence, he took his permit and several friends on a circuitous route, leaving Bethlehem through the main Israeli checkpoint and coming around to his land from the Israeli side. "Four or five minutes after we entered the land, the soldiers aimed their rifles at us and asked, 'What are you doing here?'" Atik said. "I told them I had an official permit. But the commander told me, 'This is a military area. You are not allowed to be here. Go home.'" Atik complained that he was home. This was his backyard. Yet he was forced to leave and did not return. "Anybody from Jerusalem can enter my land from the other side and pick my olives. But I can't go there."

In building the barrier, Israel faced a problem. There was no way to construct it with clean, straight lines because the 120 West Bank settlements were scattered throughout the territory. Over the years, settlement sites were selected for many reasons, but geographical continuity was not one of them. The army carefully picked hilltops for their military value. Some settlements were constructed because they were within easy commuting distance of major Israeli cities such as Tel Aviv or Jerusalem. In other instances, settlers claimed sites that had religious or historic significance to Jews. Sometimes, settlers simply seized a convenient hilltop and started building.

When you look at the settlements on a map, it seems as if they were sprinkled throughout the West Bank almost at random. Some Palestinians said that was exactly the point. Israeli settlement builders did not want them clustered together in neat, tidy blocks. Instead, they were built in every far-flung corner of the territory. The settlers needed to be protected, and the patchwork of settlements created a reason for the Israeli military to be present everywhere in the West Bank. As long as all of the settlements remain in place, it will be difficult, if not impossible, to establish a contiguous Palestinian state.

In some instances, new Israeli settlements were wedged between two existing Palestinian villages. This greatly annoyed the Palestinians and also meant that the Palestinian villages had little or no room to expand as their populations grew. This created major hardships when the barrier went up. In several places, Israel looped a fence around these Israeli settlements, making it extremely difficult for Palestinians to go about their everyday lives. The barrier cut off many Palestinians from their farmland. Others were not able to travel easily to the towns and the cities where they have worked, shopped, and studied for generations.

In addition, tens of thousands of Palestinians were trapped in a no-man's-land, living just to the east of Israel's 1967 border but to the west of the barrier. They could not move freely in either direction. Going to Israel, where many had once worked, became virtually impossible because Israel has barred entry to most Palestinians in recent years. Travel to other parts of the West Bank was often restricted. Israel has built gates to allow the Palestinians in and out, but the hours and the routes were not always convenient.

Israel called the barrier a "security fence" built to keep Palestinian bombers out. Ariel Sharon even invoked poet Robert Frost's reassuring notion that "good fences make good neighbors." The Palestinians called it the "apartheid separation wall," a phrase that managed to simultaneously evoke racist South Africa and the famous barrier that sliced Berlin in half for decades. Although many of these language disputes were a matter of perspective, the disagreement on the barrier seemed to be a question of observation: is it a fence or a wall? Actually, it is both.

More than 90 percent of the barrier is a chain-link fence that includes electronic sensors to detect attempted breaches. There are trenches, military patrol roads, and coiled razor wire running parallel to the fence in many places. Guard towers and cameras are spaced along the route. "The word 'fence' unites Israelis who just want security," said Ruvik Rosenthal, who wrote a language column for the Israeli newspaper *Maariv*. "If you call it a wall, it just sounds ugly."

Yet in places where Israelis and Palestinians live side by side, there tends to be a high wall of gray concrete, and it is indeed a blight on the landscape. The wall is particularly monstrous where it divides Jerusalem and Bethlehem. Before the barrier was built, Palestinians considered Jerusalem and the West Bank towns of Bethlehem and Ramallah to be a single metropolitan area. It was common for a Palestinian to live in one of the cities and work in another. The wall, however, cut off the two West Bank cities from Jerusalem.

Bethlehem's local economy has always been hugely dependent on tourism, and it used to be easy for visitors to Jerusalem to make the trip. In the late 1990s, dozens of buses streamed into Bethlehem daily and delivered tourists to the Church of the Nativity, which had been built in the fourth century CE to mark the grotto where, according to tradition, Mary gave birth to Jesus. The tourists would often stay for lunch and buy nativity scenes carved from olive wood in the countless tourist shops.

Tourism was at record levels in 2000 when the Palestinian uprising delivered the first body blow to the industry. Not only were the tourists scared away, but the town's educated, middle-class Christian population began to emigrate. Bethlehem was about 90 percent Christian at the time of the 1948 Israeli-Arab war. In the decades that followed, the town's Muslim population grew much more rapidly than the Christian community did, but the town was still 50 percent Christian when the 2000 uprising began. Within five years, Bethlehem was barely one-third Christian. The Christian emigrants tended to be quite successful and rarely looked back after reaching Europe, the United States, or Latin America. In one striking example, the two top candidates in El Salvador's 2004 presidential election, Tony Saca, the winner, and Schafik Handal, the runner-up, were both descended from Catholic families in Bethlehem.

Christians have left Bethlehem for multiple reasons, including increased friction with what is now the Muslim majority. Yet for some of Bethlehem's Christians, the Israeli wall was the final straw, removing any hope of a solution in the near future. "Christians all over the world need to know this reality," said Hanna Nasser, a Christian who was the mayor of Bethlehem when I visited for the subdued Christmas celebrations in 2004. "If there is not a break-through in the peace process, this trend will continue. Imagine the town of Bethlehem without Christians."

To go from Jerusalem to Bethlehem required driving up to the wall, where Israelis security officials checked your documents. Once approval was granted, a giant garage-style door opened, allowing vehicles in and out. Traffic was sparse. Foreign journalists, aid workers, and tourists used the hole in the wall to go back and forth, but most Palestinians were prohibited. Many kids in Bethlehem had never been to Jerusalem and its holy sites, although they were only a few miles away.

On the Jerusalem side of the wall, the Israelis painted a sign that read, "Jerusalem-Bethlehem, Love and Peace." There were colorful, flowery scenes depicting two neighborly cities. The Palestinian side of the wall was covered with spray-painted graffiti, and the unifying theme was a deeply unflattering portrait of Israelis.

The Palestinians have challenged the barrier in court. The International Court of Justice at The Hague sided with the Palestinians in 2004, although the ruling was advisory, not binding. The court said that all portions of the barrier built in the West Bank, past Israel's 1967 borders, were illegal and should be torn down. The court said that Israel had "the right, and indeed the duty, to respond in order to protect the life of its citizens." But the judges said that the barrier had effectively annexed Palestinian land. Fourteen of the fifteen justices endorsed the ruling, with an American jurist the lone dissenter. The majority found that the barrier "cannot be justified by military exigencies or by the requirements of national security."

Greg Khalil, a thirty-year-old American lawyer of Palestinian descent, was part of the Palestinian team that argued the case at The Hague. The ruling did not come until weeks after the court proceedings, and Khalil received word while walking on the street in Ramallah. "I was very excited and started talking about what a big impact this could have," Khalil recalled. "A couple of guys overheard me and asked me about the decision. I started to tell them that we won, and one of them said, 'When are you going to wake up and realize the language of the law doesn't apply to us? We are weak. The only time people see us is when we make noise.'"

"I realized I didn't really have an answer to that," said Khalil, who was suddenly deflated. The Israeli government rejected the court's jurisdiction, and the building continued.

24

AMERICANS IN THE HOLY LAND

The tarmac at Ben-Gurion International Airport near Tel Aviv was so sizzling, it seemed to be melting. I could feel the heat through the soles of my shoes and with every breath I drew. This July morning in 2004 was no day to be outside. Yet Prime Minister Ariel Sharon was on hand, in a navy blue suit and a tie, along with members of his cabinet. The pomp and circumstance and security all suggested a state visit. Yet no kings or presidents were landing on this day. Sharon had ventured to the airport to greet four hundred North American Jews who were immigrating to Israel.

An El Al jumbo jet brought the new arrivals directly from John F. Kennedy Airport in New York, and not a one fit the immigrant stereotype of a poor, desperate soul seeking a better life in a far-away land. These were educated, middle-class professionals from the United States and Canada.

Their mass migration had no real parallel. There was no other country, not even a peaceful, prosperous one, that could persuade a jet full of Americans to relinquish their comfortable existence at home and immigrate en masse. These immigrants were coming to, not fleeing from, a state in the throes of a violent uprising. In relocating, they would encounter many challenges. Their standard of living and their career opportunities would drop a notch, at least for the first few years. Most of them did not speak much Hebrew. Some were headed directly to Jewish settlements in the West Bank on the front lines of the conflict, and at least a few of the younger ones faced the prospect of mandatory military service. The traditional motives for immigrating simply did not apply.

The new immigrants were jet-lagged and giddy after an eleven-hour overnight flight. They were ushered directly from the steaming tarmac to a stifling hangar, where the prime minister welcomed them and urged them to bring their Jewish friends. "We have to bring hundreds of thousands of Jews from America to Israel," said Sharon, his face bright red from the heat. "We need them here. It is important for you. It is important for us."

Sharon's ambitions were inflated. North American Jews have not and will not come in the numbers he hoped. They have been migrating to Israel at a steady rate of three thousand to five thousand annually for more than a quarter century, according to Israeli government figures. Still, the mass migration speaks to the extraordinary bonds between American Jews and Israel and to the larger relationship between the United States and Israel.

The planeload that arrived on that summer's day in 2004 was sponsored by Nefesh B'Nefesh, or Soul-to-Soul, a private group that seeks to increase migration to Israel from the United States and elsewhere. It is just one of many groups that work tirelessly to further develop the bonds between American Jews and Israel.

Dr. Jonathan Paley, an orthodontist from Cedarhurst, New York, on Long Island, landed with his wife, Sarah, and their five children, ages eleven years to four months. Dr. Paley, thirty-three, planned to quickly settle the family in Jerusalem and then commute to New York for two weeks each month to keep working at his old practice until he established himself in Israel. "It's not easy, but this is something very important to all of us," Dr. Paley said. "I first came to Israel when I was eleven, and I've been dreaming about this ever since."

Israel rolls out the welcome mat for most Americans. Any American can land at the airport in Israel and get a three-month tourist visa.

Any Jew from America or any other country can get citizenship in Israel. Yet the advantages of being American can evaporate rapidly for Americans of Arab descent or those who express strong sympathies for the Palestinians.

Sam Bahour, an American of Palestinian descent, would seem to be the kind of neighbor the Israelis would welcome. Bahour, who was in his midforties, grew up in Youngstown, Ohio, where his father ran a supermarket. The Oslo Accords in 1993 inspired him to move to Ramallah in the West Bank, with the dream of helping build a Palestinian state.

He and his new bride, a Palestinian woman, soon had two daughters. The energetic Bahour earned a master's degree in business from Tel Aviv University through a joint program with Northwestern University. He set up a business consulting firm and helped bring the first private telecommunications company to the Palestinian territories. Then he established a $10 million shopping center, anchored by a gleaming, U.S.-style supermarket.

Bahour is a friendly, persuasive, and persistent man. Yet for all that he was able to accomplish, there was one crucial thing he could not easily get: a Palestinian identity card that would allow him to live permanently in the West Bank. Israel technically relinquished control of Ramallah and other West Bank cities in the 1990s, but Israel still controlled the Palestinian population registry and therefore decided who could and could not live in the occupied Palestinian areas. Bahour was not seeking permission to live or work in Israel— he simply wanted to be with his family in the West Bank. Yet Israeli bureaucrats controlled his fate. Every time he left the West Bank, he risked being denied reentry when he returned.

He managed to live in the West Bank by repeatedly renewing his three-month tourist visa from 1993 to 2006, but Israel then said that it would stop granting renewals, because Bahour and others like him were clearly not tourists. Bahour faced a tough predicament. "If I leave, I may not be able to come back here, which is where my life is," Bahour said in 2006 after the Israelis announced the policy. "If I stay, I will be here illegally."

The Israelis effectively froze immigration to the Palestinian areas after the Palestinian uprising began in 2000. In the years that followed, tens of thousands of people, the vast majority of them of Palestinian descent, applied without success to immigrate to the West Bank or Gaza to join relatives.

Israel argued that it was under no obligation to help the Palestinians at a time when Palestinians were trying to kill Israelis. The Palestinians, meanwhile, saw it as another example of Israel's "collective punishment," whereby Israel imposed punitive measures that affected many or all Palestinians, regardless of their guilt or innocence.

Bahour acknowledged that he was fortunate enough to have a range of options. His daughters were also American citizens, and his wife had a Green Card that allowed her to live and work in the United States. He and his wife owned a second home in Youngstown, and his profession as a business consultant was portable. Yet the family was committed to building a life in the West Bank. "People ask why I don't just leave," Bahour said. "I tell them it's because I want to make a contribution here." Bahour was in frequent contact with Israeli officials, but they repeatedly refused to give him a formal answer to his original application, made in 1994.

"You know what happens, Shlomo comes from Brooklyn and Sam comes from Youngstown. Shlomo is allowed to enter with no questions asked. Not only is he offered Israeli citizenship, he can get in a taxi at the airport and go to the illegal settlement next to my house in the West Bank," Bahour said. "When I come, I am interrogated. I run the risk of being denied entry. I am only allowed to be here as a tourist for a short period of time. We want the Israelis to set a clear policy in line with international law so we can plan. How are we supposed to build a state while we cannot plan to be here physically, how can we build an economy, a university, a business?"

In May 2009, some fifteen years after Bahour applied for a Palestinian ID, he finally received approval from Israel. Bahour was thrilled that he could now be a legitimate, full-time resident in the West Bank and would no longer have to worry about being kicked out and separated from his family. Yet when Israel decided to recognize Bahour as a Palestinian, it effectively stopped recognizing him as an American, although Bahour retained his U.S. citizenship. This had a dramatic impact on his life.

"Now, instead of being worried about entering the West Bank, I'm totally confined to the West Bank," Bahour said. When he was an American on a tourist visa, he was free to travel in Israel. That disappeared the instant he officially became a Palestinian.

"I no longer have access to Jerusalem. I no longer can visit Tel Aviv University, where I graduated. I can no longer take my girls to the sea," he said. "I learned overnight what it means to be classified as a full Palestinian. It is a suffocating feeling of living in a large prison with little hope of release."

25

FOLLOW THE MONEY

To understand Israel's evolution from a poor, socialist, agri-cultural state surrounded entirely by hostile neighbors to a free-market, middle-class, high-tech economy surrounded by mostly hostile neighbors, a good place to start is Stef Wertheimer's kitchen porch, circa 1952.

Wertheimer's family fled Nazi Germany and landed in British-ruled Palestine in 1936, when he was only ten years old. Wertheimer was smart and ambitious but had little use for formal education. He dropped out of school at age fourteen to start working. As a young man, he was caught up in the passions of the times. When World War II broke out, he first joined the British military to fight the Nazis and then enlisted in the Palmach, a Jewish militia trained by the British in Palestine. After World War II, he helped make weap-ons for the Haganah, the largest Jewish militia prior to statehood, and after Israel's independence in 1948, he served in the company that made arms for the newly established Israel Defense Force.

In his midtwenties, Wertheimer began to look for a new outlet for his natural manufacturing talents. The young Jewish state was imbued with socialist ideals that glorified communal efforts and was indifferent to, if not a touch disdainful of, individual pursuits such as running a private business. Yet Wertheimer was undeterred and launched a tool-making shop on the porch of his modest home in the quiet town of Nahariya, on the Mediterranean coast in northern Israel, just a few miles south of the border with Lebanon.

Wertheimer tended to his business in this remote outpost, fabricating metal-cutting tools used by companies that made everything from cars to kitchen appliances. Year by year, the reputation of Wertheimer and his firm, the Iscar Metalworking Company, steadily grew. As his business expanded across Israel and into international markets, his firm seemed to outgrow the small community that served as his base. Yet he coveted his independence and kept his operation in northern Israel, where it continued to prosper as a private concern. He repeatedly spurned offers to take the company public on the Tel Aviv Stock Exchange. He intentionally kept his distance from Tel Aviv, the business center, and was also wary of a government that played a leading role in the economy but generally managed it poorly.

Despite his efforts, Wertheimer could not insulate himself entirely from the region's political and economic turmoil. Yet out of these upheavals, Wertheimer, along with other Israeli businessmen, learned valuable lessons. First, crises were a fact of life in Israel. Second, these crises often created unforeseen opportunities.

Wertheimer had learned his manufacturing skills in Israel's first major war, at independence. He then found another grand opportunity in the wake of the 1967 war. Israel effectively won the war on the morning of June 5, the first day of battle, when the Israeli air force's French-made Dassault Mirage III fighter planes carried out a surprise attack and decimated both the Egyptian and the Syrian air forces while their planes were still on the tarmac. This gave Israel undisputed control of the skies and paved the way for the ground attack that followed.

Yet the stunning victory produced fallout. France imposed a military boycott after the war, and Israel's air force suddenly found itself cut off from the spare parts supplier for its Mirage fighters and in desperate need of an alternative. Wertheimer's company had never crafted airplane parts but agreed to try. It turned out that the company made them very well. So well, in fact, that it also began to produce parts for commercial aircraft. From this business born of necessity, the Wertheimer family built a new company, Blades Technology. Today, in partnership with Pratt & Whitney, Blades Technology is one of the world's leading manufacturers of fan blades for jet airplane engines. In other words, every time you get on a commercial flight, there is a decent chance you are on a plane with fan blades supplied by Wertheimer's firm.

In 1983, Wertheimer's businesses were thriving, when another trauma intervened, this one personal. Wertheimer was in a serious car accident and suffered a severe concussion. He eventually recovered but decided to turn the family business over to his son Eitan, who expanded on his father's success.

Eitan Wertheimer is a modest, unassuming man who is unfailingly polite and friendly. He has maintained a low profile by choice, and on the rare occasions when he seeks attention, it is usually related to his philanthropic efforts. We met Eitan Wertheimer occasionally at social events, although he rarely volunteered much about himself or his work and was clearly more comfortable when the spotlight was on someone else.

In the spring of 2006, however, more than a half-century after the family business was founded on the kitchen porch, Eitan Wertheimer became front-page news in Israel. American billionaire investor Warren Buffett paid $4 billion to buy 80 percent of the Wertheimers' metalworking company Iscar. The deal was Buffett's first major acquisition outside of the United States. Wertheimer initiated contact with a letter to Buffett, who was so impressed when he examined Iscar that he plunked down his money after only a few meetings with Wertheimer in the United States. Buffett did not even bother to visit Iscar's hilltop headquarters in the thinly populated Galilee region until months after the deal was finalized. The Wertheimer family maintained ownership of the remaining 20 percent of the company, valued at $1 billion, and Eitan Wertheimer continued to run it much as he did before Buffett's purchase.

The Wertheimer family appears annually on the Forbes list of the world's billionaires, and the Wertheimers' success is perhaps the leading example of how Israelis have transformed their economy, despite relentless turbulence. In many ways, the conflict has forced the Israelis to find new and creative solutions to their economic challenges.

Consider Israel's high-tech industry, which, beginning in the 1990s, modernized and reshaped an economy larded with many inefficient, state-run companies. The high-tech sector is centered in Herzliya, a suburb to the north of Tel Aviv, and is known as Silicon Wadi—*wadi* being the Arabic term for a "valley" or a "dry riverbed."

The industry has established a reputation for producing nimble and innovative start-ups that often have ties to the United States.

Israelis point to several factors in the industry's success. The mandatory military service that is required of Israeli men and women after high school provides many with intensive training in computers, aircraft, and high-tech military equipment that later leads to civilian careers. The conflicts with the Arab neighbors have also driven homegrown military technologies that have been converted into successful international companies. One example is Elbit Systems, which makes night-vision equipment that is sold around the globe.

And in a country made up of immigrants, Israelis are comfortable working with the rest of the world, and in particular, the United States. More than seventy Israeli companies are listed on NASDAQ, a figure no other country outside the United States can match. Israel has also lured top U.S. high-tech firms to set up shop in Israel. The country's leading private employer is Intel, which has some six thousand employees in Israel. Many of them work in the southern desert town of Kiryat Gat, just a few miles from the Gaza border. A new plant there, known as Fab 28, is one of the most advanced computer chip–making facilities in the world.

News from the Middle East inevitably focuses on violence and political turmoil and often gives the impression that both the Israelis and the Palestinians are neck deep in economic problems. Yet Israel's economy is significantly larger, more robust, and more sophisticated than it was when the Palestinian uprising began a decade ago. Israelis have jobs, they own homes, and they look to the future with the expectation that their standard of living will improve, even as the conflict with the Palestinians grinds on.

In contrast, the defining feature of the Palestinian economy was the free fall that started the day the uprising began. The two economies were both expanding and becoming ever more integrated back in 2000. They quickly decoupled. Binding the economies together will make the conflict easier to resolve, while the economic divisions that have developed over the past decade make it that much harder to solve.

To be fair, it is not an apples-to-apples comparison when looking at the two economies. As an independent country, Israel controls its economic destiny. It has an educated population and a web of trading relations with all of the most prosperous places

on the globe—the United States, Europe, and Asia. The Palestinians lack economic sovereignty in the same way they lack political
sovereignty. Israel controls the West Bank border with Jordan and
effectively controls Gaza's border with Egypt. Israel has closed the
Palestinian airport in Gaza and has not allowed the Palestinians to
build a seaport. This means the Palestinians have to work with and
work through Israel, rather than making their own decisions. With
a few simple security measures, Israel can choke off the Palestinian
economy whenever it chooses.

In the past few years, Israel has eased some restrictions in the
West Bank. This, combined with the leadership provided by Palestinian Authority prime minister Salam Fayyad, has led to a limited
economic revival in that territory. In Gaza, Israel still keeps tight
control on the flow of goods in and out of the coastal strip, and the
economy limps along just a notch or two above subsistence levels.

To show how dramatically the Israeli and Palestinian economies
have diverged, consider just one year: 2006. Both the Israelis and
the Palestinians faced political upheavals with potential economic
consequences. In January, Prime Minister Ariel Sharon suffered the
stroke that put him in a coma and threw Israeli politics into turmoil.
The Palestinians were working their way through their own political
transition following the death of Yasser Arafat in November 2004.
In January 2006, Palestinian voters elected Hamas, tossing out
Fatah, the party of Arafat that had dominated Palestinian politics
for decades.

As both sides struggled to come to grips with the changes in leadership, their economies charted very different courses. The Israelis
were experiencing their third straight year of strong growth. The
Palestinians were undergoing new levels of economic hardship and
financial misery on an almost daily basis.

In the spring of 2006, the U.S. Treasury took the simple step
of publicizing the fact that it was a crime under U.S. law to provide funds to a terrorist group, a not-so-subtle reference to Hamas.
Throughout the world, even small local banks tend to have a U.S.
banking partner to help facilitate dollar transactions. When the
Treasury Department issued its notice, banks in the Middle East
abruptly stopped handling even basic wire transfers from Arab

countries to the Palestinian areas. The banks feared they would run afoul of the U.S. authorities and lose their U.S. partners. "No bank wants to risk being cut off from international transactions," said George Abed, the governor of the Palestinian Monetary Authority, which effectively served as the Palestinian central bank. "This is oxygen for banks. If you are a bank, and you shut yourself out of the United States and Europe, what are you going to do—conduct all of your transactions in rupees?"

Many Arab and Muslim states wanted to send assistance to the Palestinian Authority but could not find a bank willing to carry out the transfer. The Hamas-led government needed about $150 million a month to run the Palestinian Authority, but its revenue stream was heavily dependent on foreign donations and on taxes collected on its behalf by Israel. Those monies largely stopped flowing when Hamas came to power. "The problem is not with raising money," said Ismail Haniya, the Hamas leader who served as the Palestinian prime minister at the time. "The problem is how to transfer this money to the Palestinians."

Hamas officials soon undertook desperate measures. The lone exit available to Palestinians in Gaza, including the Hamas leadership, was the Rafah border crossing with Egypt. The Hamas leaders used the opening to visit sympathetic countries, such as Syria and Iran, and pursued an economic recovery plan based on stuffing as much donated cash as possible into their pockets and suitcases.

Hamas spokesman Sami Abu Zuhri was returning from a regional tour in May 2006 when he was stopped and checked at the Rafah Crossing. The European Union inspectors who assisted the Palestinians at the crossing found more than 600,000 euros (roughly $800,000) tucked in Abu Zuhri's money belt. Abu Zuhri was allowed to enter Gaza with the cash because he was not breaking any rules as long as he declared the money. It soon became clear that this cash-and-carry operation was the main mode of public finance for the Palestinian Authority.

In December 2006, Haniya, the prime minister, took the same approach on a much more ambitious scale. By this time, however, Israel was reasserting its authority over the border and intervened to prevent Haniya from entering the territory he supposedly governed. The Israeli government said that he was carrying tens of millions of dollars in cash. The Israeli media put the figure at $35 million and said it was stuffed in suitcases. It was not clear who gave Haniya the money, although his regional travels included a stop in Iran, which had pledged a quarter-billion dollars in assistance.

Israel did not have troops on the Gaza-Egypt border, but it did have army bases nearby in southern Israel, just a few miles away. Israel apparently passed on intelligence to Egypt and asked the Egyptians to close down its side of the border, which it did. During Haniya's lengthy wait on the Egyptian side, dozens of angry gunmen from his Hamas movement shot up the border crossing, clashing first with Palestinian security forces on the Gaza side of the border and later with Egyptian security officials on the Egyptian side. At least fifteen Palestinians were hurt. After hours of negotiations, Haniya was allowed back into Gaza, while his aides took the money to El Arish, Egypt, for safekeeping, according to Hamas officials. As Haniya reached the Gaza side—without his suitcases— another round of shooting broke out, this time between rival Palestinian factions. One of Haniya's sons was injured, and one of his bodyguards was killed. If the money Haniya raised ever reached Gaza, it was not enough to make a difference.

As Palestinian conditions worsened by the day, the Israeli economy just kept getting brighter in 2006. The front pages of Israeli newspapers were filled with political turmoil, but the business pages were a sunny and happy place. The stock market was hitting record highs. Unemployment was at a ten-year low. The shekel continued to strengthen against the dollar. Foreign investment was reaching levels never seen before. Tourists once again clogged the streets of Jerusalem's Old City. This cheery economic news was capped by Warren Buffett's purchase of the Wertheimers' firm.

We traveled to see Eitan Wertheimer at his hilltop headquarters in northern Israel's Tefen Industrial Park shortly after the announcement. Eitan Werheimer had just moved into a new office, and packing boxes were still scattered around the floor.

His new digs featured a large glass window and a deck that offered a commanding view of the rolling hills that marked Israel's border with Lebanon.

Like his father, Eitan Wertheimer had little use for formal education. He bested his father by making it through high school but never attended college, aside from a few management courses at

Harvard Business School in the 1980s. In his understated way, he said that his "main job is not to disturb anybody." He was happy to chat about his dealings with Buffett, who shared his low-key, hands-off, "aw-shucks" approach to managing multibillion-dollar operations, but what Wertheimer really wanted to do was show off the Tefen Industrial Park.

The Tefen Park is one of several industrial complexes the Wertheimers have built, and each is intended as a sort of "capitalist kibbutz," in the words of Stef Wertheimer. The Wertheimers invite other manufacturers to set up shop at the parks, and they center around factories in a range of industries. Yet they are also large-scale philanthropic ventures that include much more than factories. There are museums and sculpture gardens and occasional concerts, as well as classrooms where businesses hold training sessions. The Tefen Industrial Park in northern Israel draws about a quarter-million visitors a year. These amenities are intended "to give respectability to industry," Eitan Wertheimer said. "Jewish mothers don't like their kids working in factories. They think they are dirty, they don't smell nice, and they don't pay well. But if we can make them look like a place you want to visit, then maybe industry doesn't look so bad to the Jewish mothers."

Through the industrial parks, the Wertheimers have spread their belief that economic prosperity will lead to Arab-Jewish coexistence. "This area doesn't have much experience in industry, but this is what it needs to get on its feet," Stef Wertheimer said. "The idea is to put people to work, get them off the street, and end the quarreling about land and religion. I think everyone should be working during the day. In the evening, everyone can have their religion."

In the 1970s, Stef Wertheimer thought he might be able to bring this about through politics and got himself elected to the parliament. "I went to the Knesset nearly thirty years ago to try to convince the government we had to develop this region industrially," he said, but he soon grew frustrated with the political process. "I left the Knesset in 1981 and decided to build industrial parks. I have followed through in a systematic way."

His experience was telling. His first industrial park, Tefen, which serves as Iscar's headquarters, has been a huge success. It has attracted many Israeli companies and Arab workers from northern Israel. Iscar was just one of sixty companies that employed some four thousand workers at the park, which resembled a college campus, with manicured lawns and rose gardens. It was one of three such complexes in the Galilee, and there was another in the Negev Desert in southern Israel. All were flourishing and accounted for a large share of Israel's industrial production and exports. In 2005, Wertheimer also opened an industrial park outside Istanbul, Turkey's business capital, which has shown great promise. "I made my money in Iscar," Stef Wertheimer said. "I spend my money on the industrial parks."

One industrial park that never got off the ground, however, was in Gaza. Harvard economists helped the Wertheimers draw up the plans in the 1990s for a park in Rafah, on Gaza's border with Egypt. Stef Wertheimer met Palestinian leader Yasser Arafat and with Israeli leaders. Both governments pledged support, but the Palestinians and Arafat never quite followed through, and the project was shelved after the violence broke out in 2000.

The episode was just one example of the Palestinians' seeming indifference to their own economic development. Given the chance to work with a world-class businessman who had successfully built office parks that nurtured dozens of companies and provided thousands of jobs, the Palestinian leadership let the opportunity slip away. When I spoke by phone to Stef Wertheimer in 2006, he was visiting his industrial park in Turkey. An industrial park in the Palestinian areas could have a much greater impact than one in Turkey, a country that already had a large, dynamic economy. Yet Wertheimer was there because Turkey welcomed his project. "These industrial parks could work for the Palestinians, but perhaps the time is not right," Stef Wertheimer said.

Just two months after we visited the Tefen Industrial Park, Israel and the Lebanese guerrilla group Hezbollah were at war. Hezbollah fired rockets from across the border, and one slammed into the park, shutting it down briefly. Many more rockets crashed nearby. Some of Eitan Wertheimer's workers moved their families farther south, out of Hezbollah rocket range. After relocating their families, however, the workers themselves chose to stay on the job during the thirty-four-day war. While much of northern Israel was evacuated, Iscar maintained its production schedule and did not miss a deadline. "It took us a brief time to adjust, but we didn't miss a single shipment," Eitan Wertheimer told me after the fighting stopped. "For our customers around the world, there was no war."

Israel could have taken a big hit economically, but after so many upheavals over the years, the war was only a hiccup. The northern city of Haifa, home to the country's largest port, came under almost daily rocket attacks, and ships stopped docking. The southern ports of Ashdod and Eilat picked up the slack, and some exporters sent their goods by air at much greater expense in order to meet deadlines. The Tel Aviv Stock Exchange shrugged off the war and was slightly higher at the end of the fighting in August than on the day it started in July.

The war caused one rough economic quarter in an otherwise prosperous year. By the end of 2006, Israel's economy was again in full swing. The economy grew by a strong 4.8 percent for the entire year—down from the 5.5 percent that had been forecast before the war. "Israelis look at the economy, and they've essentially been through these disturbances in the past, and they know the economy is pretty robust and it tends to come back," said Stanley Fischer, the governor of the Bank of Israel. "Things that happen here have a smaller impact on markets than I think they would abroad."

26

MISERY BY THE SEA

For once, the Israelis and the Palestinians agreed.

As Israel was preparing to pull out of Gaza in the summer of 2005, it faced the question of what to do with the roughly sixteen hundred homes belonging to the departing Jewish settlers. It seemed like a no-brainer. Israel could simply leave the houses in place, and the Palestinians could use them as they liked. The settlers lived in clusters of heavily guarded settlements scattered throughout the territory. Most homes were modest, cookie-cutter, single-family stucco structures with red-tile roofs on small plots of land. The Palestinians, in turn, desperately needed all of the housing they could get in a territory where overcrowding was endemic. It seemed like a bit of cosmic justice that Israel would be leaving behind homes similar in number to those that the military had destroyed during the previous few years of fighting. Making the decision even easier, the Israeli military wanted to get out of Gaza as soon as possible. The military was reluctant to keep soldiers in Gaza for several additional weeks to tear down the houses of Jewish settlers and thereby expose the troops to potential attack from Palestinian militants.

Because the Israelis and the Palestinians agreed on so little, any meeting of the minds would seem like cause for celebration. Yet even this rare convergence of agendas only seemed to highlight the perverse logic that often drives the conflict and leads both sides to choose the irrational over the rational. Faced with an obvious solution, the Israelis and the Palestinians agreed . . . that every last Jewish home would be torn down.

The Israelis and the Palestinians both had their reasons for making this choice. As the Jewish settlers prepared to abandon the homes, many said they could not bear the thought of Palestinians moving in and raising their flags in triumph. The Israeli political and military leadership wanted the settlers to cooperate during the withdrawal and were concerned that they would put up widespread resistance. Hoping to win the acquiescence of the settlers, Israeli leaders agreed to accommodate their wishes by tearing down the homes immediately after the settlers left—and before the Palestinians could claim them.

For very different reasons, the Palestinian leadership also wanted the houses gone. The Palestinians did not feel that the homes were appropriate for their needs. While Israeli families in Gaza typically consisted of a couple with three or four children, the Palestinians had extended families that often included three generations and a dozen or more members. The Palestinians also felt that the single-family homes took up too much space, and they wanted to use the land for a variety of purposes, including schools, parks, and factories. And in a territory where the vast majority was impoverished, the Palestinian leadership would face the impossible task of allocating the homes to sixteen hundred lucky families, while many thousands would be disappointed.

As a result, the Israeli settlers were removed, and the Israeli military stayed on in Gaza for several additional weeks to bulldoze every Jewish home in the territory, reducing them to piles of concrete and mangled rebar. The Israeli leadership did not want to be seen tearing down Jewish religious sites, so synagogues and a few public buildings were left standing.

So everyone was happy, right? Well, not exactly. This loss of the dwellings did not sit well with homeless Palestinians such as Ibrahim Abu Shatat. If Gaza is a place where almost everyone has a hard-luck story, Abu Shatat had enough material to write an entire book. Not one, but two of his homes had been destroyed by Israeli troops. He once had a good job in Israel as a welder but lost that in the Palestinian uprising. He was forced to find shelter in the storage room under Rafah's soccer stadium with his wife and eight children.

During the fourteen years that he worked in Israel, Abu Shatat spent the work week there and returned to his family in Gaza on weekends. He saved enough money to build a large, three-story home in Rafah, just fifty yards from the border with Egypt. Yet the Palestinian uprising undid all of his hard work.

Rafah has long been a smuggling town, with underground tunnels running between the Palestinian and Egyptian sides of the border. In times of calm, the contraband was mostly commercial, ranging from cigarettes to prostitutes. The smugglers even drugged young lions and monkeys, placed them in cloth sacks, and transported them from the Egyptian side into Gaza as zoo attractions. "Without the tunnels, I couldn't have done this," Shadi Fayiz, who managed the zoo in Rafah, told the AP.

The tunnels have been a leading source for the import of Palestinian weapons and ammunition since the fighting began in 2000. A tunnel often began inside a home on the Egyptian side of the border and emerged inside a Palestinian home on the Gaza side of the frontier. Abu Shatat's front-line neighborhood became one of the main battlegrounds in the almost daily shoot-outs between Palestinian militants and Israeli troops on the border. Abu Shatat insisted that he was not in the smuggling business and that Palestinian gunmen had never used his home to fire on Israeli soldiers. Why, he said, would he risk his job in Israel, his home, and the safety of his children?

As the fighting increased in Rafah, the Israelis systematically bulldozed homes near the border. In 2001, Israeli bulldozers demolished the home of Abu Shatat's neighbor and, in the process, inflicted collateral damage on Abu Shatat's house, leaving it uninhabitable, he said.

The Abu Shatat family rented another house a few blocks away. As Israel tore down each row of homes, however, Palestinian gunmen would retreat one street and continue firing from the new front line. By 2004, Abu Shatat and his family again found themselves facing Israeli troops. Not long afterward, the bulldozers came calling again and knocked down his home once more as part of a large demolition campaign.

By this time, Abu Shatat was broke, and there was an acute housing shortage in Rafah. The only shelter he could find was the storage room under the Rafah soccer stadium. The family ate, slept, and passed the time sitting on thin mats on a concrete floor. There was enough electricity to allow for a refrigerator and a bit of light cooking. The stadium's toilets served as the family bathroom. They were intended exclusively for men, but Abu Shatat's wife and daughters used them when they were empty. "It hurts us to be here, because nobody respects you when you live like this," Abu Shatat said.

Israel's home-demolition policy, a source of controversy for many years, was particularly far-reaching during the second Palestinian uprising. It consisted of tearing down individual homes belonging to Palestinian militants in the West Bank and the wholesale demolition of neighborhoods in Rafah and other areas. In 2005, Israel said that it was halting the demolition of the homes of Palestinian militants. Major General Udi Shani, who headed a committee that reviewed the issue, said he concluded that the policy had caused Israel more harm than good by generating hatred among the Palestinians. "House demolitions are just one measure of deterrence, and at present, it doesn't play the same role it did previously," another military official told the *Haaretz* newspaper, noting that attacks against Israel had dropped substantially by this time.

In the four years prior to the Israeli announcement, the military had torn down more than twenty-five hundred homes in Gaza and the West Bank, according to B'Tselem, the Israeli human rights group, and other organizations that also tracked the issue. Rafah was by far the hardest hit, with more than fifteen hundred houses flattened in the area. For Abu Shatat and his neighbors in Rafah, the Israeli announcement was filled with bitter irony. The Palestinian homes had been knocked down to create a buffer zone to protect the Israeli troops serving on Gaza's southern border. Now the Israelis were leaving, but their final act was to knock down the perfectly good settler homes, any one of which would have comfortably housed the Abu Shatat family.

The Israeli departure gave Abu Shatat hope that he and his neighbors could finally rebuild, but he still faced many obstacles. The Israelis greatly restricted the import of building materials to Gaza. The Palestinian leadership was unhelpful. Money was scarce.

Yet Abu Shatat was doggedly persistent. He lobbied the Palestinian Authority to build replacement homes. He set up a committee for the homeless in Rafah and made himself a nuisance at government offices in Gaza City, particularly at the Land Authority. "I told them that if they did not give us land, we would start living in their offices," he said.

When I caught up with him in February 2007, he was still living under the soccer stadium, which had been his home for three years, but he had some good news. The Palestinian leadership in Gaza had finally allocated land to accommodate the homeless families in Rafah. It was a barren patch of sandy soil in southern Gaza that used to be a no-man's-land just outside the vacated Jewish settlement of Rafiah Yam.

I asked Abu Shatat whether he would take me there. It was only a couple of miles from his stadium dwelling. As we discussed it, I found out that his wife, Maha, had yet to see it. We all piled into a taxi and drove to the construction site, which consisted of twenty cinder-block homes whose foundations had been set. The plans called for simple detached houses of two or three stories, with one family living on each floor. "I'm so excited," Maha said, as her face lit up. "Now I finally believe it is happening."

Abu Shatat still lacked a job and depended on charity to feed his eight children. The Palestinians were fighting among themselves. Israel was imposing an embargo on the territory and carrying out periodic air strikes. Yet in Gaza, this was as close as I ever got to a happy ending.

Most of our trips to Gaza led to the discovery of new forms of human frustration—like the time I went to one of Gaza's border crossings with Israel at 3 a.m. to witness Gaza's truly bizarre rush hour.

Gazans speak obsessively about a sense of suffocation, and much of it stems from Israel's tight restrictions on the territory's three main crossing points to the wider world. Gaza is so small and so poor that it comes to a grinding halt when people and goods are not flowing in and out. The territory is self-sufficient only when it comes to sand and angry young men, and it is dependent on Israeli imports for almost everything else. Yet Israel sees Gaza as a hopelessly messy problem that it would prefer not to deal with, and the overarching goal is to prevent Gaza's pathologies from seeping out. Since the Palestinian uprising began in 2000, the Israeli military has frequently closed or greatly limited access to the three crucial crossings: Erez in the north, which is used for people going to and from Israel; Karni, to the east, which handles the import and export of goods with Israel; and Rafah to the south, which is for travelers going to and from Egypt.

On a cold night in February 2006, I traveled to the Erez crossing. Until 3 a.m., the crossing was mostly empty and silent, manned by a small number of Israeli security guards on the northern side and by a few sleepy Palestinian counterparts on the southern side. They were separated by a no-man's-land that stretched for a half-mile. To cross it, you had to travel through a tunnel that had concrete blast walls on either side, a corrugated roof above, and an overpowering scent of urine from one end to the other.

When the clock struck three, the silence turned to pandemonium as hundreds of yellow Mercedes taxis descended on the Palestinian side of the crossing and disgorged thousands of bleary-eyed workers who were just beginning a marathon morning commute. From a distance, the men were ghostly, all but invisible in the darkness and the fog that rolls in from the Mediterranean in the winter. Many were visible only by the puffs of vapor that marked their every breath in the chill.

The workers were a scruffy lot, most of them in clothes stained from yesterday's labor. As they reached the Palestinian checkpoint, they smoked cigarettes, sipped coffee, or wolfed down plain bread while waiting in a line that was soon several thousand men long—and not moving. Even on a good day, the men still had several hours before they would clear Israeli security, get a ride on the Israeli side of the boundary, and reach the factories, the construction sites, and the auto repair shops where they toiled in Israel.

It would be heartless to describe anyone in these wretched circumstances as lucky. Yet the middle-of-the-night scene at the Erez crossing was a sterling example of how nasty and brutish life was in Gaza. The cruel truth was that these workers were much better off than the vast majority of Gazans. At this time, they were among the fortunate five thousand Gazan men who still held work permits from Israel, despite the years of violence that led Israel to drastically reduce their numbers. As long and harsh as their days were, these men were able to escape the confines of Gaza and earn about forty dollars a day. This was several times what they would make in Gaza, if they could find work at all in a territory where unemployment was rampant. If a Gaza worker ever tired of the numbing commute and decided he would like to see the sun when he woke up, thousands of unemployed Gaza men were itching to replace him. Many Gazans hate Israel, but few would pass up the chance to work there.

Yousef al-Masri, an auto mechanic and a father of fourteen, said that he rose every working day at 1 a.m. in order to be at Erez an hour later. A good day meant getting to his job in Tel Aviv, about forty miles away, by 8 a.m., although he was often late. He left work at 5 p.m. on a commute home that took a mere two hours, because Israel cared much less about what was going into Gaza than about what was coming out. In the evening, Masri grabbed dinner and saw his family briefly before dozing off, knowing he would never feel refreshed when his alarm went off. "Believe me," he said, "if there were jobs in Gaza, we would stay here and never go to Israel again." The frequent closings at Erez meant that he often did not make it to work at all, and Masri's boss said that he was training an Israeli mechanic with an eye toward replacing Masri.

As the minutes passed with no movement in the line, the mounting sense of frustration was palpable. Around 4 a.m., the seething crowd suddenly surged past the hapless Palestinian guards and raced down the long, grimy tunnel toward the Israeli checkpoint. A metal gate topped with coiled razor blocked the Palestinians as they neared the Israeli end. Several workers grabbed the bars of the gate with both hands and shook it with frustration. Their howls of anger echoed off the tunnel walls. Feeling cheated out of a day's pay, they cursed Israel before the first rays of sunlight.

Many workers gave up and returned home, believing that Israel would keep the crossing closed for the day, as it often did. Around 5 a.m., however, the Israeli security staff decided that their unidentified security concerns had been allayed, and they opened the doors. Some twenty-four hundred workers entered Israel, about half the number that would on a normal day.

A few hours later, the scene at the Karni crossing, the focus of Gaza's imports and exports, was equally miserable. More than a hundred Palestinian trucks, most of them packed with tons of fruits and vegetables, were backed up in a line that stretched nearly a half-mile. Ayman Badwan was the last in line on the Palestinian side. His truck

was loaded with eight tons of cucumbers and sweet peppers. He
had not moved in four hours and was calculating his waiting time
in days. "I have waited as long as a week," Badwan said. "I feel lucky
when I can do this in just one day."

This delay was not merely a headache for the beleaguered truck
drivers; it had a direct impact on every Gazan. The territory gets
every drop of its gasoline from Israel. Gaza imports its dairy products from Israel, so even a closure of a few days means milk supplies
can run short in a place where homes typically have a half-dozen
kids. In addition, Gaza's leading exports—fruits, vegetables, and
flowers—are perishable and rot rapidly in the heat and the dust.
When the Karni crossing shuts down, Gaza shuts down.

In the years before the Palestinian uprising, Palestinian and
Israeli truck drivers drove right through the Karni crossing to make
pickups and deliveries on both sides of the frontier. That system
was an early casualty of the intifada, however. Once the shooting
began, no Israeli drivers dared to venture into Gaza, where their
distinctive yellow-and-black Israeli license plates would have made
them very large targets. And Israel stopped allowing Palestinian
drivers into Israel, fearing that a bomb could be hidden in a crate
of strawberries.

By this time, Palestinian trucks could only travel up to Karni's
thirty-foot-high concrete wall, which has thirty cargo bays and runs
about a quarter-mile along the border with Israel. On the Gaza
side, the Palestinians backed their trucks up to the bays, and the
Israelis did the same on their side of the wall. Under this back-to-
back arrangement, the goods were unloaded from the back of one
truck, rode a conveyor belt to the other side, and then went directly
onto the rear end of another truck. Both sides simply shoved their
goods through the hole in the wall and then let the other side deal
with them. This allowed Israel and Gaza to trade with each other,
while having virtually no face-to-face contact. I once saw cows walk
backward—a bovine version of Michael Jackson's moonwalk—as
they were forced off an Israeli truck and had to reverse themselves
directly onto a waiting Palestinian truck.

On a good day, about three hundred Israeli trucks and fifty
Palestinian trucks sent their loads through the wall. The numbers
were uneven because the Palestinian needs were great, and they
tended to import much more than they exported. Also, the goods
being unloaded from the Palestinian trucks had to go through an

X-ray scanner and were often checked by hand before entering Israel, a process that could sometimes take hours, if not days. This system survived several years of fighting, and it seemed as if the two sides were doomed to cooperate, even when they were busy shooting.

Yet the delivery system had become terribly erratic. Gazans frequently faced shortages of imports, and Gaza's anemic economy depended heavily on the export of its short-lived crops. "I call the Israelis when I arrive every morning, but I never know if they will let us open," said Walid Abu Shouga, who was in charge of Palestinian security. It was 11 a.m., three hours after the terminal was supposed to open, but the Israelis said they had security concerns. As it turned out, the Israelis did have reasons to be jittery. Several hours later, a mysterious explosion rocked an area on the Gaza side of the Karni crossing. No one was hurt, but Israel responded by shutting the crossing for an extended period.

The Karni crossing, like all of the Gaza crossings, came under frequent Palestinian attack. In one instance in 2004, two Palestinian suicide bombers hid inside a container on a Palestinian truck and managed to escape the notice of the Israeli security team as the container was transferred to the Israeli side and placed on an Israeli truck. When the Israeli truck reached the nearby port of Ashdod, the bombers emerged and detonated their explosives, killing ten Israelis.

If Israel locked up Karni and threw away the keys, Gaza would be out of food, fuel, and medicine within weeks, creating a humanitarian disaster. When Karni was open, however, the Israelis working there were targets.

During the Palestinian uprising, the Rafah crossing at the southern end of Gaza, on the border with Egypt, was just as tense, if not more so, as every other place where Palestinians came into contact with the Israeli military. But the Palestinians took control of the Rafah crossing in the fall of 2005, shortly after Israel pulled out of the territory. This had huge symbolic and practical significance. For the first time since Israel had captured Gaza in 1967, Gazans could enter and exit their territory without having to go through Israeli security checks. "I think every Palestinian now has his passport ready in his pocket," President Mahmoud Abbas said at the ceremonial opening. "Let them come to cross this terminal whenever they want." In excess of a thousand Palestinians were soon passing through Rafah daily, and it was a model of efficiency. A steady flow of Palestinian travelers passed in both directions. The atmosphere was relaxed. "This is so much better than any other checkpoint, because it's our checkpoint," said Naal Kishawi, a Gaza businessman returning from Cairo with his teenage son, who had undergone treatment for a hand injury.

As I watched Palestinians come and go freely, I realized what a strange sight this was. For years, Palestinians had not been able to travel more than a few miles in Gaza or the West Bank without running into an Israeli soldier blocking the path and demanding documents. At the Rafah crossing, the Israeli presence had been reduced to wall-mounted video cameras scattered around the terminal. Israel received the video feed at a monitoring center several miles away, outside Gaza's border.

The contrast between Rafah and Gaza's other crossings could not have been greater.

This begged an obvious question: which model would win out? It seemed that either the Rafah crossing example would spread, and life throughout Gaza would become a bit more tolerable, or the tension elsewhere in Gaza would poison the atmosphere in Rafah.

It did not take long to get the answer. Palestinian militants continued to fire rockets into southern Israel. The Israelis countered with air strikes. The final straw came four months after my visit, when Hamas militants dug a tunnel under the border and kidnapped an Israeli soldier, Gilad Shalit, in June 2006. Israeli troops charged back into Gaza and effectively took control of the Rafah crossing. In recent years, Israel has kept the crossing closed for weeks at a time, reopening it for only a day or two when a large backlog of Palestinian travelers develops.

Shortly after Israel shut down Rafah in the summer of 2006, my *New York Times* colleague Taghreed El-Khodary planned to return to her home in Gaza City after spending the academic year in the Nieman Fellow program for journalists at Harvard University. Taghreed flew to Egypt and intended to cross into Gaza via the Rafah crossing. Yet she was repeatedly turned back and eventually retreated to Cairo. She was more fortunate than most of her fellow Palestinians, and could afford a hotel. Many poor Palestinians simply camped out near the crossing in the summer heat. In an experience that has become all too common for Palestinians, Taghreed waited thirty-nine days before the Israelis briefly reopened the Rafah crossing, allowing her and other Palestinians back home.

27

INTO THE ABYSS

The sunrise over the Gaza Strip on September 12, 2005, marked one of the few auspicious moments in the last decade. With deafening roars and suffocating blasts of diesel fumes, the final convoy of Israeli tanks and armored personnel carriers rumbled out of the Kissufim crossing on the eastern side of Gaza. We were among the pack of journalists watching from the Israeli side of the chain-link fence. As the last vehicle passed through the gate and entered Israel, the soldiers staged a brief flag-lowering ceremony and padlocked the gate. For the first time in thirty-eight years, no Israelis were in Gaza.

The Israeli pullout proceeded far more smoothly than anticipated. The Israelis wrangled among themselves, but there was virtually no friction with the Palestinians, who stood by, holding their fire as the Israelis left. The Israeli departure touched off a frenzy of celebrating—and scavenging—by the Gazans. Palestinians entered the abandoned Jewish settlements and ripped out ceiling fixtures, window frames, and anything else salvageable at synagogues and community halls. Then they set the buildings on fire. At mosques, loudspeakers hailed the "liberation" of Gaza. The Palestinians could not wait for sundown to rejoice; they set off fireworks all day long. My colleague Steve Erlanger was inside Gaza, where Palestinian women stood at the side of the road in long robes and headscarves, waving Palestinian flags and praising Allah. One village leader told Steve, "I feel freedom today."

The pullout created a rare opportunity. The Israelis and the Palestinians were now completely separated physically in this corner of the conflict, and there was reason to hope that this flash point could enjoy at least a bit of calm. The withdrawal also tested the most fundamental claims of both sides. The Palestinians argued that the conflict was all about the Israeli occupation. The shooting would stop when the occupation ended, many Palestinians said. Many Israelis predicted that the Palestinians would always find an excuse to keep attacking. No Israeli concession would ever be enough, they said.

The Gaza withdrawal was not a perfect experiment. Israel claimed that its occupation of Gaza had ended, while the Palestinians insisted it had changed only in style, not in substance. The Palestinians had not received statehood. The Israelis remained in control of Gaza's entrances, exits, and coastal waters. Israel ruled Gaza's air space and did not allow the Palestinians to reopen their airport. Diana Buttu, an adviser to President Mahmoud Abbas, said with a wry smile, "Israel never acknowledged there was an occupation. Now that they're leaving, they're saying the occupation is over."

In the West Bank, the Israelis and the Palestinians were still shooting it out daily. It seemed entirely possible that the West Bank would be the focus of the conflict, while Gaza might quietly tend to its own business. This would not be easy, given Gaza's history of bloodshed, poverty, and unsettled politics, but the Palestinians did have some choices. Reasonable and thoughtful Palestinians viewed Gaza as a potential mini-state that would prove the Palestinians were capable of handling full statehood. "The most important step after the withdrawal will be how we rebuild," said Abbas. Shortly after the Israelis left, Abbas asked the armed Palestinian factions to stop brandishing weapons in public as the first step toward restoring order. The factions agreed, although Hamas said it first wanted to hold a series of celebratory parades.

One of those parades was winding its way through the Jabaliya Refugee Camp, on the edge of Gaza City, on September 23, just eleven days after the Israelis left. As thousands looked on and cheered a convoy of Hamas vehicles, rockets in the back of a pickup truck exploded. They unleashed a massive fireball that killed fifteen people and wounded eighty, most of them spectators. Body parts were scattered along the route. People who survived the inferno unscathed dragged the wounded into cars and rushed them to hospitals.

All of the evidence suggested that the blast was exactly what it appeared to be: a monumental blunder by Hamas. The Palestinian factions have never read the safety manuals on handling explosives. All have miserable track records when it comes to "work accidents," the derisive Israeli term for these unintended detonations. Yet this was perhaps the worst disaster ever, both in casualties and in timing.

Hamas claimed the rockets in the truck were dummies and did not contain live explosives. The group alleged that an Israeli air strike had caused the blast. Yet no reliable accounts emerged of Israeli aircraft in the skies over Gaza, despite the thousands of spectators in the streets. Even the Palestinian Authority placed the blame on Hamas, calling on the group to "shoulder its responsibility" for the explosion, "instead of making accusations against others."

In a cynical attempt to save face, Hamas cut loose with a barrage of rockets into southern Israel. In an instant, the fighting picked up where it had left off before the Israeli pullout. With the Israelis gone, neither side had anything to gain in a new round of fighting. Israel wanted to wash its hands of Gaza, but it played into the hands of Palestinian extremists by leaving behind a poor, isolated territory that could not function on its own. The Palestinians, in turn, should have been preoccupied with figuring out how to make Gaza work. Led by the extremists, however, the Palestinians gave in to their worst impulses, picking a pointless fight with Israel and quarreling among themselves. The shooting match resumed, and the opportunity was lost.

In the West Bank, Palestinians undermined their cause by sending out suicide bombers. The Palestinians in Gaza achieved the same end with rockets. Because Israel had built a fence on Gaza's borders in the mid-1990s, Palestinian militants found it virtually impossible to make it out of the territory to attack Israel.

Shortly after the beginning of the second intifada, Palestinian militants in Gaza started to construct short-range rockets in garages and metal workshops. The so-called Qassam rockets initially traveled only three miles. To call them inaccurate was a grave understatement. In the early days, the launching tube was often a street-light pole that had been torn down and sawed into several parts. The main target was almost always the Israeli town of Sderot, home to about thirty thousand working-class Israelis who lived just a mile or so beyond Gaza's border fence. Yet often the rockets missed not only the town, but all of Israel. A fair number never made it out of Gaza and menaced the Palestinians who lived in the northeast corner of the territory. Some landed in the Mediterranean. The Israeli military made enormous efforts to prevent the rocket launches. There were radar systems, blimps, and drones that sought to detect and track every launch, yet still the Israelis could never manage to follow all of the unpredictable rockets. On a typical day when the rocket fire was at its peak, the military might report six launches out of Gaza but could confirm only three landing in Israel. The rest, the military assumed, landed somewhere in Gaza.

All of the armed Palestinian factions, including Hamas, Islamic Jihad, the Al Aksa Martyrs Brigades, and the Popular Resistance Committees, participated in the rocket launches. The rockets made life miserable in Sderot and a few other communities, forcing residents to dive for cover when they were alerted by air raid sirens. Fatalities were rare, though. From 2001 through 2009, the Palestinians fired more than twelve thousand rockets and mortars and killed fewer than twenty Israelis. The damage inflicted by the Israelis in response to the rocket attacks was massive. The Palestinian dead and wounded numbered in the thousands, towns in northern Gaza suffered widespread destruction, and good agricultural lands, including many citrus groves, were flattened. The count could not have been more lopsided, yet for years it was the rare Palestinian who openly denounced the folly of rocket attacks.

The Palestinians offered a host of reasons for firing rockets, all based on the emotion of the conflict, rather than on the logic of warfare. "We know we can't achieve military equality," Salah Bardawil, a Palestinian legislator from Hamas, told me during the summer of 2006, when the Palestinian rockets had prompted Israeli bombardments. "But when a person suffers huge pain, he has to respond somehow. This is how we defend ourselves. This is how we tell the world we are here."

Palestinians often spoke about their rockets and suicide bombings creating a "balance of fear" with Israel, even if they could not match Israel's weaponry. "Why should we be the only ones who live in fear?" said Muhammad Abu Oukal, a student at the Islamic University in Gaza City. "With these rockets, the Israelis feel fear, too. We will have to live in peace together or live in fear together."

With Hamas leading the way, the Palestinians in Gaza embarked on this self-destructive course that sabotaged the effort to rebuild Gaza before it even began. Israel made its contribution, greatly restricting the flow of goods and people in and out of the territory as it pressured Hamas. Israeli soldiers were entrenched on the borders, and aircraft watched from the sky, keeping Gaza under constant surveillance. Israel and Hamas lacked a forum for discussing grievances and defusing tensions, giving every incident the potential to escalate rapidly. Gaza has been the scene of all of the major crises in recent years, and it is a good bet that turmoil in the coming years is likely to revolve around Gaza's festering problems. Some of those confrontations will feature Israelis and Palestinians; others will pit Palestinians against one another.

The Palestinians have a long tradition of feuding among themselves. Even when Yasser Arafat was at the height of his powers as the unquestioned leader of the Palestinians, he often struggled to keep the Palestine Liberation Organization (PLO) in some semblance of order. These feisty internal battles were often nasty, but at the end of the day, the Palestinians managed to patch up their differences and direct their collective anger toward Israel. It helped that the multiple factions in the PLO, including Arafat's Fatah movement, tended to have at least a few things in common. The leaders were secular; their goals were nationalist.

In the late 1980s, however, just as Arafat and the PLO were moderating their positions and moving toward talks with Israel, Hamas emerged with its uncompromising calls for the elimination of Israel. As Arafat pursued negotiations in the 1990s, he managed to keep Hamas in check. Yet in the turmoil of the second Palestinian uprising, the rivalry between Fatah and Hamas began to spin out of control. A turning point came when Israel confined Arafat to his West Bank compound in 2002. After that, Arafat never returned to Gaza, leaving the territory essentially ungoverned.

One spring day in 2003, I tried to find out if anyone was in charge of Gaza. I went to Arafat's seafront headquarters in Gaza City. I knew Arafat would not be there, but I expected to discover at least a few Palestinian Authority officials. Instead, the compound was all but abandoned. I approached the front steps, where journalists had often waited for Arafat following his regular midnight meetings. Arafat would bid good-bye to his guest and then take a few questions from reporters. But those days were gone. After restricting Arafat to the West Bank, Israel bombed and partially damaged his Gaza headquarters. The front door was missing, and I was able to gaze into the banged-up interior and look straight through the missing back door to the placid waters of the Mediterranean. The only people present were a few bored security guards sitting and smoking beneath the shade of a palm tree. Their only concern was a flyspeck on the horizon, which they said was an omnipresent Israeli naval boat.

Unable to find any leaders at Arafat's compound, I tracked down Muhammad Dahlan, the former Palestinian security chief in Gaza, who had resigned from his post a year earlier. He was still considered the most powerful man in Gaza, pulling strings from behind the scenes. I asked him whether he was running Gaza. "Right now, only God is in charge," Dahlan said. "The Israelis have greatly weakened the Palestinian Authority, and Hamas is gaining more support. Is this the result Israel wants?"

At that time, everyday life still carried on. Schools were noisy with students. The hospitals still had supplies to tend to the ailing, and policemen stood on most street corners. Yet ominous signs were multiplying. "Sometimes I wonder how we are functioning at all without a central government," said Salah Abdel Shafi, who ran the Gaza Community Mental Health Program, which offered a range of services throughout the territory. "The young guys carrying guns are dominating the street. Various groups are all trying to impose their own agenda, and no one really has control." In the absence of a central government, Gazans were turning to their extended families to solve disputes, he said. Even murders and other serious crimes were now handled by families and clans, without the intervention of the police or the courts. This had occurred occasionally in the past but was becoming increasingly common as the Palestinian Authority became weaker and less visible.

Hamas surveyed this vacuum of authority and decided to take the plunge into electoral politics. The Islamist group had shunned elections previously, saying it would not be part of a Palestinian Authority that had been created through negotiations with Israel. Hamas did boycott the Palestinian presidential election in January 2005, which was held to replace Arafat, who had died two months earlier. Arafat's longtime aide Mahmoud Abbas won easily. Later in the year, though, Hamas entered municipal elections and made a strong showing throughout the Palestinian territories. Its strength in Gaza was expected, but it also did surprisingly well in the West Bank, the traditional stronghold of Fatah.

The local elections were mostly symbolic. The big test came the following year in the Palestinian parliamentary elections in January 2006. Abbas was reluctant to hold the elections because the Palestinian territories were so unsettled; however, the Bush administration saw elections as an important part of its plan to democratize the Middle East and insisted that the balloting go forward. Fatah, after all, was strongly favored to win, an assessment backed by multiple opinion polls. It seemed as if Hamas might capture Gaza. Yet no one was predicting an outright Hamas victory—not even Hamas.

My colleague Steve Erlanger and I stayed up most of the night monitoring the results. We were as shocked as everyone else when early the next morning it became clear that Hamas had won. The overall voting was close, with Hamas winning 44 percent of the vote to 41 percent for Fatah, but Hamas won a large majority of seats in part because it exhibited discipline where Fatah had none. In one winner-take-all election district, ten candidates were on the ballot. Nine were from Fatah and one was from Hamas. The Fatah candidates split the vote among themselves, and the Hamas candidate captured the seat.

The Palestinian election, which was free and fair by all accounts, was a seminal event on the Palestinian road to civil war. Fatah had been the dominant Palestinian political force for decades, but now Hamas would lead the elected government. Neither side would accept a subservient role. The showdown the Palestinians had long avoided was coming to a head, and Gaza would be the battleground. "The Gaza Strip is full of thugs these days," Mkhaimar Abusada, a political science professor at Al Azhar University in Gaza City, told me. "As a Palestinian I'm ashamed to say that, but it is part of the problem."

Just weeks after taking over, the Hamas government defied President Abbas and deployed a new security force in Gaza. The force was made up of members loyal to Hamas, as opposed to the existing forces, which were tied to Fatah. The new forces were distinguished by their black uniforms, and most members had thick beards, a sign of religious devotion. The Palestinians already had about a dozen ineffectual security force branches, and the Palestinian Authority was so broke, it could not afford to pay them. Yet Hamas was determined to have its own branch. Said Siam, the new interior minister from Hamas, said that the new force was being deployed to end the "state of chaos and anarchy and the increasing assaults on our people." He had a point—but having rival security forces was a recipe for disaster.

Another ominous sign came when Hamas and Fatah militants fought in a place that had always been considered sacrosanct: the two leading universities in Gaza, which stand side by side in Gaza City. Al Azhar University was a traditional bastion of Fatah support, while people at the Islamic University were known for backing Hamas. The students were on their winter break in February 2007, and the institutions were largely deserted, but their tall buildings presented militants with high ground from which to attack their opponents. The shooting lasted three days. I toured the campuses shortly after the battle ended. The computer center in the Islamic University's library was ankle-deep in ashes, and the few computers that survived a grenade attack and fire were misshapen and melted, as if painted by Salvador Dali. Just next door, at Al Azhar University, a rocket mangled the protective metal bars as it crashed through the window of the president's office, destroying his desk and pocking his walls with shrapnel.

Gazans were shocked that the street violence had spread to the universities, which were among the few places that offered hope of a better life for people in the territory. The two universities are separated by a single concrete wall on Thalathini Street, a main thoroughfare in Gaza City. The Islamic University had nearly twenty thousand students, a majority of them women, and catered to those who sought a religion-based education. All of the women wore black abayas, or long robes, as well as head scarves, and some had full veils. Many Hamas leaders in Gaza had links to the university.

Al Azhar had more than twelve thousand students, and most offices featured a large photo of Yasser Arafat. "I have two sisters and many friends at the Islamic University," said Rasha Nejem, twenty-two, a pharmacy student at Al Azhar. "But when I visited to see the damage, one girl told me, 'Get out of my university. You have no business here.'"

The clashes at the universities showed that any sense of restraint was vanishing. From that moment on, a full-scale battle loomed. It came just four months later, in June 2007. The Fatah fighters were mostly members of the security forces. They had years of training and access to a large store of weapons, and they controlled the security force compounds that were among the leading symbols of the Palestinian Authority. Yet this provided little in the way of advantage. The Hamas gunmen were better organized and more effective from the moment the battles began.

As Hamas began to gain control of the streets, it targeted the security force offices and systematically ousted the Fatah members in shootouts that consisted mostly of automatic gunfire and rocket-propelled grenades. In tit-for-tat episodes that captured the nastiness of the fighting, Hamas seized a Fatah member who belonged to the Presidential Guard and threw him off a fifteen-story apartment building, the tallest in Gaza. Fatah retaliated by tossing a Hamas militant to his death from another building. As Hamas gained the upper hand, its members looted a house that once belonged to Arafat and dismantled a villa that was owned by Muhammad Dahlan, the former security chief who was responsible for the arrests of Hamas leaders a decade earlier.

After a week of blistering urban battles in Gaza City and other towns, the fighting was over. Hamas controlled the government buildings, the compounds belonging to the security forces, the main roads, and everything else of consequence. Fatah had been completely routed. More than a hundred Palestinians had been killed and in excess of five hundred were wounded. Hamas quickly began to consolidate its hold, rounding up weapons that belonged to Fatah members.

. . .

This decisive battle, long in the making, will define the Palestinians for years to come. The battle cemented the split between Hamas and Fatah, making reconciliation extraordinarily difficult. Neither group will easily relinquish the territory it controls. Yet if the Palestinians cannot bring the West Bank and Gaza under single management, there is virtually no hope of holding meaningful negotiations with Israel.

Since the split, both Fatah and Hamas have worked diligently to protect their fiefdoms. Both see the other as destroying the Palestinian cause. Fatah says that Hamas does not understand that negotiations with Israel will be necessary to create a Palestinian state. Hamas believes that Fatah is engaged in discussions with Israel that are a waste of time. Israel exploits the cleavage by talking to Fatah and isolating Hamas. The United States has pursued a similar policy. Yet Hamas is now a full-fledged equal to Fatah and will not be easily dislodged.

Within Hamas, power is shared, somewhat uneasily, between leaders in Gaza and those in exile. Khalid Mishal, who has lived outside the Palestinian territories for more than three decades, has established himself as the single most important Hamas figure. In the West, he is largely unknown because he maintains a relatively low profile from his base in Damascus, where he resides in a heavily protected enclave that is reserved mostly for the Syrian elite.

Mishal was born in the West Bank and went into exile as a youth with his family. He has bounced around the Arab world for much of his life. Like almost all Hamas leaders, he is well educated. He received a physics degree from Kuwait University in 1978. He was the senior Hamas figure in Jordan in 1997 when Israeli Mossad agents, disguised as Canadian tourists, injected him with a slow-acting poison on a street in the capital, Amman. The bumbling Israeli agents were then captured. Jordan's King Hussein, who had signed a peace treaty with Israel three years earlier, was livid. He demanded that Israel provide the antidote, which it did, thus saving Mishal's life. This made Mishal a legendary figure in Hamas, the so-called martyr who would not die.[1] Mishal, who has salt-and-pepper hair and a matching beard, tends to issue hard-line pronouncements and has shown little willingness to make compromises. Yet those who have met him say that he always seems up-to-date on the details in the Palestinian territories, despite his decades-long absence.

The Hamas leaders in Gaza tend to be a bit more practical, particularly since they assumed power and have the unenviable task of running the failing territory. The most prominent Hamas figure in Gaza is Ismail Haniya, who became the prime minister of the short-lived government after Hamas's 2006 election victory. He is soft-spoken and mild mannered and has a strong bond with ordinary supporters. "The local Hamas leadership, especially Ismail Haniya, is more pragmatic than the external leaders because they see how tough Palestinian life is on the streets here," said Mkhaimar Abusada, the political science professor at Al Azhar University in Gaza City. "When Khalid Mishal is in Damascus talking about continued armed struggle, he doesn't see the level of suffering that has taken place here."

Haniya was born and still lives in the congested Beach Refugee Camp in Gaza City. Although he now has a comfortable three-story stucco home, it is squeezed between the cinder-block homes that dominate the area. Like most Hamas leaders, he has a large family that includes eight boys and four girls. And like other Hamas leaders, he has spent time in Israeli prisons. Haniya was arrested at least three times by Israel and was once deported to Lebanon for more than a year. He received a degree in Arabic literature from the Islamic University in the mid-1980s and spent many years there as an administrator. Haniya, who became prime minister while still in his early forties, has an air of authority about him and could be the public face of Hamas for years to come.

So, how will the Israeli-Palestinian conflict be resolved if Hamas remains in control of Gaza? No one has offered a plausible scenario. Israeli leaders have often pointed to Hamas as a reason that full-fledged negotiations are not possible. And it is not simply that Israel has refused to talk to Hamas; the Islamist group has also refused to speak to Israel. Israel has dealt with the more moderate Fatah leadership in the West Bank, and conditions there have been more stable.

One possible scenario envisions Israel and the West Bank Palestinians reaching some sort of arrangement that will improve life for Palestinians in that territory and demonstrate that Hamas is taking the Palestinians in Gaza down the road to ruin. Yet the Hamas leadership and many in Gaza would see this as an unholy collaboration between Israel and the West Bank Palestinians, and it would almost certainly deepen the rift between the Palestinians in the two territories.

Optimists have raised other possibilities that could potentially break the deadlock over Gaza. First, they argue that Hamas is not as unyielding in its positions as is often portrayed, and second, they say that Israel could negotiate indirectly with Hamas.

When pressed, Hamas says it will accept a Palestinian state along the 1967 borders and is open to a long-term truce with Israel. This is the line that Hamas offers to Westerners, although the group talks about it much less among its own supporters. Even if Hamas is sincere, this arrangement would not fly in Israel. Israeli political and military leaders have repeatedly said that the country will never return to the 1967 boundaries, arguing that it would leave the country too vulnerable to attack. In addition, any deal on a Palestinian state would have to be a full-fledged peace agreement that permanently ended the conflict. Israel says that Hamas is simply trying to eliminate Israel in stages.

Israel and Hamas have experimented with indirect negotiations, and the result was not a happy one. In the summer of 2008, Egypt served as the go-between in arranging an informal, six-month truce. The shooting between the Israelis and the Palestinians across the Gaza border declined but did not stop altogether. When the cease-fire expired at the end of 2008, neither side showed much enthusiasm for an extension. Israel, citing the Hamas rocket fire, then unleashed a three-week bombing campaign on Gaza, the most intensive the territory has ever endured. Despite the massive loss of life and destruction, Israel's Operation Cast Lead did not shake Hamas's hold on Gaza.

The greatest threat to Hamas in Gaza may be its own incompetence. Hamas has followed down the path of radical Islamist governments in Iran, Afghanistan, and elsewhere that have abysmal track records in administering the affairs of state. The Israeli restrictions have made it impossible for anyone to run Gaza effectively, but Hamas has proved quite capable of failing on its own.

Hamas has not, as some feared, imposed strict Islamic law in Gaza. The territory was already extremely religious and conservative, and Hamas has largely abided by a pledge to use persuasion, rather than force, in shaping social customs. Yet Hamas has only a limited understanding of the world beyond its own borders, and perhaps its greatest long-term challenge is its own economic illiteracy.

Gaza had already achieved full-fledged beggar status by the time Hamas took full control in 2007. Still, Hamas leaders have offered no plausible plan for economic revival. Hamas's inability to improve living standards seems destined to cut into its popularity over time, but this is a slow-motion process that could take years, if not decades. Even if Hamas is weakened, that does not mean it will lose power. And even if it loses power, that does not mean it will vanish from the scene. Even a diminished Hamas requires only a small band of zealots to undermine any future negotiations between Israel and the Palestinians.

28

ALONE ON A HILL

For anyone wondering how difficult it will be to remove large numbers of Jewish settlers from the West Bank, a visit to Shlomo Mor's mountain is highly instructive.

Back in 1999, Mor, a retired Israeli army colonel, scoured the scrub-brush hills in the southern part of the West Bank and parked his caravan on one with a commanding view. He then began building a ranch, something he had dreamed of since watching John Wayne's Westerns decades earlier.

"I like being alone in the mountains. I like the quiet. I like the night and the stars," said Mor, a rugged man with a full white beard and a face reddened by the desert sun. "If it's what you want, this place is a treasure." He insisted that his decision to build a homestead was a personal act that flowed from his love of wide-open spaces. Yet in the contorted politics of this conflict, his vision had much larger ramifications. His outpost, which stretched over some eight hundred empty acres, was strategically located between two existing settlements. Mor had effectively established a new Jewish settlement with a population of one.

Mor received help from multiple sources to establish his private settlement, including a letter from the Ministry of Defense and financial assistance routed through the World Zionist Organization.

He got a water system, a large generator, and a one-lane blacktop road, more than a mile long, that serves as his front driveway and connects him to the nearest Jewish settlement, Tene. For a while, the army even sent soldiers to guard him against attack by Palestinians. He also received assistance to establish a dairy farm that produced goat milk.

It all started quite nicely. About a year after he moved in, his dairy farm was in operation, and Israeli clients began to come from far away to buy his milk, which was popular among those who cannot tolerate cow's milk. Mor was a regular visitor in the nearest Palestinian town, Dhahariya, where he sold some milk and did his shopping. His dairy operation was just beginning to prosper, sometimes bringing in as much as $1,000 a day in sales, when the Palestinian uprising began in 2000. Concerned for their safety, Israelis abruptly stopped coming to his outpost, and Mor himself could no longer safely travel to Dhahariya.

When I met him in 2002, Mor and his son Avi, then twenty-three, were the only residents of Mor's mountain. Mor said his wife was not interested in such an isolated existence and had left him. That meant the civilian population was outnumbered by the three soldiers who kept guard. Shortly before I visited, Palestinian gunmen had twice fired on Israeli cars traveling on a road that was visible from Mor's ranch and had injured four people.

As the conflict dragged on, things got worse. An Israeli government report in 2005 identified his homestead as one of dozens of small outposts that had not been authorized. The government did not act on the report, but soon afterward, Mor's support dried up on all fronts. "When I came here, I was sure I was legal. I have signed documents from the Ministry of Defense, and lots of people came here with me to choose the spot, to bring the caravan, to build the road. They sat here and ate and drank with me," Mor said, as we sipped tea at a plastic table in front of his mobile home in the spring of 2007. "But then the government decided I came here by myself, and that I'm not legal, and now no one wants to talk to me." The soldiers were removed, leaving Mor and his son to take turns staying up all night to guard against attack. They patrolled with night-vision goggles and rifles slung over their shoulders as they drove a yellow dune buggy around the periphery of their ranch. "I've become a soldier again," said Mor, who also carried a nine-millimeter pistol tucked inside the back of his blue jeans. "I came here to establish a farm; instead, we have a fortress."

Mor was no zealot. His political views were very much within the Israeli mainstream, and he was philosophical about his personal predicament. He said he was ready to leave if the Israeli government would compensate him for his life savings, which he had plowed into his outpost. "I would prefer that all of this land be part of Israel. But it's clear we can't live together with the Palestinians. No matter who will be prime minister, he will have to give this land to the Palestinians. There will be no choice. We will have to live in our small country."

Yet the government had neither demanded Mor's departure nor offered to help him leave. "No one is asking me to go," Mor told me. "The people who used to help me are just saying, 'We're not going to help you anymore. It's your problem.'"

So there he sat on top of his mountain, feeling bitterness toward the military that once protected him, frustration with the government that would not bail him out, and anger at the private Jewish groups that cut off funding. Yet he could not leave because he was deep in debt, surviving on a military pension of about a thousand dollars a month.

Mor's tale showed how complicated it was to remove a single West Bank outpost consisting of a father and a son in a mobile home who were willing to leave. Israel has built 120 West Bank settlements that have been authorized by the government, and there are dozens more like Mor's that are considered unauthorized. Collectively, they pose one of the greatest challenges to any peacemaking attempt.

The relentless expansion of Jewish settlements also illustrated how the peace process has, in some respects, been marching backward. Before the 1967 war, no Israelis were living in the West Bank or Gaza. In the 1970s and the 1980s, the settlement movement began to expand significantly, particularly when the right-wing Likud Party was in power. Still, the numbers were small enough that the settlements could theoretically be dismantled as part of a peace agreement. Yet at some point, the West Bank settlers reached a critical mass, and removing all of them, or even most of them, became massively complicated. It is a political problem, a land issue, a security question, a financial dilemma, and a logistical nightmare, all wrapped into one.

Any Israeli leader who takes on the well-organized settler movement risks being driven from office. Therefore, no Israeli leader is likely to consider a wholesale pullout of settlers unless it is part of a full-fledged peace agreement with the Palestinians. Yet because there are now so many West Bank settlers, it has become ever more difficult to envision a peace agreement that will create a viable Palestinian state. This Catch-22 is reinforced on a daily basis. In a typical year, the settler population in the West Bank increases by ten thousand to fifteen thousand, a combination of new arrivals from other places in Israel and babies born to the young families who are already living in settlements. For this reason, it is harder to forge a peace agreement this year than last year, and it will be harder still next year.

Even the most moderate Palestinians insist on a state that would include Gaza, the West Bank, and a capital in East Jerusalem. Israel has left Gaza, but there is no prospect of a quick exit from either the West Bank or East Jerusalem.

When the Israeli-Palestinian negotiations began in 1993, the West Bank settlers had topped a hundred thousand. By the year 2000, when the peace talks were at a make-or-break stage, the settler population was hovering around two hundred thousand. Despite the fighting of this last decade, with settlers being among the most vulnerable to attack, the settler population has increased at a much faster rate than in Israel as a whole. The settlers now number around three hundred thousand.

As the settlements have grown and evolved, many have became suburban, middle-class bedroom communities. Today, many settlers are politically moderate, middle-class Israelis who chose to live in settlements purely for reasons of lifestyle. Housing is cheaper, it comes with government subsidies, and young families are much more likely to have a detached, single-family home with a yard, compared to Israeli cities, where the vast majority live in apartments. If the settler movement attracted Jews based only on religion and political ideology, the settlements would have remained relatively small, but the settlements have grown large and powerful because they have successfully lured Israelis who are very much part of the country's mainstream.

Settler leaders have mastered the art of steadily expanding settlements and buying time, regardless of the political climate, a policy known as "creating facts on the ground." As years pass and the settlements grow bigger and more entrenched, it will be ever more difficult to reverse the process. "It is important that these arteries of life are reinforced—shopping centers, gas stations, cash machines," said Pinchas Wallerstein, one of the top figures in the YESHA Council, the main settler organization. "The more you make these communities seem accessible and normal, the more people will be encouraged to live here, and the more people will think of them as a part of Israel just like any other."

Even if all of the Israelis living in the West Bank woke up one morning and decided to leave voluntarily, it would pose a staggering logistical challenge. Israel would have to accommodate this wave of citizens returning to the country's 1967 borders. In such a tiny country, it would be a huge burden to find new homes, schools, jobs, and services to replace the ones they would be abandoning.

Even the most liberal Israeli politicians, such as the former justice minister and peace negotiator Yossi Beilin, have acknowledged that Israel is likely to keep the largest settlement blocs by drawing the borders to accommodate them. Beilin and others in the liberal camp say that the solution is a land swap. Israel would get something in the order of 3 percent of the West Bank land to make the largest settlements a permanent part of Israel. In return, the Palestinians would get an equal amount of Israeli territory. This is perhaps the most realistic scenario in play, but it is fraught with difficulties. Israel would have to relinquish part of its internationally recognized territory, a proposal that is certain to face strong internal resistance. The Palestinians might entertain a land swap in principle, but the details would not be easy to work out, particularly when it comes to territory in and around Jerusalem.

Israel has shown that it can retreat when it comes to settlements, but those examples also illustrated that it is wrenching process. Ironically, Ariel Sharon, the driving force behind the spread of the settlements for decades, was also directly involved in the two major settlement withdrawals. The first came in 1982, when Sharon, as Israel's defense minister, oversaw the dismantling of the Yamit settlement and the withdrawal of its five thousand residents in the Sinai Peninsula as part of a peace agreement with Egypt. The second came in Gaza in the summer of 2005.

When Sharon first announced his Gaza "disengagement plan" in December 2003, many found it hard to believe, given his history. Yet as aggressive as Sharon had been in building settlements, his real obsession was always Israel's security. Viewed through this prism, his Gaza plan made sense and demonstrated that settlements were not necessarily permanent. Gaza was an albatross for the Israeli security forces as they tried to protect the roughly eight thousand settlers scattered from one end of the territory to the other in twenty-one separate settlements. They accounted for less than 1 percent of Gaza's population. In addition, Sharon was facing pressure from the United States and the rest of the international community to negotiate with Yasser Arafat under the Road Map peace plan introduced in the summer of 2003 by the Bush administration.

For Sharon, the Gaza withdrawal had the beauty of simultaneously addressing several problems. In leaving Gaza, he believed that he would be relieving the security forces of a major burden. He could carry out the withdrawal unilaterally, allowing him to control the game. Compared to the overarching goals of the Road Map, the Gaza pullout was a small, tactical maneuver. For Sharon, however, it succeeded in placing the Road Map in formaldehyde, as one of his aides put it. And finally, with the focus on Gaza, Sharon could work to consolidate Israel's hold on the West Bank settlements, which were far more important in Sharon's mind. As an added benefit, the Gaza pullout was widely praised by the international community. Even the Palestinians could not oppose the pullout itself, only the unilateral way in which it was done.

The big downside for Sharon was facing the wrath of the Israeli settlers, his traditional allies. Yet Sharon was well prepared to deal with the settlers he had helped send to Gaza in the first place. Ever the tactician, Sharon placed the settlers in an extremely awkward position. If they staged routine, peaceful protests, they would show themselves to be reasonable citizens playing by the rules, but they would not be able to stop Sharon. If they resorted to illegal actions or violence, they would come across as extremists and lose broader public support. Dressed in orange, in a nod to the citrus grown in Gaza, the settlers and their supporters staged huge demonstrations, bringing tens of thousands of supporters to the streets in Jerusalem, in Tel Aviv, and to the sandy fields just outside Gaza. They snarled traffic and burned tires to grab the attention of the Israeli public.

Sharon merely shrugged off the protests. As evacuation day approached in August 2005, the one remaining question was, how would the settlers respond when Israeli soldiers came to pull them from their homes? The answer was important not only for the Gaza withdrawal, but also as a precedent for any future pullout.

On the first day of the Gaza evacuation, Greg and I found ourselves in the living room of Yuval Unterman, thirty, a bearded community leader in the settlement of Morag, which consisted of only thirty-nine families. A succession of military officers attempted to bring Unterman out of his home. Initially, an earnest army captain tried to persuade him to leave the tan stucco house. Then a soft-spoken major gave it a shot, followed by a cajoling colonel. After three hours of protracted negotiations, an empathetic general placed his arm around Unterman's shoulder and explained that he had no choice but to say good-bye to his two-story house in Morag, which was considered one of the most religious and ideological settlements.

Unterman's wife, Michal, confronted the soldiers on the front walkway. She snapped photos of the soldiers. "Our children will look at these pictures of you every day," she said. The couple had six children, and they, too, joined in. "You can refuse orders," one of the young boys told the soldiers. "Many soldiers are doing it. If you lived here, you wouldn't want to leave either."

In the end, Mrs. Unterman approached the soldiers while carrying the couple's two-month-old son, Maoz, whose name means "fortress." "You've been brainwashed," Mrs. Unterman told the soldiers. "Look in my eyes, and remember for the rest of your life that you threw me out of my home." She then handed Maoz to one of the officers. The baby began to cry and so did Mrs. Unterman, but she and the kids were eventually escorted to the family's beat-up gray Subaru station wagon. Her husband remained in the tiny living room, decorated with religious images, as the Israeli officers and Unterman kept talking past one another.

"We want to do this in the most respectable manner," one officer said.

"Expelling Jews from their homes—there is no way to do this respect-fully," countered Unterman.

Eventually, five policemen carried the burly Unterman out the front door as he shouted, "Morag, Morag!" He was deposited next to the car, where the rest of the family was waiting. "I've been here ten years, and the terrorists and the rockets didn't drive me out," he told the soldiers. "But now you are kicking me out." As he was about to drive away, we asked Unterman where he was going, suspecting that he would resettle in the West Bank. But he did not give anything away. "I don't know," he mumbled before getting in his car and driving out of Gaza for the last time.

Unterman exemplified the passive resistance that many Gaza settlers displayed during the pullout. As Israeli soldiers systematically emptied out the settlements in Gaza during that sweltering week, however, they reached some of the last holdouts in Kfar Darom, an isolated spot in the southern part of the territory. There, about 150 young protesters, many from out-side Gaza, chose to make the most forceful stand against the evacuation.

Like so many confrontations in the larger Israeli-Palestinian conflict, there was history at Kfar Darom. Jews had acquired the land in 1930, and a small community was living there when the 1948 Arab-Israeli war erupted at Israel's independence. After a prolonged siege by the Egyptian army, the Jews abandoned Kfar Darom, and Egypt came to control all of Gaza. Yet nearly two decades later, Israel drove the Egyptian forces out of Gaza in the 1967 war. The Israeli military set up an outpost at Kfar Darom, and a Jewish settlement followed. It was no accident that the strongest settler resistance took place at Kfar Darom in the summer of 2005.

Jewish youths barricaded themselves in the settlement's synagogue and battled to keep out the Israeli security forces. The protesters took to the roof and taunted police and soldiers, pelting them with paintballs. Greg and I were among the large crowd of journalists who gathered, and I took a paintball in the seat of my pants while live on air.

The protesters secured the front doors with chains and put oil and grease on the floors and the stairways to make all of the approach routes slick. On the roof, the holdouts had metal shields to guard against water cannons and long poles to push back security force members who tried to reach them by ladder. As members of a police unit worked their way up the ladders, the settlers poured buckets of oil and a caustic blue liquid on them, followed by garbage, eggs, and spray foam.

Special police units wore black coveralls and visors and carried riot shields but had no weapons. The police broke through the front doors on

the ground floor, but the door leading to the roof was barricaded. Ulti-
mately, the police reached the roof in two shipping containers that were
hoisted by giant cranes.

Before the officers emerged from the containers, the protesters doused
them with paint, turning their coveralls to white. The scuffling lasted for
hours, but eventually the protesters were rounded up and placed inside
the shipping containers that had brought the policemen. Dozens of police
officers and soldiers were injured, most of them lightly.

This confrontation illustrated the depth of the anger among the
settlers, but it also showed the limits of their opposition. Twenty months
passed from the first time Sharon spoke of withdrawing from Gaza until
the final settler was removed.

The rhetoric was incendiary, with the settlers comparing Sharon and
the security forces to the Nazis, but the settlers and their supporters could
assemble only limited numbers to resist. No shots were fired by either side.
And once removed, the settlers did not return to Gaza. There is no guar-
antee that such restraint would hold if a major evacuation was under-
taken in the West Bank, but the Gaza withdrawal illustrated that even
the deeply committed settlers could not bring themselves to use lethal force
against the Israeli security forces.

There was another important lesson to be gleaned from the Gaza
withdrawal. For all of the noise, the overall settler population was
larger at the end of 2005 than it had been at the beginning of the
year. The new West Bank settlers that year outnumbered the eight
thousand who had been withdrawn kicking and screaming from
Gaza. In fact, some of the new West Bank settlers *included* those
dragged out of Gaza.

Such as the Untermans. The Unterman family spent five hours
in the family's hot, cramped station wagon as they drove out of
Gaza and across Israel. Then they reached the West Bank around
nightfall, and they were settlers once again.

I caught up with the Unterman family five days after their Gaza
eviction. They landed in Ofra, a large settlement where twenty-
three of the thirty-nine families from Morag had taken temporary
shelter. The Untermans said they had not yet decided where to put
down roots. "We feel very welcome here," said Michal Unterman.
"The reception has been very kind, and they have provided us

with everything. We have hot meals. They are taking care of our laundry. They have provided us with everything from soap to toothbrushes."

Ultimately, the Untermans moved to the West Bank settlement of Tene, along with more than a dozen other families that came from the same settlement in Gaza. Unterman described his new life in the West Bank as difficult but tolerable. "We struggle to make a living. In general, it is worse than it was. But life is going on," Unterman said in 2008. "I used to work in a community center with computers. Now I work as a magician. My wife used to work as a teacher. She changed her profession to graphic design. We can work anywhere with these jobs." The Unterman children still talked about their old home, although "they were not traumatized. They miss it. They look at the pictures. But they are not stuck there."

Yet Unterman said that he and the other Gaza settlers would not go so easily if the government tried to move them from Tene, a relatively small settlement that is well beyond Israel's separation barrier. It is exactly the kind of place that would be evacuated under any peace deal. "We were very naïve about moving [from Gaza]," Unterman said. "There were things I would have done completely differently. Unfortunately, we didn't fight as we should have for our home."

Could he tell us how he would respond next time? Unterman chuckled and said, "No, I prefer not to. The struggle [in Gaza] was managed by people whose motto was, 'Love Will Win.' We didn't agree with the decision, but we cooperated. The people won't behave the same way next time."

29

THE TRAITOR

Dror Etkes brought his white Mazda pickup to a stop on a rutted dirt path, several hundred yards outside the perimeter fence of Karmei Tzur, a West Bank settlement south of Jerusalem. If any one Israeli symbolized the antisettler movement, it was Etkes. An energetic man who speaks at a machine-gun pace, Etkes worked many years for the Peace Now advocacy group, which monitors settlement building, before moving to another organization, Yesh Din, where he does similar work. He has spent countless days crisscrossing the West Bank in his truck, bouncing up and down dirt roads as he tracked the formal Jewish settlements and the informal outposts. Most were in full expansion mode when Etkes took me for a daylong drive in the spring of 2007.

Etkes stopped on the outskirts of Karmei Tzur to show me a common point of friction. Just outside the fence that surrounded the Jewish settlement was a Palestinian grape vineyard that had belonged to Palestinian farmers for generations. Due to the violence, however, the Israeli military had barred the Palestinian owners from the vineyard because it was considered too close to the settlement. The settlers feared that an armed Palestinian could use the vineyard as cover to approach the settlement undetected, and Karmei Tzur had indeed come under attack.

We had been parked for less than a minute when the settlement's security guard recognized Etkes's truck from the settlement's front gate. The guard jumped into his own pickup and came racing toward us in a manner that was self-explanatory. As he neared, he slammed on the brakes, kicking up a cloud of dust as he pulled up next to us. He rolled down his window and greeted Etkes. "Don't come any closer, or you'll get your ass kicked," he snarled.

I told Etkes that I had been turned away from settlements on occasion but never in such a hostile manner. "You have to understand that I'm considered a traitor," Etkes said. "In his mind, I should know better."

Etkes was raised in an Orthodox Jewish home in Jerusalem, and his upbringing gave him insight into the thinking of settlers and their supporters. Indeed, his own sister became a settler. Israeli society has many fault lines, and one of the deepest splits is over the question of settlements. From afar, it may appear that Israelis are of one mind when it comes to settlement building. Yet even when the Israeli-Palestinian fighting was at its worst, polls consistently showed that a majority of Israelis were willing to relinquish many, if not all, of the settlements in exchange for genuine peace. The settlers and their supporters have been able to keep on building, however, even when public opinion is divided or running against them.

Settlers have never been fond of Etkes poking his nose in their business, and as his reputation grew, these confrontations became more frequent. "The hard-core settlers know me, and many others know my name. But not that many know me by face," said Etkes. "Some just ignore me. Others say something nasty. And some are dangerous." He has been physically attacked three times by settlers, and the police have warned him to stay away from the more radical outposts for his own safety. Aside from being a general nuisance, Etkes can point to several achievements that certified him as a leading enemy of the settlers.

Peace Now produced a report in 2007 revealing that 32 percent of the West Bank settlement land was on private property, almost all of it owned by Palestinians. This undermined one of the fundamental arguments put forth by the settlers and their supporters. They have long said that the West Bank is disputed territory, claimed by both the Israelis and the Palestinians, but that it does not currently belong to any country. Over the centuries, the Ottomans, the British, and Jordan have held sway in the West Bank, but no one was recognized internationally as the legal sovereign. Therefore, the settlers said, they were not taking land from any country or individual. The settlements were going up on empty land, they argued, whose legal status was still to be determined. The Israeli government often said that it respected private Palestinian property, that the military took such land only when it felt compelled by security reasons, and that those seizures were temporary.

Yet Peace Now filed a lawsuit seeking the land records, and, after a protracted battle, the Israeli courts ruled that the Israeli military had to hand over the paperwork. Peace Now found that the Israeli military was fully aware that many settlements were built beyond the boundaries authorized by the Israeli government and on private land owned by Palestinians, many of whom had documentation dating back to the Ottoman period. "For the first time, we have the official boundaries of all of the settlements," said Etkes.

In another case, Etkes and Peace Now filed a petition to have the West Bank outpost of Atmona removed on the grounds that it was illegal under Israeli law. The court ruled in favor of Peace Now, and one of Prime Minister Ehud Olmert's first moves in office was to tear down the outpost. It consisted of only nine buildings, but the operation involved a daylong battle in February 2006 between the security forces and the settlers. "Before this case, many settlers didn't like me, but they thought I wasn't very harmful," Etkes said. "But then they learned that I had used the system to beat the system."

During our tour, Etkes was rebuffed several times. When we drove to the entrance of the Adora settlement near Hebron, Etkes asked whether we could enter. A security guard with an automatic rifle came out of his hut and said he would have to check with his supervisor. He returned ten minutes later to tell us that "management does not authorize a visit." This happened often to Etkes, and it reflected what many settlements had become: fortresses surrounded by a hostile Palestinian population, guided by a bunker mentality, and so suspicious of outsiders that they refused to open their gates to fellow Israelis.

In his work, Etkes was essentially a detective in a world full of hostile witnesses, and every day was a battle of wits to glean nuggets of information on where the settlements were expanding. One of his favorite methods was to pick up, or at least chat with, Israeli hitchhikers in the West Bank, where they were common. He freely offered rides, the longer the better, because it gave him a captive audience and helped him ferret out information he could rarely get by knocking on doors. During our drive, a young woman was waiting on the side of the road in the southern West Bank, and Etkes immediately began to grill her: Are all of the houses occupied? Is anyone moving in or moving out? Is anyone trying to sell a house? What is the mood in the community?

A bit later, we visited Kiryat Arba, a large settlement next to Hebron. Etkes saw a billboard advertising new apartments for about $125,000. Etkes called and inquired about the apartments as if he were a prospective buyer. The willingness of a builder to negotiate was often a guide to the state of a given settlement. When the violence was bad, buyers could be hard to find. At this time, however, the settlements were booming. As we walked through Kiryat Arba, home to some of the more radical settlers, Etkes could not help but nervously look over his shoulder and check his truck repeatedly. "I have to keep eye contact on the car," he said. "If my car is recognized here, the tires will be slashed in a second."

We visited close to a dozen settlements and outposts during our tour of the southern West Bank, and construction was taking place in almost every one. Just outside Jerusalem, the government had authorized the building of a road that would link several settlements directly to the city. Etkes pointed out one of the great ironies of the settlement-building enterprise: virtually all of the laborers were Palestinians who desperately needed the jobs. In this case, the workers were building a road on which they would not be allowed to drive. For years, Palestinian laborers had built homes in the settlements. They often tended the gardens and performed other manual jobs inside the gates until the uprising.

Etkes knew better than anyone how fast the settlements were growing. Yet he believed that several factors could slow or reverse the trend. In his view, the withdrawal of the Gaza settlers and the building of the barrier in the West Bank were clear signs that the settlers would, at minimum, eventually retreat behind the barrier. This had already affected the settlements beyond the barrier. Few Israelis were willing to buy homes there. "You see lots of houses that are empty. Many projects are not finished. Basically, these are communities with no future, even if they are being left in place today."

Also, the settlers had become more diverse as their numbers increased, and these divisions could be exploited, he said. A large secular settlement, such as Maale Adumim, just outside Jerusalem, regarded itself as a typical Israeli suburban community. The residents tended to be middle-class and in the political mainstream. They commuted to Jerusalem for work, served in the military, voted for a range of parties, and felt completely connected to the broader Israeli society.

These settlements were very different from several large, fast-growing settlements near Jerusalem made up entirely of ultra-Orthodox Jews. The ultra-Orthodox were not traditionally part of the settler movement, but with their large families and limited resources, they welcomed settlements that offered them affordable housing close to Jerusalem.

And then there were the "hilltop youths," the deeply religious, intense kids with tousled hair who refused to play by anyone's rules but their own. They were often the children of the first generation of settlers but saw their parents as having gone soft. Filled with religious fervor, they considered themselves modern pioneers who built new settlements that began with a single caravan on a remote West Bank hilltop. They routinely rejected the authority of the state. They demonstrated their disregard by setting up outposts wherever they chose and scuffling with the security forces on the rare occasions when soldiers came to take down those outposts. Engaging them in conversation was not easy—their long list of perceived enemies included the media—but they often saw the Israeli government and its military as their main opponents, surpassing even the Palestinians.

Jennifer and I witnessed the hilltop youths in action on one of our first days in the region in 1999. We went to Ma'on, outside Hebron, to observe the Israeli military taking down an outpost that consisted of several cinder-block and corrugated-tin buildings on a barren hill. The security forces and the scruffy youths battled for hours as the kids tried to prevent the soldiers from reaching the homes. Some youths took to the corrugated-tin roofs and had to be removed individually and dragged onto buses. For an outsider, it was impossible to see the value of this empty patch of scrub brush. And yet, this was only round one. The settlers rebuilt the outpost, and the Israeli security forces returned to take it down again several years later. In the fall of 2009, settlement monitors reported that new caravans had been moved into Ma'on, and it was larger than ever.

These very different groups of settlers—the suburbanites, the ultra-Orthodox, and the hilltop youths—have very different agendas, Etkes noted. If Israel decided to remove the relatively small settlements beyond the separation barrier, those facing eviction would include the hilltop youths and other hard-core settlers who could resist mightily. Yet the more mainstream settlers would probably welcome the departure of the fringe elements, believing that this would help solidify the large, suburban-style settlements.

In the view of Etkes, Israel has for decades avoided the fundamental contradiction of the settlements, but demographics could soon force some tough decisions. "The settlements are the single biggest state project since the State of Israel came into existence," he said. "At the same time, there hasn't been a single day when Israel seriously considered annexing the West Bank entirely or faced the other question—what do you do with the Palestinian population? You can't claim you are a Jewish, democratic state and have 2.5 million people who are under occupation. You have to give up something."

For this reason, Etkes believed that Israel was "not yet at the point of irreversibility. The main reason is demographics, which is always a factor in Israeli politics. Those on the left favor two states, and those on the right have different ideas, but the barrier shows that they are now working off the same principle: maximum land, minimum Arabs. The rationale is the same on the left and on the right. Jews and Arabs can't live together and must be separated."

30

GRAPES OF WRATH

In the spring of 1996, we covered a brief battle with major consequences. Israel and the Lebanese guerrilla group Hezbollah had been fighting for more than a decade at this point, and the hostilities were usually confined to a small patch of territory in southern Lebanon. In April of that year, however, the shooting escalated and included Hezbollah rocket fire across the border into northern Israel. Israel's prime minister, Shimon Peres, was better known for his peace plans than for his military strategy. Yet he was facing an election battle in which his security credentials were being questioned, and he opted for a forceful response.

Operation Grapes of Wrath, as the Israeli military called it, was an asymmetrical battle—the only kind of combat that Israel has waged for decades. Israeli F-16 fighter planes came screaming over southern Lebanon, low and hard, unleashing missiles at the small bands of Hezbollah fighters darting around the hills and the villages of southern Lebanon. The militants shot off rockets and then quickly disappeared.

We were based in Cyprus at this time and flew to Lebanon to report on the fighting. Because southern Lebanon lacked reliable communications, we stayed at a hotel in Beirut. This meant we had to take a nerve-jangling drive down the Mediterranean coastal road every day to the war zone in southern Lebanon, then return in the evening to file our stories. The most harrowing stretch was at Sidon, where a pair of Israeli warships were waiting about a mile offshore, their guns directed at a small piece of exposed coastal road.

When approaching the vulnerable spot, Lebanese drivers would pull to the side, get out, and squint at the glinting Israeli gunboats. The drivers often waited for a few minutes, allowing other cars to go first to see whether these drew Israeli fire. When the Israelis cut loose with several shells, the drivers would then count off the seconds between firings, trying to calculate whether they would have enough time to slip past between rounds.

Our driver had his own, less scientific, method. Before running the gauntlet, he would hold up his right index finger, declaring it his "lucky finger," which had protected him during the many years of fighting in his homeland. Then he hit the gas. Somehow, we made it up and down the coast each day, speeding past the carcasses of vehicles that were not so fortunate.

The deadliest single episode of the war took place farther south, in the sun-baked town of Qana. In a scenario that played out all during the fighting, Hezbollah fired rockets, and Israel responded with a barrage of artillery rounds directed at the source of the fire. Yet this time, the Israelis were well off the mark and hit a large group of Lebanese civilians who had sought shelter at a United Nations compound. More than a hundred Lebanese were killed, many of them women and children. When we attended the mass funeral in Qana a few days later, it seemed that all of southern Lebanon was present, wailing for the dead.

Until that point, the fighting had been seen as a mostly localized skirmish. In Beirut, a city of many sects, Lebanese Christians and Sunnis often expressed an almost casual indifference to the battle, viewing it as just another round in the endless quarrel between the Shiites of Hezbollah and Israel. The slaughter in Qana, however, created an outcry that reverberated throughout Lebanon and the Middle East and to points far beyond.

Israel came under tremendous pressure to halt its operation. The United States helped broker a truce shortly after the Qana killings. Like most Middle East battles, the fighting did not produce a clear winner, and the outcome was open to interpretation. No land was won or lost. No political problem was resolved.

In the years that followed, whenever I mentioned Operation Grapes of Wrath, Greg would roll his eyes. He said that hardly anyone recalled the battle itself, much less the silly name supplied by the Israeli military, which presumably came from the biblical reference and not the John Steinbeck novel.

Yet Grapes of Wrath, and the Qana killings in particular, had far-reaching ramifications. Israel was effectively forced to end its offensive before it wanted to, and it had not weakened Hezbollah as it had hoped. The myth of Israeli invincibility suffered a setback. Hezbollah claimed that it had fought Israel to a standoff, a boast that resonated throughout the Arab world. The Lebanese group was emboldened. In Beirut, Hezbollah became a more potent political force. In southern Lebanon, it rearmed and became even more entrenched, winning the loyalty of villagers as it handed out cash to those who had lost loved ones or had their houses damaged by the fighting. Most important, the inconclusive fighting during Operation Grapes of Wrath made another big Israeli-Hezbollah clash all but inevitable. This forecast did not require a crystal ball, only common sense.

31

RAINBOW OF ROCKETS

On the morning of July 12, 2006, a decade after the previous war, Hezbollah infiltrators slipped through Israel's northern border fence and ambushed two armored Israeli Humvees on a patrol road that ran parallel to the fence. Hezbollah killed three Israeli soldiers and seized two more. Israel sent troops charging into Lebanon in search of the missing soldiers and also launched air strikes. Before the sun set, Israel and Hezbollah were once again at war.

We both raced to Israel's northern border, where we were greeted by a powerful sense of déjà vu. Back in 1996, we had walked along the same front line, just a mile or so away on the Lebanese side of the hilly frontier. Now we were on the Israeli side, where the incoming rockets were courtesy of Hezbollah, instead of Israel.

We wanted to set up camp close to the fighting, but Hezbollah's random rockets made it hard to find a secure location. Get too close, and you risk your life. Stay too far away, and you miss the story. It was always a tricky balance.

Yet we quickly found an unlikely sweet spot in the scenic farming village of Metulla, at the northernmost tip of Israel's panhandle. Metulla had been settled in the 1890s by several dozen farming families on land purchased by a representative of Baron Edmond de

Rothschild, a member of the French banking dynasty and a strong supporter of Zionism. Metulla had only one main street, where several of the original stone buildings still stood. The town offered a sweeping view of villages in southern Lebanon, which were separated from Israel by a modest chain-link fence. At first glance, it appeared to be one of the riskiest places to stay. Metulla seemed an obvious target. It had less security than a gated community in an upscale American suburb. You could be shot through the fence with a pistol.

In the calculus of this strange war, however, Metulla was relatively safe precisely because it hugged the border. Hezbollah guerrillas operated several miles back from the frontier, and its Katyusha rockets were wildly inaccurate. If Hezbollah aimed at Metulla, misfires would have endangered villages on the Lebanese side of the border. Rather than risk hitting fellow Lebanese, Hezbollah aimed its rockets over Metulla, targeting towns deeper inside Israel. In turn, Israeli tanks and big artillery guns were several miles south of the border, tucked away in valleys, and they, too, fired over Metulla as they targeted Hezbollah sites inside Lebanon.

For the entire war, Metulla was under this rainbow of rockets screeching overhead in both directions. Most Metulla residents fled, along with the vast majority of civilians in northern Israel, but the journalists piled in. The village had drawn its share of tourists during quieter times and had three serviceable hotels and an excellent steakhouse that remained open for the duration of the war. It was one of those scenes that cropped up in every war we covered: at least a couple of hoteliers and a few restaurateurs braved the conflict and reaped a financial bonanza. Rockets were slamming into northern Israel around the clock, inflicting casualties on a daily basis among the few residents who remained. Yet every evening, the steakhouse was so busy we sometimes had to wait for a table. The sizzle of sirloins on the flaming grill helped muffle, though it could never fully suppress, the whine of Hezbollah rockets coming from the north or the rhythmic pounding of Israeli artillery launches to the south.

We spent much of the war in Metulla, although our schedules were so contradictory that we had to take adjoining rooms at the Cedars Hotel, and we rarely saw each other. Jennifer worked through the entire night, local time, in order to synchronize her schedule with Fox's primetime evening shows in the United States.

She would end her working day at dawn and then return to the hotel to sleep all morning and into the afternoon.

I would head out early in the morning and spend the day reporting, then usually return in the afternoon to begin writing while Jennifer was still asleep next door. We went days without seeing each other awake. On the weekend, one of us would make the four-hour drive back to Jerusalem to see our daughters.

In Israel's 1982 invasion of Lebanon—which led to the birth of Hezbollah—Israeli troops faced only limited resistance as they rolled north, needing just two weeks to reach the outskirts of the capital, Beirut. Yet that early success turned into a quagmire, and Israel did not withdraw its soldiers from southern Lebanon until 2000. No one in Israel wanted to repeat that experience.

The goal in 2006 was much more limited. It was restricted to driving Hezbollah out of rocket range in the south, yet it proved far more difficult. Hezbollah had spent years preparing for this battle. Its fighters were well concealed in bunkers and tunnels. They emerged to fire automatic rifles, rocket-propelled grenades, and antitank rockets and then quickly vanished.

As the fighting dragged on, it became increasingly clear that this battle would follow the script written in 1996, marking yet another inconclusive conflict. Israel flexed its muscles and bombed Lebanese villages at will. The Israeli artillery rounds saturated southern Lebanon with high-powered explosives. The air force struck throughout the country, hitting Hezbollah's strongholds in the suburbs of Beirut, the Beirut airport, the Bekaa Valley in the east, and major roads connecting southern Lebanon to the rest of the country. The Israeli navy imposed a blockade. Lebanese casualties were high, and many of the dead were civilians. Yet Israel never came close to rooting out all of the Hezbollah fighters hiding in the nooks and crannies of southern Lebanon.

Many Israelis were surprised, if not a little shocked, at how difficult the fighting was, but they should not have been. Israel's swift, sweeping victory against Arab armies in the 1967 war looms large in the collective Israeli psyche, but it was an anomaly. Israel spent almost all of the 1980s and the 1990s in southern Lebanon trying to exterminate Hezbollah, and the group only grew larger and stronger. During those years, the Israeli troops were based in southern Lebanon and worked with a local proxy force, the South Lebanese Army, which gave Israel a broad presence and a solid intelligence network. After Israel pulled out in 2000, Hezbollah took control of the territory. With considerable help from Iran and Syria, Hezbollah stockpiled an arsenal and dug in along the border.

By 2006, it was completely unrealistic for Israel to send its army back into southern Lebanon and assume that it could crush Hezbollah in a matter of days or weeks. Israeli troops had been pounding the overmatched Palestinians in recent years in the West Bank and Gaza. When Israeli armor rolled into Palestinian cities, the soldiers faced only limited resistance. These skirmishes did not prepare the Israelis for a much tougher fight in the rugged hills of southern Lebanon, where the mobile and elusive Hezbollah fighters were much better trained and armed than the Palestinians.

Israel sent a limited number of ground forces into southern Lebanon during the first few weeks of the fighting, and those troops were not able to stop the Hezbollah rockets. In the final days of the war, an increasingly frustrated Israel sent some ten thousand soldiers several miles into southern Lebanon in an attempt to crush Hezbollah or at least drive its fighters out of rocket range. The ground assault was risky, and Israel suffered its heaviest losses of the war.

During the fighting, Israeli casualties were flown by helicopter from the Lebanese battlefield directly to the Rambam Health Care Campus Hospital in the northern Israeli port city of Haifa, about twenty miles south of the border. The hospital is on the coast, and rockets were landing all around the city—and near the hospital. From the coastal side of the hospital, I watched as the helicopters came in over the sea to deliver the wounded soldiers.

From their hospital beds, Israeli troops were unanimous in describing intense fighting by a fierce, well-organized enemy. For tank gunner Sergeant Or Bar-On, the war lasted all of ninety minutes, yet his wounds would last a lifetime. A week into the war, Bar-On's tank crew was sent about a mile into Lebanon to rescue soldiers in a military bulldozer that had been hit by Hezbollah fire. Yet before his crew reached the stricken bulldozer, a rocket pierced the tank's armored skin and shredded both of Bar-On's lower legs. "I was gushing blood, and I felt pain like I've never felt before," Sergeant Bar-On said. He screamed for help and crawled out the back of his tank. He was dragged to safety by fellow soldiers and delivered by helicopter to the hospital, where he arrived with extreme blood loss. "I wanted to pass out, but I knew if I did, I would die."

He survived but lost both legs just below the knee. I met Sergeant Bar-On three weeks after he had been wounded and while the war was still going on. Rockets were still crashing in the neighborhood near the hospital, but Bar-On's mood was upbeat. A female friend was visiting, and he strummed his guitar while sitting in bed in his tiny hospital room. His most immediate goal, he said, was to return to performing in his heavy metal band, Vendetta.

In Kiryat Shmona, the northern Israeli town most often targeted by Hezbollah, rockets whistling in from Lebanon had been a recurring presence in Eli Ben-Abo's life for more than three decades. As he waited out a barrage on the last full day of the war, he was sure the truce was not a permanent solution. "I've been listening to these rockets from 1970 until today," said Ben-Abo, fifty, who was squeezed into a tiny, sweltering cinder-block shelter on the ground floor of his apartment building. It was just large enough for his extended family. His wife, two daughters, and four more relatives were packed inside a space that resembled the sleeping quarters on a submarine. "We keep hoping it will end, but it never does."

The shelters are simple concrete boxes with minimal facilities that usually include bunk beds that fold out from the walls, as well as a toilet and a sink. Electricity allows for cooking on a hot plate, watching television, and running a small fan. Most larger apartment buildings typically have communal shelters in the basement.

All of the communities in northern Israel had a well-practiced game plan for coping with rockets. The town halls had twenty-four-hour hotlines. Municipal workers in flak jackets carried food, water, medicine, and even diapers to families running low on supplies. The elderly were moved to senior citizens' homes farther south, out of rocket range. Towns organized activities inside the shelters to keep residents from going stir-crazy. Singers from around the country gave impromptu concerts. Artists set up craft centers for painting and woodworking. Soldiers were sent to entertain children.

Yet these efforts could only do so much to relieve the tedium. When the warning sirens stopped, the Ben-Abo family stepped outside for a breath of air that was merely hot and sticky, not suffocating. The lethargic family members rarely strayed more than a few paces from the shelter, knowing that the siren would inevitably cry out again. A moment later, another rocket came crashing down. Ben-Abo retreated to the shelter and took a moment to recount his long history with the rockets.

His first taste was at age thirteen, back in 1970, when the Palestine Liberation Organization, led by Yasser Arafat, began raining rockets on the town. In 1982, Ben-Abo was a soldier who fought in Lebanon for nearly a year in the operation that drove the PLO out of that country. That raised the hope that Israel would have quiet on its northern border. Yet the Israeli incursion spawned Hezbollah, which proved to be a much more formidable foe. In the 1996 fighting, a Hezbollah rocket slammed into Ben-Abo's apartment, causing extensive damage. He and his family were in a shelter, however, and were unharmed.

Over the years, he had taken cover in the shelter more times than he could remember, but the 2006 fighting marked the longest period ever. Money was tight, and the family could not afford to leave. The only break during the five-week rocket barrage was when the Israeli government bused several hundred residents to the southern tip of Israel in Eilat, on the Red Sea, for a brief respite. "It was so nice to just get away," Ben-Abo said. Yet the vacation was all too brief, and he predicted that the truce would end the same way. "This will all happen again in another couple of years. In Kiryat Shmona, I don't think we'll ever have peace."

Of course, there were optimists, even in Kiryat Shmona. Freddy Misika manned his bright-orange lottery kiosk on the town's main drag, promising winning tickets for all during the fighting, although Kiryat Shmona had become a virtual ghost town. "I was here from eight in the morning until the evening, even when the rockets were falling," he said cheerfully. Business was down sharply, but he pulled out a pile of receipts from winning tickets, some for ten thousand shekels, or more than two thousand dollars. "That's just good luck," he said. Apparently, if you are going to roll the dice with your life, you might as well also play the lottery. Misika closed only on Saturdays, when the country shut down for the Jewish Sabbath. As it turned out, that too was lucky. Hezbollah, which had little regard for the Jewish day of rest, fired a rocket one Saturday that dug out a large chunk of pavement just twenty yards from Misika's kiosk, shattering windows up and down the street.

I asked Misika whether he believed in bad luck. He acknowledged that his wife and one of his sons had been injured by a rocket twenty years earlier, and that their apartment was damaged by another one six years back. Yet these episodes had not dented his belief that on the whole, the scales were tipped in favor of good fortune over bad. He didn't have a shelter at home, and neither he nor his wife had given any thought to leaving town. "I'm working and bringing home money, so she's happy," Misika said.

To stage even this brief war in Lebanon, Israel had to call up large numbers of reserve soldiers who had not waged this kind of combat in years. Reservists were summoned from their civilian jobs and received only a few days of training before they were dispatched to Lebanon. Until the day the war broke, the main battle facing a typical Tel Aviv businessman in his thirties was the oppressive traffic that separated him from his home and the modern glass-and-steel tower where he worked. Just a few days into the war, however, many such businessmen found themselves in armored vehicles on the front lines of battle in a foreign country. Many reservists complained that they were woefully underprepared. Their skills and equipment were rusty, they said. Basic logistics, including food, water, and ammunition, were in short supply.

Michael Oren, a historian and an author in his early fifties, was a former paratrooper. He put on his uniform once again to serve as a military spokesman during the war. Oren, who became Israel's ambassador to the United States in 2009, wrote an authoritative and best-selling book on the 1967 war, *Six Days of War*, and has written frequently about Israel's military campaigns. One day near the end of the 2006 conflict, he joined me as we made our way up a rocky, scrub-brush hillside to look across a border fence into southern Lebanon. At this point, the war was a month old, and there was still shooting going on within sight of the border. It was a striking example of how difficult it was for Israel to clean out the small, pesky groups of Hezbollah fighters.

Oren cited several reasons for the Israeli shortcomings in the war. "One is the historical, psychological layer," he said. "No one wanted to go back into Lebanon. We spent eighteen years there. There was a fear of being bogged down." In Israel's 1982 invasion of Lebanon, Israel was expecting a short, successful campaign. The Israeli soldiers were actually greeted as liberators in southern Lebanon, where the poor, neglected Shiite communities felt that their territory had been overtaken by Yasser Arafat's PLO. Israel thought it could remake Lebanon but was quickly dragged into the chaos of the country's ruinous civil war. In southern Lebanon, Hezbollah began as a group of ragtag fighters, but with revolutionary Iran providing weapons and training, the Shiite guerrillas of Hezbollah became increasingly sophisticated.

"Then there is the diplomatic, strategic layer," said Oren. Aside from the United States, Israel did not have any real security partners, and it was particularly wary of the United Nations. Israel was concerned about getting stuck in Lebanon and being forced to work out a diplomatic solution at the United Nations, an arena that Israel always preferred to avoid. "We could go in and wait for an international force, but what if the international force doesn't come?" he asked. After Israel withdrew unilaterally from Lebanon in 2000, it had no appetite for a renewed occupation.

"The third layer is technical and economic. You can't do this without reserves," Oren said of the Israeli operation in Lebanon. "And very few combat reserves have undergone maneuvers. It's been years since the reserves were used to any great extent. The reservists haven't done this kind of training. You can't just throw them into battle. You have to give them time to practice maneuvers."

Oren noted that his military training bore little resemblance to that of his son, who had recently been wounded during an operation directed at Palestinian militants in the West Bank. "I was trained to take out Syrian tanks. He was trained to go into Hebron at two in the morning and grab a terrorist in a house."

There was at least one additional reason the war did not go well for Israel. The Israeli military once again bombed the town of Qana and once again slaughtered civilians. This time the Israeli air force dropped two bombs on a three-story apartment building on the edge of town, killing twenty-eight Lebanese on the night of July 30. Most of the dead belonged to two families who were sleeping in an underground garage, hoping that this would keep them safe. The Lebanese were outraged by the killings that rekindled the terrible memories of the 1996 Israeli attack.

Israel said it was unaware that civilians were in the building, and that the apartment block was targeted because Hezbollah militants were believed to be using it as cover for their rocket fire. Yet these mass killings of civilians have become a recurring feature of major Israeli military actions. Israel faces the difficult challenge of fighting militants who intentionally operate from civilian areas. The militants hope the civilians will serve as a shield, discouraging Israeli attacks. If Israel does strike, the inevitable civilian casualties provide a propaganda coup for the militants. Israel has fallen into this trap time and again and has suffered for it.

At the beginning of the 2006 war, Hezbollah was seen as the aggressor and came under sharp criticism, even in some parts of the Arab world. But the Israeli strikes soon inflicted heavy civilian casualties, which quickly turned international opinion against the Jewish state. The bombing in Qana, with its parallels to 1996, again put massive pressure on Israel to call off its operation. Israel suspended air strikes for forty-eight hours after the 2006 bombing in Qana. After this brief hiatus, Israel resumed its attacks. By this time, though, it was becoming clear that Israel would not score a decisive victory, and that a stalemate was once again the likely outcome.

In purely military terms, the 2006 war between Israel and Hezbollah was a marginal event. After thirty-four days of fighting, neither side could point to any significant gains. Israel seized Lebanese territory during the battle, yet such conquests had no real value. Israel did not want to reoccupy southern Lebanon, and the Israeli troops in their lumbering armored vehicles were easy targets for the stealthy Hezbollah fighters. In addition, Hezbollah could continue to launch rockets from forested hillsides or small farming communities and vanish before Israel could respond. For the Israeli military, it was an endless and seemingly futile task. Israel discovered yet again that conventional military superiority did not guarantee victory when fighting a foe that was prepared to absorb extensive casualties.

After the fighting, life in Israel quickly returned to normal. The economy recovered, and, for the first time in years, Hezbollah stopped firing rockets. Israel probably bought itself a few years of calm on its northern border. In the cycles of Middle East warfare, spasms of violence are generally followed by periods of relative quiet.

Lebanon, meanwhile, suffered another convulsive shock to the economy and its fragile political system. Many towns and villages in southern Lebanon had been flattened, and great damage was caused to apartment buildings, roads, communication lines, and the airport in Beirut. The Lebanese government and the Lebanese population were all much worse off after the war.

Yet even if Lebanon lost, Hezbollah could claim victory. Hezbollah's goal was not to defeat Israel militarily; it was simply to battle Israel for a limited period and to survive. Afterward, that would translate into increased political support. In practical terms, Hezbollah expended much of its arsenal and suffered heavy casualties.

That, however, was not how Hezbollah assessed the war. Hezbollah, like many others in the region, measured it in psychological terms. By this standard, the war was a significant boost for Hezbollah and its supporters in the Muslim world and a setback for Israel. Most important, Israel's deterrence suffered a blow. The Jewish state had to accept that it could not swiftly crush an enemy, despite its military superiority. Hezbollah showed that an Arab fighting force could bedevil Israel. As the postmortems took place, Israelis were virtually universal in expressing disappointment, while Israel's most radical enemies were greatly heartened.

Israel has waged three major military operations in the last decade, all with similar results. In 2002, Israel's West Bank incursion, Operation Defensive Shield, marked the moment that Palestinian suicide bombings started to decline, and they stopped almost completely within a couple of years. In 2006, the war with Hezbollah put an end, at least temporarily, to the rockets being launched from Lebanon. And in December 2008 and January 2009, an intensive three-week bombing campaign in Gaza greatly reduced the number of Palestinian rockets flying out of that territory.

Israel dealt effectively with the immediate threat in all of these instances. Yet none of these military actions gave Israel a real sense of victory. The operations did not solve the political problems in the West Bank, Gaza, or Lebanon. The groups that Israel targeted can still attack. Israel suffered political fallout at home and abroad. Inside Israel, many citizens wondered why Israel had not scored a decisive win. In the international arena, Israel faced heavy criticism for the extensive damage and the civilian casualties it inflicted.

As Israel's military planners look to the future, they see similar challenges. Hamas and other militant groups in Gaza have been working to improve their arsenals. Israel says that Iran has resupplied Hezbollah with powerful rockets that can reach major Israeli cities. And in the eyes of most Israelis, the greatest threat of all is Iran's nuclear program.

This is the ultimate Israeli nightmare, the prospect of a new Holocaust unleashed by a suicidal leadership in Tehran. The likelihood of attack by Iran is considered minimal, because Iran would face devastating retaliation, certainly from Israel, and most likely from the United States. Yet because the potential consequences of an Iran attack are so great, Iran and its nuclear program will be the obsession of the Israelis for years to come. Making predictions in such a fluid situation is folly, but Chuck Freilich, a former member of Israel's National Security Council, summed it up well. "First, the good news. It is difficult to imagine a practical scenario in which Iran would initiate the actual use of nuclear weapons against Israel," he wrote. "Now for the bad news. . . . When God is invoked, all bets are off. We cannot simply dismiss the possibility that the divine objective of destroying Israel is, somehow, worth the price, especially given the regime's apocalyptic character."

32

WHAT TO DO
WHEN FRIENDS
ARE KIDNAPPED

Lorenzo Cremonesi, a veteran reporter with the Italian newspaper *Corriere della Sera*, covered the Middle East for nearly
two decades and was as well connected as any foreigner in
the Gaza Strip. Yet as Gaza slid into anarchy, those credentials did
nothing to protect him.

One afternoon in September 2005, Lorenzo had just finished
interviewing Palestinian gunmen in central Gaza and was leaving
when a yellow Mercedes-Benz taxi pulled up and blocked the road
in front of his taxi. Three armed men jumped out, seized Lorenzo,
and threw him in the back of their vehicle. The first few moments
were tense. Then the atmosphere calmed. Soon it turned to farce.

The kidnappers, members of the Al Aksa Martyrs Brigades,
were clearly novices. They flailed about as they tried to decide
where to take their captive. They drove Lorenzo to several houses
before settling on one in the town of Deir al-Balah. After several
fractured conversations in English and Arabic, Lorenzo and his kidnappers discovered that it was easiest for them to communicate in

Hebrew. Lorenzo explained to his captors that it was crazy for the Palestinians to seize Western journalists who had come to tell the Palestinian story. The kidnappers repeatedly reassured him. "Don't worry, it's nothing personal. It's not against you, it's not against the press," they told him. They offered Lorenzo a Coca-Cola and told him to relax.

As the initial tension subsided, Lorenzo's reportorial instincts took over. He knew his capture would make a good story when it was over, and he asked the kidnappers whether he could take some notes. The kidnappers consented. Lorenzo then pressed a bit more and began to interview them, asking what they wanted. The aim was simple, the kidnappers said: they were unemployed and wanted jobs in the Palestinian security forces. Lorenzo would be their bargaining chip.

Lorenzo said he could help but would need to make a phone call. The kidnappers again granted permission, allowing Lorenzo to use his cell phone to call his newspaper in Italy. He explained to an editor that the story he had planned to write might be a little late, but he had a good excuse. He then detailed his predicament, and within moments of the call, Lorenzo's kidnapping was posted on *Corriere della Sera*'s Web site. From there, Al Jazeera and the other pan-Arab satellite channels picked it up. The kidnappers were thrilled. They had received far more attention than they ever imagined. A flurry of phone calls ensued as the kidnappers made contact with the Palestinian Authority over the terms of Lorenzo's release. Less than six hours into the kidnapping, a deal was struck, and Lorenzo was to be set free.

The three kidnappers took Lorenzo to an olive orchard, where they waited for a car that would liberate him. First, though, they had to scale a six-foot fence. Before the first kidnapper climbed over, he handed his AK-47 rifle to the second kidnapper. As the second gunman prepared to climb, he handed the two rifles to kidnapper number three. And when the last gunman was ready to climb, he handed all three rifles to . . . Lorenzo.

"It was such a joke," said Lorenzo. "There I was holding all three Kalashnikovs. I passed them over the fence, then I climbed over myself. As you can imagine, I didn't really feel in danger."

As the gunmen had promised, Lorenzo was released a short while later. He was mostly amused by the episode, and instead of leaving Gaza, he decided to stay and work on some more stories.

Two days later, he was taken to the Gaza City offices of President Mahmoud Abbas. "I've been waiting for a long time to interview you," Lorenzo told the president. "I didn't know it would take a kidnapping to get it." Lorenzo also asked, out of curiosity rather than vengeance, what would happen to the kidnappers. Abbas dodged the question, but Lorenzo later heard from other Palestinian sources that his captors had received their wish and become policemen.

When Western journalists and aid workers first started to get kidnapped in Gaza after the Palestinian uprising began, it was more often comedy than drama. The victim was a source of leverage, and kidnappers would usually keep him in the living room of a private home, where he would be offered endless cups of tea and home-cooked meals. Josh Hammer, the *Newsweek* correspondent, said after his brief confinement in 2001 that the best meal he ever had in Gaza was during his captivity. Time and again, the hostage-takers patiently explained to the hostage that he was really a "guest," and that as soon as the matter was resolved, he would be on his way, unharmed. For several years, the kidnappers kept their word, and without fail, the victims would emerge and remark on the good manners and the excellent hospitality of their captors.

About thirty Western journalists and aid workers were seized in Gaza from 2001 to 2006, and in almost every case, the kidnappers wanted one of two things: a job in the Palestinian security forces or the release of a relative held in a Palestinian jail. The rules of the game were established early on, and as long as everyone played his assigned role, the negotiations usually went without a hitch. If the kidnappers did not get greedy with their demands, the Palestinian Authority usually complied within hours. The Westerner was often free and on his way home before sundown. This acquiescence by the Palestinian Authority only encouraged additional kidnappings. Palestinian officials, however, were far more concerned about the negative publicity that would be generated by a protracted kidnapping involving a Westerner, and Palestinian leaders displayed a rare sense of urgency when dealing with these cases.

For years, we never hesitated to travel to Gaza. I averaged about one trip a month, usually for three or four days at a time. Jennifer went slightly less often but was also a regular visitor. Together, we made more than a hundred trips to the territory. We were always treated hospitably, aside from the occasional rants from finger-wagging Palestinians. When they learned we were American, they would sometimes express their anger that the United States had supplied the hardware, including Apache helicopters and F-16 fighter planes, for Israel's bombardments of Gaza.

My *New York Times* colleague James Bennet did have a narrow escape when he traveled to southern Gaza to cover a major incursion by Israeli troops in May 2004. The Israeli forces were trying to stop weapons smuggling into Gaza via underground tunnels from neighboring Egypt. The violence was intense, with dozens of Palestinians killed in the area over several days. Toward the end of one blood-soaked day, James visited the Al Najar Hospital in the town of Rafah for a firsthand look at the Palestinian casualties.

As James walked out of the hospital, he was talking on his cell phone, preparing to be interviewed by NPR in Washington. He attracted the attention of several young Palestinian men, and one approached him. James tried to politely gesture that he was busy talking, and sensed something was a bit strange. The Palestinian continued toward James and extended his hand to shake. James hesitated, but as he began to reciprocate, the man and an accomplice grabbed James and tried to shove him into the back of a nearby Mercedes sedan parked in front of the hospital. James resisted and shouted for help as the would-be kidnappers kept trying to push him inside.

James's plea came through loud and clear to the NPR studios in Washington as they prepared to tape him, but the Palestinians milling about in front of the hospital did not respond immediately. After about a minute of scuffling and shouting between James and his assailants, Palestinian policemen came to the rescue and pulled James away. The policemen then scolded the kidnappers and slapped one of them in the face. Yet no one was arrested. The police placed James in the back of their squad car and sped away at an alarming rate of speed. This was the most unnerving part of the entire episode, according to James, whose only injury was a sore throat from yelling. James played down the episode, mentioning it only briefly at the bottom of the article he wrote that day about the fighting in southern Gaza.

This was still the era of amateur kidnappings. Yet they were becoming too frequent to ignore, and the potential for a misstep was growing. We saw the kidnappings as a barometer of Gaza's steady descent into anarchy. Despite the territory's many problems, Gazans had always treated foreigners as honored guests. In addition, the political leadership and the educated elite in Gaza understood the need to court foreigners in order to draw international attention to the plight of Gaza. As Gaza unraveled, however, extremists gained the upper hand. They viewed Westerners merely as bargaining chips and were not concerned about how the kidnappings reflected on the Palestinians in the wider world.

In June 2006, Palestinian militants dug a long tunnel under Gaza's border fence, emerged on the other side, and assaulted an Israeli military post. As was mentioned previously, the attackers from Hamas and other factions killed two Israeli soldiers and kidnapped a third, Gilad Shalit, who was dragged back into Gaza. The kidnapping of an Israeli was far more serious than the taking of a Westerner. Even at this date, a Westerner could expect to be freed unscathed, but the Palestinians were sure to make the most of a captured Israeli soldier, and as of this writing, Shalit has remained in captivity.

Despite these conditions, Jennifer and I still considered it safe enough to travel to Gaza. I made several trips during the summer of 2006, although I took some special precautions. Previously, I had stayed at hotels along Gaza's seafront, but kidnappers had recently seized several Westerners from these hotels. So I began to stay in the high-rise apartment belonging to George Azar, an Arab American photographer who was living in Gaza City and working with the *Times*.

As I wrapped up a visit to Gaza in August, one of the last Western journalists still working in the territory was Jennifer's Fox colleague Steve Centanni. When I was leaving, I ran into Steve, who was reporting from Gaza's northern border with Israel. I wished him well and told him to turn out the lights when he left Gaza.

Less than two weeks later, Steve and Fox cameraman Olaf Wiig wrapped up their working day in Gaza City and got in their armored car to head back to the nearby Beach Hotel. They had traveled only a few blocks when a green Toyota pickup truck pulled in front of them, and several masked gunmen jumped out. They seized the two Fox journalists, stuffed them in the second row of the pickup, and placed hoods over their heads.

As the truck sped off, Steve asked, "Where are we going?"

"To hell," said one of the kidnappers.

On that day, August 13, many Western journalists, including Jennifer and me, were on Israel's northern border, covering what was the final full day of the war between Israel and Hezbollah. It did not take long for the news from Gaza to reach us.

We received a phone call from Gaza during the afternoon while we were sitting in the makeshift Fox workspace in an apartment building. Our camera was set up to broadcast from the building's roof, which overlooked the border with Lebanon. We had endured weeks of Katyusha rockets, and our nerves were fried. Every time I heard a thud, I tried to determine whether it was incoming or outgoing. Back-to-back thuds meant it was an outgoing Israeli artillery shell. A single thud meant an incoming Hezbollah rocket. It was often difficult for me to distinguish initially, but my Israeli team, all of them military veterans, knew instinctively. A cease-fire had been reached, and it was set to begin the following dawn. I worked through the night, as I had all during the war, and finished up at 5 a.m., shortly before the cease-fire went into effect. As advertised, the guns went silent. Fox's bureau chief Eli Fastman and I then drove straight to Gaza.

Eli had worked in Gaza many times previously but was putting himself in great danger by going to the territory at this sensitive moment. He carried both a U.S. and an Israeli passport. Yet for the Gazans, the Israeli nationality was the only one that counted, and Eli would be a huge prize for kidnappers in the territory. As a woman, Jennifer felt that she was less likely to be kidnapped than a man, regardless of nationality. They were soon joined by Olaf's wife, Anita McNaught. She, too, was a journalist and had received the news of her husband's kidnapping while working in Damascus. She traveled overnight by road from Syria, going through Jordan and Israel to reach Gaza the following day.

Jennifer and her colleagues first stopped at the office of Abu Askar, a Gazan who ran a media center and had worked closely with the Fox journalists for years. He knew all of the key figures in the territory. In New York, Fox News chairman Roger Ailes agreed to let Jennifer and her colleagues pursue their contacts in Gaza, while he pressed the State Department, the FBI, and others in the government to seek the release of the journalists.

Yet soon there were signs of trouble. The kidnapping was rumored to be the work of a man named Mumtaz Daghmush. Gazans who had known him since his school days described him as extremely dangerous but not very bright. He also had one lazy eye that wandered. He was the shadowy leader of the Daghmush clan, a poor family that had become rich and powerful by mastering a range of illegal activities. The clan smuggled guns and other contraband through tunnels that ran beneath the Gaza-Egypt border. They carried out killings and performed other favors for Hamas, although that relationship was fraying as Hamas became more powerful and the Daghmush clan felt inadequately compensated for its services.

We thought we might be able to resolve the kidnapping quickly, using our contacts on the ground. We wanted to avoid the prospect of an outside group, such as the Israeli military, staging a raid that would likely involve shooting. We tried to put the pieces together to see who might have Steve and Olaf. We met with our Palestinian assistant who had been working with Steve and Olaf at the time of the abduction. The assistant learned that the kidnappers' vehicle had been seen at an ice cream shop shortly beforehand, and he went to talk to the employees. There was a bank next door, and we requested the videotape from the security camera. In the meantime, the FBI called and wanted to do a credit card check. It seemed like a preposterous notion in a place like Gaza, where no one used credit cards, but the Fox bureau in Washington tracked down Steve's and Olaf's credit card numbers just in case the kidnappers had taken their cards and had started to use them.

Meanwhile, Steve and Olaf faced much harsher treatment than any previous Western hostages ever did. The kidnappers were extremely hostile during the first few hours. They kicked Steve and Olaf and hit them with pistols. The two men were blindfolded, with their hands cuffed behind them so tightly that their shoulders burned from the strain. They were taken to an industrial building and forced to lie facedown on a dirty concrete floor.

Later they were moved to another building, which seemed to be part of a mosque. They could hear the call to prayer and were told to take off their shoes. The kidnappers eventually took Steve's and Olaf's clothes and gave them track suits to wear. Communication was difficult. Steve and Olaf spoke only a few words of Arabic, and none of the kidnappers spoke English well. One of them, a man named Abdullah, ranted at them in pidgin English: "U.S., Israel kill Palestinians. America kill Islam. Bush kill Islam in Iraq."

On their second day of captivity, the kidnappers drove Steve and Olaf to a house where they would spend the duration of their kidnapping. The two men thought they were somewhere north of Gaza City, but it was only a guess. They tried to determine the identity of their kidnappers and their motives, but little was clear. Unlike other kidnappers, these men did not talk about getting jobs as policemen. Rather, they were obsessed with radical Islam. The kidnappers said they did not like any Palestinian factions. Instead, they praised Osama bin Laden. "Osama is good. Osama is king," one kidnapper said.

When the kidnappers brought Steve and Olaf a Toshiba laptop computer that featured an English-language presentation on Islam, the screensaver was a portrait of bin Laden. The kidnappers also supplied a steady stream of books and pamphlets on Islam, ranging from the Koran to *Islam Forbids the Free Mixing of Men and Women*.

Olaf began Islamic Studies 101 with great zeal, looking for theological ammunition he could use to tell the kidnappers that it was against Islam to hold hostages or to harm them. He read nearly one-third of the Koran in one day, finishing his studies on page 178. Steve, a reluctant student, reached page 22. Olaf reminded his kidnappers when prayer time was approaching, and he let his blond beard grow, hoping it would make him appear more pious. Steve remained clean-shaven.

We met one shadowy Palestinian leader after another but began to feel as if we were hitting a brick wall. Some Palestinians genuinely wanted to help. They realized that holding Western journalists was not serving their cause. But we were getting nowhere. So we opted for a more public approach. Abu Askar, our Palestinian colleague, called Palestinian reporters in Gaza and arranged for them to demonstrate outside the Palestinian

Interior Ministry in Gaza City. One of our many meetings had taken place there with the interior minister, Said Siam of Hamas. At the demonstration, Olaf's wife, Anita, made an emotional appeal to the women of Gaza for help. "There is no good reason for these two men to be held. They are friends of the Palestinians. They are here telling the Palestinian story," she told the gathering of about 150 people. It was broadcast in Gaza, in Israel, and across the West Bank. In some ways, we were trying to shame the Palestinian mothers and sisters of the Daghmush clan to pressure their relatives or neighbors to release Steve and Olaf. The response from the Palestinian public was positive, but it was not clear whether it had any impact on the kidnappers.

The Fox team continued to hold endless meetings with every influential group in Gaza. They shuttled between Hamas leaders and Fatah officials, security force officers, and Egyptian intelligence officials who had contacts with all of the main players in the territory. Yet no one seemed to have hard information or a clear way out of the crisis.

A crucial meeting came late one night at the upscale apartment of Muhammad Dahlan, the former security chief in Gaza who had been a close ally of Yasser Arafat. With Dahlan's many bodyguards also in attendance, the discussion became increasingly tense. It also became clear that Eli and Dahlan could communicate most easily in Hebrew.

Dahlan, like many Palestinians, had learned Hebrew in an Israeli jail. Since arriving in Gaza, Eli had been speaking exclusively in English to disguise the fact that he was Israeli. Speaking in Hebrew exposed Eli to even greater risk, but he felt the need to be absolutely clear with Dahlan. "You're the big guy. This is your territory. Why can't you sort this out?" Eli Fastman said to Dahlan.

The meeting lasted until close to midnight, but the evening was just getting started. Dahlan told his bodyguards to take me and my Fox colleagues to another meeting. We were getting paranoid. We didn't know whom to trust. As we entered the elevator to leave the apartment, we did not know exactly where we were being taken. I quickly and quietly sent an e-mail on my BlackBerry to John Moody, Fox's vice president of news in New York, describing our location just in case something happened to us.

Dahlan's drivers, traveling in a caravan of SUVs, delivered us to the home of another Fatah leader, Ahmed Hilas. The Palestinian men greeted one another with kisses on both cheeks. We were invited to sit under a tin-roofed garage attached to the apartment building. The chairs were arranged in a circle, and all of the major Palestinian factions were represented. It was pitch black because there was no electricity in the neighborhood. Israeli war planes had knocked out Gaza's power supply in the recent weeks of fighting. The headlights from pickup trucks were turned on and provided the only light. The ubiquitous bodyguards, with AK-47s slung casually over their shoulders, stood watch on the periphery.

It was a very strange scene. The old, bearded Palestinian men played with the worry beads in their hands. They sat silently, avoiding eye contact. Then there were the three of us—an Israeli man and two women. The meeting was uncomfortable, and, to add to the anxiety, we could hear the buzz of an Israeli drone overhead. The sound grated like gnats that you could hear but not see. Israel relied on the drones to track militants and fire missiles. A drone usually tracked one militant at a time; a garage full of them would have been a bonanza for the Israeli air force.

The meeting went poorly. No one volunteered information, and everyone claimed ignorance regarding the whereabouts of our two Fox colleagues. Eventually, I could not take it anymore. I was boiling as I listened to the excuses in Arabic and watched the men tiptoe around the issue, not looking me or Anita in the eyes. I lost patience and stood up. "Gentlemen, we are your guests in Gaza," I began. "Anita's husband is being held by one of your groups. I do not care about your internal politics. You know where these men are. Mumtaz Daghmush has them, and you can get them out."

After my impromptu speech, one of the Palestinian men picked up his cell phone and, in front of the entire group, called Mumtaz Daghmush, whose bodyguard answered on the first ring and gave the phone to Daghmush. "Mumtaz, do you have the two journalists?" the caller asked in Arabic. That much I could understand. "La." "No," said Mumtaz.

Ahmed Hilas turned to the group and said to us in English, "He says he doesn't have them."

"Bullshit," I said. I was seething. The circle of Arab men were not used to hearing a woman speak like that—women usually did not speak at all. The meeting ended abruptly, and there was no breakthrough in sight. Eli could no longer pretend to be just an American, and soon after that midnight meeting, he left Gaza, rather than risk becoming a kidnapping victim himself.

. . .

Around this time, Steve and Olaf received ominous news. The kidnappers told the two men they would have to appear in videos. Steve and Olaf were ordered to write the scripts, and they would be filmed with Olaf's camera, which the kidnappers had stolen when they seized the two men. At that time, kidnapped Westerners were being beheaded in Iraq, and Steve and Olaf feared a similar fate. Olaf was then taken away to a darkened room to meet one of the captors. The other kidnappers called him Abu Khaled, but Steve and Olaf nicknamed him the Scary Mullah. He was dressed in black fatigues and had his face covered with scarves, except for a slit that revealed his eyes. As Olaf's eyes adjusted to the darkness, he saw two AK-47 rifles propped up behind the man and a machete on the floor in front of him.

The Scary Mullah peppered Olaf with questions. "What is Islam? What about Jesus? Do you go to church?" The Scary Mullah told Olaf, a native of New Zealand, that he could expect decent treatment because his country "didn't kill Muslims." Olaf could gain freedom by embracing Islam, he added.

Yet the Scary Mullah went on to say, "Steve is a dangerous guy. He is in the CIA and is spying for Israel to help them find Gilad Shalit [the kidnapped Israeli soldier]. He's been spying for the U.S. military in Iraq, Afghanistan, and Pakistan." Olaf spent a half-hour trying to persuade the Scary Mullah that Steve was only a journalist who had worked in all of these troubled places, but the Scary Mullah was not convinced and said that Steve would have to be killed. He then told Olaf not to speak to Steve of their discussion.

When Steve entered the room for his session, he feared the worst, but the Scary Mullah did not repeat any of the earlier accusations, and Steve left, feeling at least a small sense of relief. "I felt this was my death scene. It was the scariest freak show I had ever seen—this mysterious guy with the guns. But all I got from him was an Islamic pep talk."

When they compared notes afterward, Olaf told Steve only that they should study Islam. He did not pass on the rest of the conversation, feeling that it would make their predicament unbearable for Steve. "I'm thinking, How am I going to get Steve out of this? How am I going to get Steve to play a good Muslim boy?" Olaf said later.

Olaf, the son of a minister, had little trouble adopting a religious persona. "I told them that I saw they had a passion for their religion, they were at peace when they prayed, and I needed that in my life." Steve was much less convincing, at least to himself. "I thought they could see right through me, but they seemed to accept me at face value."

The kidnappers gave them both a crash course in Islam and showed the men how to wash themselves before prayer and the precise method of prayer, including the points of contact with the ground—the tips of the toes, the knees, the hands, and the forehead, but not the elbows. They were given Muslim names: Yacoub for Olaf and Khaled for Steve. "We are brothers now," one kidnapper told them. "When you come to Gaza next time, you can call us, and we'll help you."

After one week, it suddenly appeared that it was all over. The kidnappers told Steve and Olaf they would be freed the next day. All of the unread books and pamphlets on Islam, it seemed, were for self-directed study at a later date. The next day Steve and Olaf could barely contain their anticipation. The captors failed to say exactly when they would be released, however, so Steve and Olaf asked when the car would be coming to get them. "It will not be coming yet," one kidnapper said. "You need more time to study Islam."

It was the longest and most depressing day of their captivity. "We both sank into a terrible funk," said Steve.

Our team continued to shuttle between meetings, but after talks at the apartment of two Egyptian intelligence officers, our Palestinian colleagues, who hadn't left our side since the ordeal began, noticed that we were being trailed by a green Toyota pickup. The men in the pickup were videotaping our team, and they were identified as members of the Daghmush clan. At that point, I got spooked. We weren't making progress, and I felt that it was irresponsible to stay. I was thinking of my kids. We were hearing rumors that the kidnappers wanted to nab another member of the Fox team. I panicked and called John Moody, the Fox vice president in New York. "I'm done," I told him.

The next day, I walked down the Erez passage to the Gaza exit. I was accompanied by Anita and Ken LaCorte, a Fox executive who had flown in from Los Angeles. Also with us was our Palestinian team, including

Abu Askar, who had been so dedicated over the years. When we reached the
Palestinian immigration officers and turned in our passports for inspec-
tion, I was choked with emotion. I hugged Abu Askar and could not let
go. The tears did not stop as I kissed everyone on both cheeks. I knew I
would not be coming back to Gaza. Yet my Palestinian colleagues could
not leave, even if they wanted to. I felt as if I was abandoning them, along
with Steve and Olaf. I was filled with a feeling of defeat and despair. We
placed a call to Roger Ailes to tell him we were almost out of Gaza. All I
could say was, "I'm sorry, Roger."

Anita insisted on going back to Gaza, and Ken would not let her
return alone. The two went back the next day but limited their movements
and lowered their profile.

Steve and Olaf, meanwhile, starred in four videos, including one
that showed them dismantling and reassembling an AK-47. Not all
were made public, but one was distributed on the same day that the
kidnappers issued a sweeping demand for the release of all Muslim
prisoners held in the United States. The video showed Steve and
Olaf sitting cross-legged and barefoot, dressed in warm-up suits.
They appeared relaxed but pleaded for help. "We are alive and
well," Steve said. "We are in fairly good health. We get lots of clean
water, food every day. Access to a bathroom, shower, clean clothes,
and our captors are treating us well."

The significance of the video was open to interpretation. It suggested that the kidnappers wanted to engage in negotiations, which
was hopeful. Yet their demand for the release of Muslim prisoners
in the United States would not be met, and it showed for the first
time that this extremism might be connected to something larger
than the Israeli-Palestinian conflict.

In his own mind, Steve was contemplating the worst. He thought
that he and Olaf would remain captive until September 11—the
fifth anniversary of the World Trade Center attacks, which was only
a few weeks away. Then, Steve said, he believed that they would be
"killed in a very public way."

After the video was released, several days of silence and uncer-
tainty followed. Then, without rhyme or reason, Steve and Olaf
received a new promise from the kidnappers: they were told they
would be freed the next morning. The two men spent a sleepless

night, fearing that their hopes would once again be dashed. The morning came, and nothing happened. But at midday, the kidnappers sprang into action. They blindfolded Steve and Olaf and placed them in a car. The two men asked to be taken to the Beach Hotel, where they had been staying before they were seized. Both expected a complicated arrangement, but it proved to be as abrupt as their kidnapping was. Olaf sensed the car reversing, and one of the captors simply said, "Go."

"I didn't need to be told twice," said Olaf, "I leaped out of the car." He staggered into the hotel lobby, along with Steve, where they were immediately mobbed by well-wishers. They pushed their way up the stairs to a room. After two weeks in captivity, they were free.

Steve and Olaf were safe, but the game had changed. It was clear that Western journalists could not move freely in Gaza. After the Fox kidnappings, I made only a few brief visits to Gaza, and Jennifer did not go back.

Six months later, in March 2007, the only Western reporter living in Gaza full time, Alan Johnston of the British Broadcasting Corporation, was seized. Alan is a thoughtful, understated Scotsman with a Zen-like calm that allowed him to thrive in some of the most difficult places in the world. Yet nothing could have prepared him for the ordeal he faced.

Once again, Mumtaz Daghmush appeared to be behind the kidnapping. The strongest evidence linking Alan's kidnapping to the earlier one was a man whom all of the hostages knew as Khamis. He had a pronounced limp in his right leg and claimed that it was the result of a gun battle with the Israeli troops several years earlier. He was a sullen man who had occasionally guarded Steve and Olaf. In Alan's case, Khamis was the main guard and was even more unpredictable than during the previous kidnapping. Khamis was often moody and distant and would barely speak to Alan for days at a time. Occasionally, though, Khamis was friendly, allowing Alan into his room to watch television or to talk about politics and Islam. Alan spent four hellish months as a hostage, and moments before he was about to be freed, Khamis said good-bye by punching Alan in the face.

"It was a vast psychological battle, knowing I might be there three, four, or five years. I had to brace myself for that possibility," Alan said afterward. "It's hard to recapture the horror of that now. There is this crushing sense of captivity, this desperate desire for all of it to end. You want to be back in the place you belong, to speak to people, to walk in the sun, to eat what you want. There is the bitterness of coping, of worrying about my parents, the anxiety and fear and depression."

In the years since, Hamas has gained full control of Gaza. The daily violence has ended and the occasional Western visitors are no longer targeted for kidnapping, but the territory's larger problems remain. Israel continues to keep a constant watch on Gaza, limiting the flow of people and goods. Alan, meanwhile, returned to London to work at the BBC headquarters. He still follows the grim news out of Gaza but doesn't seek it out. "Gaza is an onrushing disaster," Alan said when I spoke with him after his ordeal. "Right in the heart of the Mediterranean is this rotten, fetid entity that is getting worse all the time. Every wall you see has posters and names of martyrs. Every house has the flag of some faction. There is this hot dry wind from the Sinai and the humid, salty air from the sea. There is always someone shouting about something. It may be the vegetable seller, people complaining about traffic, or the chanting at a funeral with gunmen firing in the air. I've never been any place in the world that is such a pressure cooker."

33

IS THERE A SOLUTION?

The longer you stay in the Middle East, the harder it becomes to imagine peace. For new arrivals, answers to the big questions appear obvious. The formula is clear: two states for two peoples, with some tweaks to the boundaries that existed before the 1967 war. Israel will have to leave most of the West Bank, although it will probably keep the largest settlement blocs. In return for any West Bank land it retains, Israel will have to give up comparable territory that is now part of Israel. The Palestinian state will include all of Gaza and most of the West Bank. The Palestinians will also get a capital in East Jerusalem, although Israelis will probably remain in the Jewish neighborhoods in that part of the city. The Palestinian refugees scattered throughout the Middle East and around the globe will be allowed to move to the new Palestinian state, though only a small minority will be permitted to live in Israel, even if they once owned land there. This is the conventional wisdom.

A million details need to be resolved, and someone with a weapon will always be plotting to undermine the peace efforts. Yet the outlines of a peace plan are not hard to fathom; it is the getting from here to there that is the problem. The conflict has quite literally become a way of life. If you date the start of the conflict to 1948—you could certainly go back earlier—this means that almost every Israeli and Palestinian under the age of retirement was born into the feud and has known nothing else for his or her entire life. Grandfathers fought in the war of 1948, fathers fought in the battle of 1967, and the sons have waged war in the last decade.

The conflict also draws in many outsiders—diplomats, journalists, and aid workers—and usually, within a few years, it drives them out, often in despair, if not disgust. "A plague on both your houses" is a popular theme at going-away parties. Many veterans of the feud tend to see only encrusted disputes and dysfunctional relations between two peoples who have learned to live, however unhappily, in a permanent state of friction. Cynicism becomes a comfortable and unassailable position. Things can always get worse, and they usually do. We battled this affliction, with mixed results. Yet without thinking very long or very hard, we came up with a list of ten major obstacles that will have to be overcome to reach a solution:

1. Peacemaking in the Middle East has a long tradition of failure. The international community has made three major attempts to resolve the conflict in the last century. Each time, it took a seismic global event to launch the process. Following World War I, the League of Nations gave the British a mandate to rule the land of Palestine. During a quarter-century of British management, the conflict simmered and occasionally bubbled over, but nothing was settled. The second big push came in the wake of World War II and the Holocaust, with the proposal for a two-state solution by the nascent United Nations. Israel got its state, but the Arabs rejected the plan, and the conflict erupted in full. The third big effort came as the Cold War wound down in the early 1990s. The Palestinians and the Israelis negotiated for most of the decade, but diplomacy ultimately gave way to bloodletting. History may not repeat itself, but it does have a lot of rhymes, as Mark Twain said. It may well take another global realignment before the world attempts another major drive for a comprehensive peace treaty.

2. The Israelis and the Palestinians both have divided societies and pedestrian leaders. There is neither an Israeli consensus nor a Palestinian consensus about how to proceed, and neither society has a dominant leader who can take it to the Promised Land. On the Israeli side, coalition politics makes it difficult, if not impossible, for an individual leader or party to take bold action. The

prime minister is constantly trying to keep his coalition patched together. Any dramatic move—such as a possible peace deal—is likely to tear the coalition apart. The Palestinians, meanwhile, cannot even agree on a single leader, as the rival fiefdoms in the West Bank and Gaza become more entrenched. The larger-than-life figures at the center of the conflict for decades, the Ariel Sharons and the Yasser Arafats, have passed from the scene. They did not make the compromises that were needed for peace. Yet ironically, leaders of their stature and clout will likely be required to forge a deal and make it stick, and these figures have not yet emerged.

3. Jerusalem—the city's fate may be the single hardest issue to resolve, due to its symbolic importance and the religious passions that are part of Jerusalem's bedrock. Both sides have a large, permanent presence in the city, and neither is prepared to relinquish its claim to Jerusalem's Old City and its holy sites. Most religious leaders on both sides reject talk of compromise and are seen more as obstacles to a solution, rather than as potential problem solvers.

4. Too many Palestinian militants have been wedded to armed struggle. Palestinian violence has been a disaster for the Palestinian cause, and never more so than in the last decade. As a society, the Palestinians have been unable to abandon self-defeating violence and contain their most radical elements.

5. Israel cannot stop building settlements. Around five hundred thousand Israelis live beyond Israel's 1967 borders, in East Jerusalem and the West Bank, and their numbers are growing by up to fifteen thousand a year. There is no way to create a viable Palestinian state if all of these Israelis remain in place. Yet every Israeli government in the last four decades has allowed the overall settlement population to expand.

6. Hamas now has a major institutional role in Palestinian politics. During the peace negotiations of the 1990s, the premise was that Arafat would keep Hamas and other radicals in line. Hamas is now too big and too strong to be suppressed. It looks set to control Gaza indefinitely, giving the Islamist group veto power over any peace plan.

7. The Israeli and Palestinian economies have been largely detached from each other. Israel has prospered and learned not only to survive, but to thrive without Palestinian labor. The Palestinian

economy, particularly in Gaza, has been crippled. Strong, integrated economies could assist the cause of peace. Divided economies and rampant Palestinian poverty make peace much more difficult.

8. The broader region is a mess. The conflicts in Iraq and Afghanistan, Western tensions with Iran, sectarian friction in Lebanon, and instability in Pakistan all contribute to a dysfunctional region that seems mired in turmoil for the long term. When Israelis look beyond their borders, they feel less secure and are therefore less willing to make concessions when it comes to the Palestinians.

9. The U.S. role has evolved in ways that have complicated peace-making. For many years, under multiple administrations, the United States has too often been uncritically supportive of Israel and has acquiesced even when Israel pursued policies that damaged peace prospects. The United States will have to be an honest broker that is willing to invoke its considerable leverage with both sides to forge a deal.

10. The Israelis and the Palestinians hate one another. This often trumps all else. After decades of fighting, both sides instinctively opt for confrontation over cooperation. No one has been able to change this psychology and break this destructive pattern. All of the best-laid plans can be undermined by the passions and the raw emotions that may boil over at any moment and that tend to erupt at the most sensitive times. Solid majorities of Israelis and Palestinians have to genuinely want peace, or it will not happen.

Faced with our own evidence, we had only one counterargument that pointed to the possibility of peace, however remote. Even on the darkest days, we encountered ordinary Israelis and Palestinians who defiantly lived their daily lives as if the feud was about to end at any moment. Like almost everyone else, they had been harmed by the conflict, sometimes grievously, yet they refused to dwell on the anguish and the heartache and behaved as if a rosy dawn was imminent.

Two individuals in particular embodied this spirit. One was Zalie Miller, our first landlord in Jerusalem. The other was Dr. Izzeldin Abuelaish, a Palestinian physician in Gaza.

Zalie lived the Jewish twentieth century. He was pushing ninety when we became his tenants in the fall of 1999 in a graceful Bauhaus building on Marcus Street in the Talbieh neighborhood. Zalie and his wife, Arline, lived right below us on the ground floor. The Israeli president's office and residence were just a block to the west, and the prime minister's official residence was only two blocks to the north. It was a lovely neighborhood, filled with grand stone houses. Zalie had reached this place after a remarkable journey, one filled with trauma and dislocation as he bounced from Europe to Africa, to the Middle East, surviving everything from war to revolution to genocide.

He was born in 1911 in the village of Ramygala, Lithuania, in what was then part of the wheezing Russian Empire. From his earliest days, Zalie had a Zelig-like knack for popping up amid the world's most monumental events. World War I erupted when he was only three. Shortly thereafter, Russia's Czar Nicholas II, whose reign was studded with anti-Semitic pogroms, removed Jews living near the Western front. In 1915, Zalie, the youngest of eight siblings, was evacuated along with the rest of his family and many other Lithuanian Jews, for resettlement deep in the Russian interior. Zalie's family was dispatched to Penza, four hundred miles southeast of Moscow. His father found work as a glazier, repairing buildings, while his mother labored in a bakery. Not only did his family spend the rest of the war in the town, they also lived through the tumult of the Russian Revolution in 1917. "The people were always talking about it," Zalie recalled. "I knew it was something big, but I was just a kid, and I didn't understand."

As we listened to Zalie's stories, they were particularly poignant in the final days of a tumultuous century because it seemed as if Zalie and his compatriots were on the cusp of peace, security, and an ordinary life. This quest for normality—*normaliyut*, in Hebrew—was a recurring theme in conversations with Israelis of any age. "When will we be normal?" and "If only we were normal," were regular Israeli refrains. The goal was to pursue everyday lives without having to worry about a suicide bomber sitting next to them on the bus. Israelis were tired of being yanked from prosperous civilian lives and sent on military duty to Gaza or the West Bank. They were weary of waking up to newspapers that endlessly debated the probability of a missile strike from Lebanon or the status of Iran's

nuclear program. Against great odds, Israel has made itself a success, but Israelis have never been able to relax and enjoy it.

Zalie seemed to be someone who had found normality. He was
active, healthy, and prosperous. He spent his days working in his
garden, and you could set your watch by his daily walks. He and
Arline were surrounded by friends in one of Jerusalem's best neighborhoods. They often spent weekends at a kibbutz, in the company
of their three grown kids and their grandchildren. Zalie was an avid
student of the country's politics and a big supporter of negotiations
with the Palestinians. Peace seemed a fitting and fair conclusion
to Zalie's long trip. "This is a historic opportunity," Zalie told me
more than once.

Zalie not only knew history, he had lived it. Zalie's family was
able to leave revolutionary Russia and return to an independent
Lithuania in 1921, when he was ten. Yet Zalie had great difficulty
fitting in because he spoke Yiddish and Russian—but virtually no
Lithuanian. "I was placed in a Lithuanian school, and I was miserable," Zalie recalled. "My father took me out after less than a year
and put me in a yeshiva, though we really couldn't afford it." Zalie
flourished at the yeshiva, where his mentor was a youth a year older
than him, Israel Brog. The two would maintain a lifelong friendship. Both would wind up in Israel, where Brog helped found a
kibbutz and fathered a son, Ehud, who changed the family name to
Barak and became a prime minister.

After graduating from the yeshiva, Zalie was conscripted into
the Lithuanian military. Serving in the armed forces of a country
with a powerful anti-Semitic streak inspired Zalie to explore the
possibility of moving to what was then British-ruled Palestine. Yet
the British had greatly restricted visas for Jews who wished to immigrate, blocking that path. Zalie bided his time, and as World War II
broke out in 1939, he was again called up to the Lithuanian army.
When he was released from duty at the beginning of 1940, he was
determined to leave but found himself trapped in a no-man's-land
between Hitler's Germany and Stalin's Soviet Union. Zalie decided
that his least-bad option was to seek a visa for the Soviet Union.
When he applied, the Soviet consul asked him why. "There is no
future for Jews in Lithuania," Zalie said, without an inkling of
the horrors that awaited Lithuanian Jewry. "He received me very
warmly but said he would not give me a Soviet visa, because I would
be stuck there." The Soviet consul advised Zalie to leave Europe,

although this would mean a trip across Germany. "It is not dangerous in transit," the Soviet consul told Zalie. "You won't have to mix
and mingle with the Germans."

Zalie and a friend left Lithuania in March 1940, and the trip
proved to be more eventful than was forecast. As they crossed Germany, they had to change trains in Berlin. "The conductor looked
at our tickets and said we couldn't get on his train," Zalie said. "My
Lithuanian companion was devastated. But we snuck around to the
other side and got on in the overflow section and sat on stools. The
conductor saw us and said he would throw us out at the next station. I offered him a pound of cheese that I had in my coat pocket.
He accepted it and let us stay. We stayed on the train all the way to
Italy." Once in Italy, Zalie boarded a ship in Genoa, aptly called the
Palestina, and left Europe behind.

Three months after his departure, in June 1940, the Soviet
army invaded and occupied Lithuania, ending its two decades of
independence. The following year, the Nazis seized Lithuania from
the Soviets and proceeded to decimate one of the most vibrant Jewish communities in Europe. Close to two hundred thousand Jews
had lived in Lithuania before the war, and more than 90 percent
were victims of the Holocaust carried out by the Nazis and their
Lithuanian collaborators. Those murdered included Zalie's parents, a brother-in-law, and several other relatives. Zalie was never
able to determine the date, the location, or the exact circumstances
of their deaths. Yet for the rest of his life, Zalie was grateful to the
Soviet consul who had advised him. "He saved my life by telling me
to leave Europe," Zalie said.

Zalie's escape from Europe took him to the port city of Durban,
South Africa, which had become a destination for Lithuanian Jews,
including one of his sisters. Zalie took up farming, and within a
decade, he was running two large farms in Margate, a few hours
south of Durban, totaling nearly one thousand acres. A 1948 newspaper story described him as the "banana king" of South Africa. As
his farms flourished, he built schools for the children of the Zulu
workers, but other whites complained, and Zalie reluctantly closed
them.

In May 1948, two seminal events took place less than two weeks
apart, and they would shape Zalie's destiny. In the Middle East,
Israel declared statehood on May 14, rekindling Zalie's dream of
moving to the Holy Land. On May 26, South Africa's National

Party, which was dominated by the Afrikaners, won elections in South Africa, which put them in power and led to the codification of apartheid.

The following year, Zalie, then in his late thirties, visited Israel for seven weeks with the intent to move there. "Israel to me was part of my religion. I loved the idea of the kibbutz, the idea of a new society, built on the land of our prophets. It's a magnificent idea. I had been planning to come to Israel since 1930," he said. "The excitement of the time was new and refreshing. We dreamed of peace. No one was thinking of war and occupation."

The new Israeli government offered Zalie more than two hundred acres near the central city of Netanya. "I wanted the farm, but I couldn't take it because I didn't have the money," said Zalie. "I was managing two farms in South Africa, and they would not let me go because I was the working partner in the operation. To develop the farm in Israel required a lot of money that was tied up in South Africa."

His dream of moving to Israel was deferred. "I stayed in South Africa, but I was bitter," he said.

In 1949, Zalie did travel to New York, however, where three of his sisters lived. Through them, he met Arline Shuck, a twenty-two-year-old student at Hunter College. "I gave him a ride to the Frick Museum, and we got married six weeks later," said Arline. They returned to South Africa, where Arline's Bronx upbringing had not exactly prepared her for living on the land. "I once planted a carrot in the ground to see if it would grow—everyone got a big kick out of that," she said.

The Millers gave up farming in 1952 and moved first to Johannesburg and then four years later to Bulawayo, Rhodesia, to help run a clothing factory owned by Zalie's brother. Yet there, too, the segregationist policies weighed on Zalie. "There was talk of a multiracial, democratic society," Zalie said. "But then [Rhodesian leader] Ian Smith said it would remain white-ruled for the next one thousand years."

In 1973, Zalie and Arline finally decided to immigrate to Israel after their daughter, Rivanna, began to study at Hebrew University in Jerusalem. They made it out of Rhodesia just before the eruption of a nasty civil war that would last seven years and ultimately bring Robert Mugabe to power as president of black-ruled Zimbabwe. They arrived in Israel just in time for the 1973 Yom Kippur war, when Egypt and Syria caught Israel by surprise. "I was stunned by the war," said Zalie. "We were in complete shock." Welcome to Israel. More wars would follow, along with Palestinian uprisings, terror attacks, and countless political upheavals.

By the time we became Zalie's neighbors, however, it seemed like those dramas might be fading into history. Prime Minister Ehud Barak, the son of Zalie's lifelong friend Israel Brog, was pursuing peace talks with vigor. A solution appeared within reach. As we set out to cover this story, the Millers were most hospitable. They invited us to their family dinners on Jewish holidays. They introduced us to their friends. Arline was forever insisting that we see the latest exhibit at the Israel Museum, where she worked as a guide. Rivanna and her husband, Simon Lichman, took us to see their project that brought Jewish and Arab schoolchildren together.

It seemed as if Israel might finally become an ordinary nation, just one of many. A country that rose out of the Holocaust, that seemed forever in crisis and carried with it a deep-rooted sense of exceptionalism, might at last become normal.

Of course, it all came crashing down. The Palestinian uprising began, the violence exploded, and the quest for *normaliyut* turned into a mirage. Jerusalem was one of the main targets for Palestinian bombers, and the streets in our neighborhood were often cordoned off as part of the increased security surrounding the residences of the president and the prime minister.

In an event we noted at the beginning of this book, a Palestinian suicide bomber killed eleven Israelis on March 9, 2002, at the Moment Café, just down the street from the apartment building where we and the Millers were living. The violence was at its peak that month. On March 27, the Millers invited us to their apartment for the traditional Seder dinner on the eve of Passover. A long table was set in the living room as the Millers' three grown kids with their spouses and children all gathered around. Early in the dinner, my cell phone rang. A Palestinian bomber had struck at the Park Hotel in Netanya, just as diners there were sitting down to the Seder meal. I ran upstairs to our apartment and began filing a story with the first fragmentary details of what was the deadliest suicide bombing ever, with thirty people killed. I went back down briefly to a much more somber affair. Here was Zalie, now in his nineties, and he still had not escaped the traumas and the upheavals that had been part of his entire life.

Several years later, shortly before we left Jerusalem, I sat down with Zalie in the book-lined study of his apartment. Despite all of the trouble Zalie had witnessed, it remained an article of faith with him that the Israelis and the Palestinians must make peace. He went even further at times, endorsing the idealistic notion that the two sides might actually be able to share a single state. "A binational state is still a wonderful idea," said Zalie, gesturing with both hands to express his passion.

Sitting next to him, his wife, Arline, rolled her eyes. She was far more skeptical but reluctantly accepted that it was probably too late in the day to change Zalie. Still, she dove into a debate that had, no doubt, played out many times. "In a binational state, what kind of flag would you have?" Arline asked.

"A flag is just a rag," Zalie retorted. "Everyone should be able to come here and pray to his own God. This is a beautiful idea, and we must hold on to it."

Arline soon gave up on Zalie and turned to me. "Zalie's very idealistic. I don't expect as much, so I'm not disappointed," she said, temporarily dropping the latest round of the discussion.

Zalie's thinking had not gone soft with age. He saw the obstacles, how violence had changed everyone's behavior in ways large and small, including his own. "When we were driving, we used to pick up anybody hitchhiking on the road—they could be ultra-Orthodox Jews or Arabs. Now we wouldn't pick up anybody. Not because we don't like someone, but because we're scared."

Zalie shook his head as he thought back over the way events had played out. "The founding fathers felt after the 1967 war that there should be peace. The occupied territories would be a bargaining chip. But it didn't work. We never thought this would happen. I'm very disappointed. There's so much bitterness. I don't know how we can turn the clock back."

Zalie Miller died in October 2008 at age ninety-seven. He was talking politics and tending to his garden until the very end. He never saw peace, but it seemed that the best way to measure his life was by how far he had come. He was born in a land where the Jewish population would be wiped out and at a time when a Jewish homeland was just a dream. He would have to travel to another continent to find refuge and make his fortune and would not reach Israel until he was ready to retire.

His spirit carried on through his three grown kids. His daughter, Rivanna, continued to run a program that allows Jewish and Arab schoolchildren to mix with one another. One son, Dovis, who also goes by "Gordon," published a book in 2008 with his own ideas on how to resolve the conflict, called *Taking the Israeli-Palestinian Conflict Outside the Box: The Bermigo Plan*. Another son, Gideon, is a successful business consultant. "The kids are all like Zalie," said Arline. The stalemate in the conflict was depressing, but several thousand years of Jewish history helps one take the long view. The world Zalie bequeathed was more hopeful than the one he inherited.

Dr. Izzeldin Abuelaish is also a man of hope. While most Gazans were quick to list their grievances, he was open, expansive, and positive, qualities that helped him to transcend the restrictions most Palestinians faced.

He was only a boy in the Jabaliya Refugee Camp when the Israelis captured Gaza in the 1967 war. Shortly afterward, the soldiers told everyone in the camp to gather in the main square. "It was the first time I saw Israelis, and I thought it was the end of the world," he recalled. Yet he was also curious about the Israelis. Before the war, Palestinians were not allowed into Israel. Under the occupation, though, Israel did allow Palestinians in to work. As a teenager, he spent his summers doing manual labor in Israel. With his outgoing personality, he got to know many Israelis.

Fast forward to 1993, and Dr. Abuelaish, an obstetrician, became the first Palestinian to work as a full staff physician in an Israeli hospital. He commuted every week from the Jabaliya Refugee Camp—where he still lived—to Israel's Soroka Hospital in the southern desert town of Beersheba. At that time, Israel had not yet built a fence around Gaza, and traveling to and from Israel was relatively easy. "Those were the golden days. I used to cross into Israel in my car, any time, day or night," Dr. Abuelaish recalled. At the Erez crossing point between Gaza and Israel, the soldiers knew him and greeted him with smiles and occasional requests. "Female soldiers would sometimes ask for birth control pills," he said.

Very few Palestinians or Israelis spent large amounts of time on both sides of the divide. Dr. Abuelaish's dual life was unusual even for the relatively calm years in the 1990s, when coexistence was the spirit of the day. Dr. Abuelaish reveled in his role. He was a natural ambassador and a one-man peace process.

Dr. Abuelaish was such a strong believer in the peace efforts that he hosted busloads of curious Israelis who came to see Gaza, many for the first time. Up to forty Jewish visitors at once descended on his home, then sat cross-legged on the floor of the large but sparsely furnished house he shared with twenty-two members of his extended family, including his wife and eight children. The Israelis sipped thick Arabic coffee and asked about life in Gaza. Dr. Abuelaish explained in his fluent Hebrew.

Although many Israelis were suspicious of Palestinians, Dr. Abuelaish was so effusive that it was impossible for Israelis not to be swept up by his enthusiasm. And while Palestinians were deeply cynical about Israel, Dr. Abuelaish returned each week from the Israeli hospital to his humble refugee camp with stories about the friendships he had built on the other side of the Gaza boundary.

Yet when I visited him at Soroka Hospital in June 2001, less than a year into the intifada, his mood had begun to darken. Dr. Abuelaish was among a dwindling number of Gazans who still had an Israeli work permit, but the weekly trip of thirty miles from his Gaza home to the Israeli hospital had become much more complicated. "I'm scared to travel now," he said. "You never know how the soldiers are going to react." The previous day in the hospital's in vitro fertilization clinic, he had discussed various options with Israeli couples. After work, he returned to his dorm room and called his home in Gaza to check on his children. His fourteen-year-old daughter, Dalal, told him that Israeli helicopters were attacking a Palestinian police station just a few hundred yards away. "My daughter said, 'We can't sleep, there's bombing going on,'" the doctor told me. "There is always anxiety. My mind is always racing."

By the end of 2002, he decided to leave the hospital and went to Harvard University to pursue a master's degree in public health policy. It gave Dr. Abuelaish the chance to escape the suffocating confines of Gaza, even though it tore him apart to leave his family behind at a time when the fighting was at its worst.

He went to one of the world's most prestigious universities, studied hard, and received an advanced degree. Yet on his return a year later, he found that the diploma was worthless in a place where conditions had only deteriorated. He renewed his relationship with Soroka Hospital, but it was limited to one day a week, where he worked on a genetic research project. The trip out of Gaza was a source of endless frustration. "The situation has completely changed," Dr. Abuelaish said. "You can't speak to the soldiers. There is no trust, only suspicion. Every time I pass through the Erez crossing, it is intimidating and humiliating."

As we prepared to leave Jerusalem in 2007, I phoned Dr. Abuelaish's home in Gaza in hopes of arranging one last meeting. One of his daughters answered and told me he was in Afghanistan. That spoke volumes about life in Gaza. Conditions were so bad in Gaza that one of the territory's most prominent doctors had left his wife and eight kids for a year and gone to Afghanistan because it offered better opportunities than the ones at home.

Over a crackly phone line, I eventually reached Dr. Abuelaish in Kabul, and he told me he was on a one-year contract with the World Health Organization to help rebuild Afghanistan's health-care system. He ached for his family but needed the paycheck to support them, and jobs in Gaza paid a pittance.

The next time I heard from him was a few months later in a plaintive e-mail. He had returned to Gaza in the summer of 2007, just in time for the internal Palestinian fighting in which Hamas seized full control of the territory. "It was beyond the imagination," he wrote. He was looking for work and asked whether I could help.

My personal recommendation, it turned out, was utterly useless for a doctor seeking gainful employment. Yet Dr. Abuelaish landed on his feet. He had the experience, the contacts, and the effusive personality to get himself hired as a senior consultant at Tel Hashomer Hospital near Tel Aviv, one of Israel's leading health facilities.

The job meant that Dr. Abuelaish would once again be serving in his role as Gaza's unofficial medical ambassador to Israel. For his new job, he left his Gaza home on Sunday and traveled to Tel Aviv, where he spent the week, before returning on Thursday evening. It meant that Dr. Abuelaish was again away from his family for most of the week, and it was a particularly challenging time, because his wife was seriously ill with leukemia.

Despite these circumstances, Dr. Abuelaish seemed to be successfully reconstructing his life. Yet within months, the unraveling began. In September 2008, his wife died of her leukemia, leaving him to care for their eight children. He managed with the help of his extended family, who continued to share the large home in the Jabaliya Refugee Camp.

Three months later, in December, Dr. Abuelaish was at home when Israel unleashed a major offensive against Gaza, Operation Cast Lead, in response to ongoing Palestinian rocket fire. Unlike previous Israeli operations, which tended to be limited in scope, Israel bombed throughout Gaza. The doctor, like most Gazans, was reluctant to leave his house. There was no way he could leave Gaza.

Yet Dr. Abuelaish was not a man who could sit still. He effectively became the correspondent for Israel's Channel 10 television. During previous Israeli incursions, foreign journalists could usually manage to get into Gaza, but this time Israel kept the journalists out, saying it was for their own safety. This left a vacuum of information, and Dr. Abuelaish stepped in to help fill it. He became a fixture on Channel 10 with his regular updates on the fighting. "I was called by Channel 10 on a daily basis," he said. "I couldn't go to the hospital—so it was like I changed my job and became a correspondent."

In the early days of the war, virtually all Israelis supported the military campaign. The military portrayed it as an effort to deal decisively with the rocket fire and weaken Hamas. Even liberal Israelis tended to favor tough action against the rockets that had been coming out of Gaza for years. The Israeli offensive, however, was much more intense than anything previously unleashed against Gaza, and the civilian toll was much greater than ever before. In Israel, information about the carnage was limited, due to the absence of foreign and Israeli journalists. For many Israelis, the only Palestinian view they received was from Dr. Abuelaish.

Dr. Abuelaish described in detail his life in a besieged neighborhood. The Jabaliya Refugee Camp was a militant stronghold and was one of the places most heavily bombed. On January 14, 2009, an Israeli tank approached his house. "When I saw the tank, I thought death was in front of me," he said. "What would my children do without parents? I started to think and then I called my Israeli friends. I gave them the location of my house. I explained everything. I called an Israeli military officer, and I gave him the details. A few minutes later, the tank moved away from my house. I thought we were safe."

After three blood-soaked weeks, the Israeli operation was drawing to a close. The Israelis had effectively run out of targets. They had pounded all of the symbols of Hamas and the Palestinian leadership in Gaza, including the parliament building and the offices of the security forces. The Israelis struck at metal workshops, where militants made rockets. The Israelis bombed the weapons-smuggling tunnels connecting Rafah in southern Gaza to the Egyptian side of the border. The Israelis tracked and killed militants, and most of those who survived had cleared off the streets and gone underground.

Many of these relentless Israeli strikes took place in civilian neighborhoods, where Palestinian fighters were taking cover, and this meant that Palestinian civilian casualties were extremely high. Israel faced enormous international pressure to halt the campaign, which seemed timed to take advantage of the U.S. political calendar. Operation Cast Lead began when George W. Bush was heading out the door and Barack Obama was not yet in office. By mid-January, with Obama's inauguration just days away, the Israelis prepared to call off the operation.

Meanwhile, Dr. Abuelaish was still providing his daily updates to Channel 10. On January 16, two days after he had seen the Israeli tank outside his home, Abuelaish was scheduled to appear again by telephone. Shortly beforehand, his house suddenly shook as an Israeli tank shell ripped through a metal grille and shattered an upstairs window, entering the bedroom where several of Dr. Abuelaish's daughters and their cousins were working on a computer. The shell exploded and pocked the room with shrapnel.

Weeping and screaming in both Arabic and Hebrew, Dr. Abuelaish called Channel 10 newscaster Shlomi Eldar. "Oh my God, my daughters have been killed! They've killed my children! . . . Could somebody please come?" Eldar held up his phone, and Dr. Abuelaish's frantic call was broadcast for more than three minutes on Israeli television.

The shell decapitated one of his daughters, Mayar, age fifteen, and killed two more, Aya, thirteen, and Bisan, twenty, along with one of his nieces. A fourth daughter, Shada, seventeen, suffered serious injuries to an eye and a hand. Dr. Abuelaish scrambled to take his wounded daughter to Gaza City's Shifa Hospital, which had been overwhelmed by the carnage since the fighting began. His injured daughter was in danger of losing an eye and several fingers, due to the severity of the injury and the limited resources at the hospital.

Dr. Abuelaish then called his hospital in Israel, and through his desperate lobbying, Shada was allowed to enter Israel. Her eye and her hand were saved.

The next day, Prime Minister Ehud Olmert announced a unilateral cease-fire in what was the deadliest Israeli operation against the Palestinians in the last decade. Some fourteen hundred Palestinians had been killed, more than half of them civilians, and in excess of five thousand Palestinians wounded. On the Israeli side, ten soldiers and three civilians had been killed. Yet as with so many other battles, nothing fundamental was resolved. The Israelis greatly reduced the Palestinian rocket fire, but Palestinians still had the capability to hit Israel and have done so occasionally. Hamas's hold on Gaza was not shaken, and the Israeli embargo on the territory was not lifted.

Several months after his tragedy, Dr. Abuelaish visited the United States on a speaking tour. He stopped in Washington, and I went to see him. He was not seeking vengeance. He did not want to assign blame. He simply wanted to tell his story, in the hope that it would somehow put an end to the fighting.

He was critical of the Israelis for not initially taking responsibility for the deaths of his daughters. The Israelis said they returned fire at militants who were shooting from Dr. Abuelaish's house, a claim the doctor said was nonsense. The military investigated and a few weeks later announced that soldiers had come under heavy fire from a house adjacent to Dr. Abuelaish's. The soldiers identified "suspicious figures" in the doctor's house and thought they were "spotters who directed the Hamas sniper and mortar fire." The army acknowledged the mistake but said that under the circumstances, the decision to fire was "reasonable."

It was no consolation, yet Dr. Abuelaish expressed no bitterness. Rather, he said the acknowledgment showed that his reports from Gaza had forced Israel and the Israeli military to reexamine their actions. "I was fighting to give the truth to the Israeli public. At first, some Israelis believed me, but others did not want to open their eyes. Then the Israeli soldiers started to speak about what happened in Gaza." The latter remark was a reference to Israeli soldiers who came forward after the war and said that they had witnessed fellow soldiers firing indiscriminately, with little concern for Palestinian civilian casualties.

Dr. Abuelaish was also critical of his fellow Palestinians for their inability to work together politically and for their continued glorification of armed struggle. "We have to take responsibility for things we have to change ourselves," Dr. Abuelaish said. "The Palestinians need to be unified. The Palestinians are suffering because we don't have this. The parties have to serve the national goal—and not use the national goal to serve their own parties."

He spoke about the miserable conditions in Gaza and the sense of futility that he and other Gazans experienced. "The situation in Gaza is unacceptable—not just for the Palestinians, but for any human beings. At least, I can cross the border. But what about the others who are imprisoned in the jail that is Gaza?" He told a story of a Gaza man who got a passport, raising his hopes that he would be able to leave Gaza for the first time. Yet he could not get permission from the Israelis, and the document expired before he could get a single stamp in it. "We all want to taste freedom," the doctor said.

For Dr. Abuelaish, this meant leaving Gaza altogether, at least for a while. He accepted a position at the University of Toronto, taking his surviving kids with him. He would not be working with Palestinians or Israelis but was still intent on spreading his message. "Arguing about who has suffered the most does not get us anywhere," he said.

The cycle is so hard to break. The fighting causes suffering. The suffering creates victims. The victims are filled with righteousness and grievances. Yet Dr. Abuelaish refused to be a link in the chain: "I am not a victim. I don't want to be a victim. I work on the things I can change. It's a waste of time to think about things you can't change. I lost three precious daughters. I can only do good things for their memory. I have five more precious children. They are the future."

AFTERWORD

Jennifer, October 2010

So, how did all of this mayhem affect us?

The Israeli-Palestinian story can be all-consuming, and we chose total immersion. We lived and breathed the assignment every day. Greg woke each morning to the reports on Israel's Army Radio and scoured the local newspapers before breakfast. I was often on my cell phone and BlackBerry at the same time, making coverage plans with my crew before I got out of bed. Come midnight, we were still tweaking the last details of our daily dispatches with editors back in New York. The appetite for stories was endless, and the news cycle had no regard for whether it was day or night, weekday or weekend. One former Jerusalem correspondent likened the job to being attached to a jackhammer that had no off switch.

Still, it was not easy for us to leave Jerusalem. It was with great reluctance that we packed our bags and moved to Washington in 2007. As much as we were attached to Jerusalem, we felt the need for a change. We had gravitated to this conflict and many others by choice, but it seemed it might be nice to wake up someplace where riots were not served with the morning cappuccino.

In Washington, where I grew up, I began to cover the Pentagon for Fox, and Greg joined NPR's *Morning Edition* program. We still observed the Israeli-Palestinian conflict but through a telescope, rather than a microscope. The distance provided some welcome perspective. The day-to-day clashes no longer felt so urgent. Even the significant developments only reinforced our belief that the two societies were trapped in a cul-de-sac. The Israelis announced a temporary freeze of West Bank settlements; the Palestinian political factions quarreled among themselves; the Israelis and the Palestinians debated whether they should hold talks about talks. The two sides had largely stopped shooting at each other, but they were making no real progress toward a resolution.

Back in 1991, as the Israelis and the Palestinians took part in the Madrid Conference, the first public meeting between the two sides, then secretary of state James Baker proved to be prophetic when he said that the United States cannot want peace more than the parties themselves do. The Americans could serve as the midwife to a peace deal but could not force it on either side.

By 2010, longtime American diplomat and Middle East negotiator Aaron David Miller aptly described the peace process as an increasingly futile exercise that was producing endless process and no peace. He said that the long-held tenets of Middle East peacemaking, including the inevitability of a two-state solution brokered by the United States, had become a "false religion." Like many other people, he did not claim to have the solution but said the formulas that had failed time and again needed to be reassessed.

From my perch at the Pentagon, I soon found myself immersed again in Middle East wars, although now the focus was Iraq and Afghanistan, and my travel agent was the U.S. military. In July 2008, I accompanied Admiral Mike Mullen, chairman of the Joint Chiefs of Staff, on a tour of these two countries. In the rugged and remote Korengal Valley, near Afghanistan's eastern border with Pakistan, I kept throwing up every time I got on the chairman's helicopter. It was embarrassing, and I thought I might be losing my stomach for these adventures. Yet I soon realized that it was a telltale sign of morning sickness. I was pregnant with our third child, Luke, who was born in March 2009.

These brief visits to Iraq and Afghanistan with senior military officials were very different from the on-the-ground reporting we had done for so many years. Still, it was impossible not to make at least some comparisons between these conflicts and the one we had covered in Jerusalem. All of these fights represented this new era of asymmetric warfare, with Western military might matched against Muslim militants in protracted and seemingly inconclusive battles. These conflicts have resisted clean, formal endings marked by peace treaties. They place a premium on intelligence, nimbleness, and endurance. The U.S. military could take a town in Iraq or a dusty village in Afghanistan, just as the Israelis could reimpose their will on a Palestinian city in the West Bank, but this did not necessarily translate into a larger success or a permanent solution. The militants often found the occupying armies more vulnerable in these circumstances. And the occupiers faced a Catch-22: if they remained, resentment by the local population often built; if they left, the militants could reclaim the territory, declare a propaganda victory, and raise their stature.

The analogies between these wars were far from precise, but there were plenty of similarities.

At the Pentagon, the main concern regarding the Israeli-Palestinian conflict was the possibility of a unilateral Israeli strike on Iran's nuclear program, an event that would unleash all sorts of unpredictable consequences. When we were living in Jerusalem, such an Israeli strike seemed highly unlikely, and Israel's eagerness to raise the scenario over and over seemed to be at least in part a calculated bluff. At the Pentagon, many were willing to take the Israeli statements at face value, and such an attack was considered a distinct possibility.

Our daughters, meanwhile, had their own unique perspective on the relative dangers of global conflicts. When we were living in Jerusalem, we often wondered what impact the violence might be having on their young minds. The fighting was a constant topic of conversation between us and our friends, but fortunately, they seemed largely oblivious to the dramas surrounding them.

By the time we moved to the United States, they had begun to develop a sense of danger. On the anniversary of the September 11 attacks in 2008, they were ages seven and five and old enough to at least partly understand the news. They saw me on television report- ing from the Pentagon's new 9/11 memorial, with floating white lights under a bench dedicated to each victim of the attack. That night, they were with me in the car as we drove past the Pentagon, and they peppered me with questions.

"Why haven't we caught bin Laden?" Amelia asked. "Who is on bin Laden's team? Where is he, and is he going to come back and get us?" The questions didn't stop. I tried to answer them as hon- estly as I could without adding to their fears, but one question led to another. The next day, Amelia asked Greg, "Why did you bring us to this dangerous country?" She was quite convinced that she had been much safer in Jerusalem.

We chuckled at the irony, but Amelia was not that far off. Trou- ble can find you anywhere. On September 28, 2009, nine years to the day that Ariel Sharon took his walk on the Temple Mount in Jerusalem, our lives took a new turn. I received a phone call at 8 a.m. from my Jewish radiologist—and I immediately knew something was wrong because it was Yom Kippur, the holiest day on the Jewish calendar. The doctors had found a nine-centimeter cancerous tumor in my breast that was growing, as I would tell my military friends, "faster than an Al-Qaeda cell in Somalia."

This was not a battle we had anticipated. I immediately began chemotherapy at Georgetown University Hospital, and it would last for seventeen rounds over five months, followed by a double mastectomy. As I began the treatment, we soon realized that our experience covering other people's wars gave us all of the tools we needed to fight this one. Our many years of living in places of perpetual conflict served us well. We began to look forward to the Friday afternoon chemo sessions as a few hours when we could work on this book together, writing and revis- ing on our laptops as the wonder drugs were pumped into my bloodstream.

I concluded my treatment with radiation in the summer of 2010. At my last session, I lay on the linear accelerator table and tried to remain still. I visualized the beams destroying any pesky cancer cells that had survived the chemo and the surgery. My doctors explained to me that there was no longer any sign of cancer that they could detect. Yet I might still have cancer cells growing inside me for the rest of my life, and the goal was to keep them in check. It can at times feel like a perpetual war, but life goes on. It is never an easy lesson to digest but one that I had already learned: some battles must simply be managed.

Acknowledgments

If the Israelis and the Palestinians were as generous with each other as they were with foreign journalists, the conflict would have been resolved decades ago. Hundreds and hundreds of Israelis and Palestinians patiently told us their stories, often at times when they, their families, and their communities were suffering great trauma. There is not enough space to thank all of them by name; we only hope we have given them their due in the pages of this book.

We are extremely grateful to the news organizations who supported us during these challenging times and remained so committed to this story. At the *New York Times* home office, those who helped us immensely included Bill Keller, Susan Chira, Roger Cohen, Ethan Bronner, Alison Smale, and Rick Gladstone. In the *Times* bureau in Jerusalem, I had the pleasure of working with two supremely talented and hugely supportive bureau chiefs, first James Bennet and then Steven Erlanger. The dedicated staff included Rina Castelnuovo, Khaled Abu Aker, Taghreed El-Khodary, Edie Sabbagh, Myra Noveck, Dina Kraft, and Gabby Sobelman.

My AP colleagues numbered in the dozens, and special mention goes to Dan Perry, Jocelyn Noveck, Karin Laub, Laura King, Mark Lavie, Mohammad Daraghmeh, Ibrahim Barzak, Jackie Larma, Laurie Copans, Jamie Tarabay, David Guttenfelder, Lourdes Garcia-Navarro, Haitham Hamad, Hadeel Wahdan, Elizabeth Dalziel, Brennan Linsley, Enric Marti, Lefteris Pitarakis, and Jerome Delay.

—G.M.

. . .

We have Fox News to thank for sending us to Jerusalem. Roger Ailes and John Moody were more than bosses. They cared deeply about us in the field and made sure we had everything we needed to tell the story. Brit Hume, Jim Eldridge, and Greta Van Susteren gave us the time and space to explain what was really happening on the ground. Jerusalem bureau chief Eli Fastman taught me the intricacies of the modern Middle East. He would be my first choice if I had to fight my way out of a foxhole. The rest of my Jerusalem team was wonderful: Mark Abrahams, Yaniv Turgeman, Mal James, Ibrahim Hazboun, Ami Shamir, Yonat Friling, Dudi Gamliel, Yoav Shamir, Dvora Olinsky, Karen Liel, Osnat Arazi-Turgeman, Yael Kuriel, Yael Bouganim, Yael Aharony, Dana Zimmerman, Gabi Goldman, Dana Karni, Uri Ravid, Ronen Shpizaman, and Saadia.

In Gaza, my colleagues included Abdel Salam Abu Askar, Nael Ghaboun, Ayman Alrozi, Muhamed Al Sousi, and in the West Bank, thanks go to Ali Daraghmeh, Fathi Natour, and Munjed Jado.

Mike Tobin was a terrific colleague, as were David Lee Miller, Reena Ninan, Shushannah Walshe, Maya Zumwalt, and Andrew Psarianos.

—J.G.

Every author should be so lucky to have an agent as supportive, enthusiastic, and persistent as Alice Martell. And Eric Nelson, our editor at John Wiley & Sons, immediately understood how we wanted to approach this book and then he patiently helped us shape it.

Several friends reviewed the manuscript at various stages, and all provided invaluable guidance. They include Monique Taylor, Joe Aceto, Michael Matza, and Sarah Williams.

At the Middle East Institute in Washington, President Wendy Chamberlain, Laurie Kassman, and Stephanie Richardson helped arrange a trio of researchers who were first rate: Gulenc Dere, Jacob Passel, and Elizabeth Perego.

Our many friends in Jerusalem included James Synder and Tina Davis, Erel and Debbie Margalit, Scott and Andrea Wilson, Andrew and Wendy Wilson, Simon and Ulrike Wilson, Phil Reeves and Mandy Cunningham, Anamarija Muvrin and Julian

Rake, Paul Nevin, James and Kerry Arroyo, James Drummond, Sarah Jessup, Betsy Erlanger, Craig Nelson and Margaret Coker, Gershom Gorenberg, Matt Rees, Larry Kaplow, Lee Hockstader and Flore de Preneuf, John Ward Anderson and Molly Moore, Danny Klaidman and Monica Selter, Gerry Holmes and Jennifer Ludden, Ken Ellingwood, Paul Holmes, Linda Breitstein, Debra Camiel, Barbara Demick, Charlie and Julie Sennott, Geoffrey and Mary Emma Adams, Joel Greenberg, Claire Kosinski, Varda and Oron Dan, Simha Cohen Stern, Safwat al-Kahlout, Nabil Feidy, Eva Aviad, Peter Kenyon, Julie McCarthy, Eric Westervelt, Dr. Drorit Hochner, Cameron Barr, Nicole Gaouette, and all the Rivkinds— Linda, Maya, Barak, Yael, and Shelly.

—G.M. and J.G.

NOTES

1 "Go to the Temple Mount"

1. Uri Dan, *Ariel Sharon: An Intimate Portrait* (New York: Palgrave Macmillan, 2006), p. 3.
2. Jeffrey Goldberg, "The Return of Sharon," *New Yorker*, January 29, 2001.
3. Arafat spoke in an interview with Mike Wallace on CBS's *60 Minutes*, November 5, 2000.
4. Deborah Sontag, "And Yet So Far: A Special Report. Quest for Mideast Peace: How and Why It Failed," *New York Times*, July 26, 2001.
5. Arafat in an interview on CBS's *60 Minutes*, November 5, 2000.
6. Al-Hayat Al-Jedida, November 9, 2000. Translated by the Middle East Media Research Institute (MEMRI), Special Dispatch No. 153, November, 17, 2000.

3 There Will Be a Bomb

1. Tovah Lazaroff, "Young Lives Lost in a Moment of Terror," *Jerusalem Post*, March 11, 2002.

4 "Hamas Doesn't Need to Recruit"

1. MEMRI, "Friday Sermon on PA TV: Blessings to Whoever Saved a Bullet to Stick It in a Jew's Head," Special Dispatch No. 252, August 8, 2001.
2. "Suicide Bombers: Dignity, Despair and the Need for Hope: An Interview with Eyad El Sarraj," *Journal of Palestine Studies* 124 (Summer 2002).
3. Ibid.
4. *The Atlantic*, "School for Suicide," May 2007, p. 33.
5. "Suicide Bombers: Dignity, Despair and the Need for Hope."

6 The Invisible Hand

1. Gershom Gorenberg, "The Collaborator," *New York Times Magazine*, August 18, 2002.

7 Double Jeopardy

1. Amnesty International Report, *Testimony from Mohammed Daraghmeh*, November 4, 2002.

8 Versions of the Truth

1. Reporters of the Associated Press, *Breaking News: How the Associated Press Has Covered War, Peace, and Everything Else* (Princeton, NJ: Princeton Architectural Press, 2007), pp. 293–294.

2. Ethan Bronner, "The Bullets in My In-Box," *New York Times*, January 25, 2009.

10 "We'll Take the Ambulance, It's Free"

1. Lee Hockstader, "Gaza Gains a Martyr, Parents Lose a Son," *Washington Post*, December 11, 2000.
2. Dr. Jehuda Hiss was removed as head of the National Center for Forensic Medicine following a 2004 controversy in which it was revealed that the center occasionally took skin, bones, corneas, and other body parts from the dead without the permission of relatives. Dr. Hiss remained at the center as the chief pathologist.

11 Soldiers to the Left of Us, Militants to the Right

1. Yola Monakhov detailed her shooting in "The Mistakes: Two Years after She Was Shot in Bethlehem, a Photojournalist Looks Back," *Columbia Journalism Review*, January–February 2003.

16 After Arafat

1. James Bennet, "Palestinian Mob Attacks Pollster over Study on 'Right of Return,'" *New York Times*, July 14, 2003.

19 "We Failed Entirely"

1. MEMRI, "Palestinian Authority TV: A Call to Avoid Extremism and Violence," Special Dispatch 824, December 7, 2004.

20 Soul Searching

1. Steven Erlanger, "Israel's Soldiers Engage in Soul Searching," *International Herald Tribune*, March 23, 2007, p. 2.

21 The New Jerusalem

1. Reuters, "Militia Sorry for Killing Arab in Jerusalem Attack," March 20, 2004.

27 Into the Abyss

1. Paul McGeough, *Kill Khalid: The Failed Mossad Assassination of Khalid Mishal and the Rise of Hamas* (New York: The New Press, 2009), p. 407.

INDEX